Death, Despair, and Second Chances

in Rocky Mountain National Park

Joseph R. Evans

JOHNSON BOOKS

AN IMPRINT OF BOWER HOUSE

DENVER

Cover and text design by Rebecca Finkel
Cover photo: "Rescue training with the military in late 1980s" courtesy of Rocky Mountain National Park.

Library of Congress Cataloging-in-Publication Data
Evans, Joseph R.
Death, despair, and second chances in Rocky Mountain National Park / Joseph R. Evans.
p. cm.
Includes bibliographical references.
ISBN 978-1-55566-440-4
1. Rocky Mountain National Park (Colo.)
2. Accidents—Colorado—Rocky Mountain National Park.
3. Violent deaths—Colorado—Rocky Mountain National Park.
4. Disasters—Colorado—Rocky Mountain National Park.
I. Title.
F782.R59E83 2010
978.8'69—dc22
                                        2010006986

DEDICATION

In appreciation of each member
of every search and rescue team
—paid or volunteer—
who has risked her or his life
in the support of those in need.

This book is also dedicated to the park ranger. Every day throughout the world, rangers put themselves in danger to protect park resources. Many are shot at, some are killed. For those rangers killed in the developing world, there is little or no safety net for their families. The Ranger Dependents Fund was created to support the families of rangers who are killed in the line of duty. This fund is managed through the International Ranger Federation (www.int-ranger.net) and the Thin Green Line Foundation (www.thingreenline.info). Any support you can offer will be appreciated.

50 percent of the author's royalties
from the sale of this book will be donated to the
Ranger Dependents Fund.

The Association of National Park Rangers (www.anpr.org) in the United States was a founding member of the International Ranger Federation and supports the work of the Thin Green Line Foundation. Please explore these websites to learn more about the work of park rangers throughout the world.

Contents

Doug Ridley and Kurt "the Master" Oliver for reading manuscripts and providing suggestions or corrections to my initial understanding of incident histories. In this same light, Debbie Hughes and Research Librarian Sybil Barnes also reviewed manuscripts. They provided sound advice on story development and gently corrected mistakes in grammar and punctuation. Thanks also to Bill Wakeman for his editing prowess. Ranger and author Butch Farabee provided invaluable advice and encouragement. My publisher, Mira Perrizo, cast a keen eye over my manuscript and tolerated numerous questions about the business of books. I could not have reached the finish line without her.

A final thank you is offered to my wife and best friend Caroline. She supported me in this effort with key, and often painful, critiques.

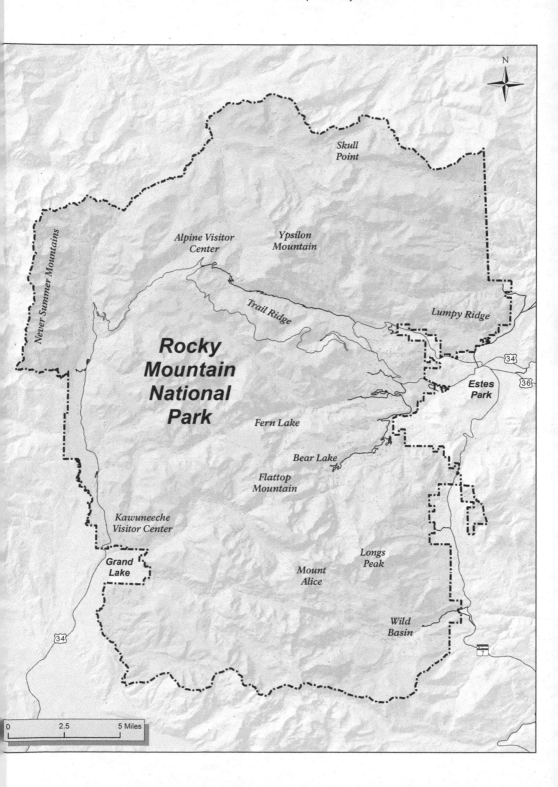

Introduction

Death is the one thing we can count on as we go about our lives. Unfortunately, the means by which people meet their demise shout out to us each day in newspapers and nightly television. Usually in the back pages of the larger regional newspapers, one often finds an article about someone who lost his or her life while out on public lands or, more specifically, in a national park. This book chronicles the 297 deaths of men, women, and children in Rocky Mountain National Park between 1884 and 2009. It is about the reasons these people died.

There is a degree of comfort in calling these deaths "accidents." However, there are few simple accidents that meet the dictionary definition of "unforeseeable incident" or "an unexpected or undesirable event." Instead, some otherwise responsible person makes a series of decisions that lead to an outcome that could be predictable and preventable. For example, a snow field is normally steep, and there are rocks at the bottom where the snow stops. If you slip on the snow, there is a high probability that you will slide to the bottom where the rocks are. That means broken bones if you're lucky, but for many it has meant death. The solution is to avoid steep snow fields.

I used the term "otherwise" to describe what is hopefully a responsible and logical person—as long as he or she is in their environment or comfort zone. What happens to many people when they visit a park is that their antennae are not fully tuned to the dangers and hazards in the area. Each hazard provides wonderful options or blood chilling ways to die or to be injured. For example, in Yellowstone National Park there are bison, grizzly bears, and boiling thermal areas, all of which can kill you. In the Grand Canyon and other southern parks, a person can die from heat stroke or dehydration. In Yosemite National Park, visitors encounter potential falls from cliffs or seductive waterfalls.

In Rocky Mountain National Park, the very altitude can be deadly. Rocky is a high elevation, vertical park! In the history of the park, heart attacks are the second leading cause of death, with 72 fatalities—or close to 24 percent of the total. If you or somebody in your group is elderly or on heart or blood pressure medication, go first to chapter five. No wait! Buy this book first, then go home—or to your hotel or campsite—and then turn to chapter five. You need to understand that in Estes Park you are at 7,522 feet (2,293 meters) above sea level; in Grand Lake you are at 8,437 feet (2,572 meters). Everything in the park goes up from there, and the reduced air pressure taxes basic biological functions. Predictable? Indeed.

People die in national parks, and there have been a number of lawsuits filed against the government for negligence and failure to sign, post, block off, fence, or close every possible hazard in the park. Fortunately, the federal courts have found that to do so would destroy the very purpose for which most national parks were established. That purpose is to preserve a piece of land as it always has been for future generations. Therefore, visitors need to visit a park on the park's terms. This does not make the hazards go away. What the courts also determined is that the National Park Service must make a reasonable effort to educate visitors and draw attention to potential hazards. In parks, this test is met through information at trailhead bulletin boards, the park's free newspaper, and information provided at visitor centers and on websites. That information is based on an analysis of the accidents and fatalities that have occurred over the years.

This book supplements the safety information provided by the park with real accounts of death and despair in Rocky Mountain National Park. Hopefully, this will encourage you to make wise decisions.

The background for these incidents comes from several sources. Rocky Mountain National Park was established in 1915, by which time superintendents were required to submit a monthly report of activities in their park to their superiors in Washington. This practice continued in to the 1960s. However, many of the early reports of a fatality are a sentence or two with minimal detail. The Colorado Mountain Club and the American Alpine Club have publications that were excellent sources of information. Local newspapers were well established prior to the creation of the park and provide a rich lode of information as a supplement to the more reliable sources of information. Background on more recent incidents was found in park press releases and Case Incident Reports available through the Freedom of Information Act (FOIA) process, as well as interviews with gracefully aging national park rangers. Despite these resources, I sometimes felt that piecing snippets of information together left me exposed to what I was certain was an inadequate story, so they are not all told here in detail. Some fatalities involve several pages. Some are briefly mentioned in the tables attached to most chapters. My degree of confidence in accurately listing all the known fatalities is in the high 90th percentiles. However, I am reasonably certain there are some deaths that I missed because the incident occurred in the park but the victim was whisked away in a helicopter or ambulance to a hospital, only to die later of complications. These need to be included in this narrative, as the original accident occurred in the park and is relevant to the prevention of further incidents. If you know of such a case, or if I missed someone, or you want to comment on a particular incident, please feel free to email me at rmnpfatalities@gmail.com.

In revisiting these incidents, I realize that I risk offending friends or relatives linked to a specific case. I apologize in advance if my narrative does not follow a particular script or touches certain sensitivities. My intention is not to fix blame. My interest is for the reader to understand decisions or circumstances that led to the fatal error and to prevent further fatalities. The challenge is to describe these incidents objectively by deciphering the information available.

When digesting the statistics in this book, I also encourage you to keep in mind that approximately three million visitors come to the park each year. On average, three people will die for assorted reasons. So, statistically, the park is a safe environment.

For each fatality, however, there are on average ten to fifteen large search and rescue (SAR) incidents and an average of one hundred minor SAR or medical incidents in which responders risk their lives to save the life of another, often in challenging conditions. A book of this nature would not be complete without a nod to those who provide the emergency response in the park. There is not a specific team in the park lounging around waiting for a search or rescue incident. There are trained people with primary jobs that are disrupted to respond to an incident. They are supported by excellent volunteer search and rescue organizations outside the park. While we may marvel at the technological toys at our disposal, such as cell phones, GPS units, and helicopters, a successful rescue still often comes down to the sweat and hard work of these many dedicated individuals.

Sprinkled throughout this book are a number of stories about people who have been given a "second chance" by the extraordinary efforts of trained staff and volunteers, blind luck, or a pretty good decision. A classic example of this is the story of the Villano rescue in chapter two, in which that fickle lady, "mother nature," failed to cooperate. Harsh weather prevented the use of a helicopter, resulting in a forty hour litter lowering and carry-out from above the Keyhole Route on Longs Peak.

The purpose of this book is to prevent death or injury to visitors and reduce the dangerous situations in which rescuers often find themselves. Similar books have been written for Grand Canyon, Yosemite and Yellowstone National Parks with the same objectives. Today, there is a sense among the park staff in Grand Canyon that the number and severity of incidents have decreased since the publication of *Over the Edge: Death in Grand Canyon* in 2001. I hope the same can be said for this book in ten years. If just one life is saved or a major search or rescue averted as a result of this book, then the hours of putting it together will have been worth it.

Please pay attention, reader. The National Park Service provides excellent information on park conditions and potential problems or dangers. Make use of it. Cell phones, GPS units, and other modern communications are helpful, but they are ultimately no substitute for adequate preparedness, proper equipment, good judgment, and common sense. That is up to you. This is a book about life, not death. By reading these stories about death, I hope you will learn to pay closer attention to the safety messages provided in national parks—and, just maybe, stay alive.

A Bit of History

The setting for the stories in this book is, of course, Rocky Mountain National Park, 415 square miles of alpine beauty anchored by Longs Peak. Before the park was established, many people contributed to the development of the park and surrounding areas. It is important to understand these early pioneers and the foundations they laid. It is also important to understand that change is inevitable, and is generally for the good. In that spirit, I have provided this summary of events in and around Rocky Mountain National Park over the decades. Woven within this history, I have included a parallel track on the development of emergency services: law enforcement, search and rescue, and emergency medicine, as practiced by a long and noble line of both national park rangers and local emergency responders. This background is intended to provide a foundation for the reader's understanding of park history and the current role and responsibilities of the national park ranger.

The prominent summits of Mt. Meeker and Longs Peak served as skyline landmarks for the Native Americans in the area. French fur trappers in 1799 referred to the twin peaks as *Les Deux Oreilles* or the Two Ears. Longs Peak is named for Major Stephen H. Long, whose expedition observed and recorded the peak from the eastern plains on June 30, 1820. Long's party did not venture into the mountain area and did not name the peak in its records. However, the name "Long's Peak" began showing up on maps as early as 1825, and the name stuck. At some point, the apostrophe was dropped. In the decades after Long's expedition, only the occasional hunter, trapper, or prospector likely wandered in or near the area. They left no mark and little record.

It was the most recent rumor of gold that brought Missourian Joel Estes and his family to Colorado in 1859. Seeing no future in mining, he settled in the Fort Lupton area, north of Denver, in late September. In mid October, Estes and his twelve-year-old son, Milton, traveled west on a hunting and prospecting trip. Originally thinking they had come to the better known North Park area (present-day Walden), they soon realized their mistake, as they found "no signs that white men had ever been there before us." Returning the next year, Estes built two log cabins and drove a herd of cattle up to the verdant mountain pastures. His family supplemented their income by hunting the abundant elk and deer and selling the meat and hides in the Denver market.

In 1864, Estes was visited by William N. Byers, the flamboyant editor of the *Rocky Mountain News*. It was his subsequent articles that attached Joel Estes' name to the Estes Valley. By 1866, Estes realized the long, hard winters were not conducive to cattle ranching, and he sold his homestead and moved to southern Colorado. Joel Estes died in 1875 in Farmington, New Mexico, at the age of 69. While credited as the region's discoverer, he and his family were not alone. In the Grand Lake area, on the west side of what is now the national park, Phillip Crenshaw, another Missourian, built a cabin around 1857 and ran a trap line for several years before returning to Missouri. In 1864, prospector Alonzo Allen homesteaded southeast of Longs Peak near the present community of Allenspark.

William N. Byers' trip in 1864 was the first indication of the potential for tourism in the area, as the editor's interest was in climbing the west peak (Longs Peak). Unable to find a route to the summit, Byers and his party climbed the east peak (Mt. Meeker). Gazing across at Longs, Byers later wrote, "We are quite sure that no living creature, unless it had wings to fly, was ever upon its summit. We believe we run no risk in predicting that no man ever will be, though it is barely possible that the ascent can be made." It is commonly believed that Major John Wesley Powell and his party were the first Europeans to reach the summit of Longs Peak in 1868. However, there is some evidence that the one armed veteran of the Civil War was not the first. The basis is found in references by many local residents, into the 1860s, who still referred to Longs Peak as the west peak and Mt. Meeker as the east peak. Byers himself, in his newspaper account of his September 1864 trip, wrote, "we were on the summit of the east peak as high as any one has ever gone ... while the main or west peak still towered hundreds of feet above our heads."

Possibly in response to Byers' 1864 newspaper account, a convincing and detailed letter from one J.W. Goss was printed in the *Rocky Mountain News* on July 12, 1865. The letter was titled "The West Peak Climbers." Goss was a prominent settler in the St. Vrain Valley and described as "one of Boulder County's honored and respected citizens." His summit partner, Robert J. Woodward, also ranched near Boulder and later served as postmaster and county superintendent. These gentlemen were not likely to be weavers of exaggerated tales.

Goss wrote that a group of seven men had traveled to the Estes Valley area and began a climb on June 16, 1865. They advanced as far as what was probably the Boulderfield before being forced by bad weather to retreat. Finally, on June 19th, Goss and Woodward claimed to have made the summit via a route that by its description would be similar to the present-day Keyhole Route. Some historians feel Goss and Woodward deserve recognition as the first to the summit. Unfortunately, they left no evidence of their climb.

What is interesting is that William Byers accompanied Powell on his 1868 ascent after tempting Powell with the honor of a first ascent. It appears Byers had conveniently forgotten the Goss story he had published in his own newspaper! Nevertheless, Powell's party bushwhacked east from Grand Lake through the blowdown and trailless area, and likely made the first ascents of Mt. Alice (13,310 ft.) and Chiefs Head Peak (13,579 ft.) en route to Longs Peak. Led by Lewis Keplinger, a student member of the expedition, the party topped out from the south side of the peak on August 23, 1868. They are still credited with the first ascent. The couloir or gully that Keplinger discovered is known today as Keplinger's Couloir. Two years later, Donald Brown is believed to have made the first solo ascent of the Keyhole Route, the route that thousands of hikers ascend today.

The east peak, or Mt. Meeker, was not named as such until 1873, when members of the F. W. Hayden Survey suggested it. This group included Anna Dickinson, the ever-present William N. Byers, and Ralph Meeker, the son of Nathan Meeker. As historic snippets suggest, this group had just made a successful ascent of Longs Peak in September of 1873.

That evening, they were enjoying a large campfire when the idea came up to name a summit for Nathan Meeker, Ralph's father. In 1869, Nathan Meeker was the agricultural editor for the *New York Tribune*. In that year, he came to Colorado and developed a farming community to experiment with his theories of cooperative agriculture. This successful community became Greeley, in honor of Meeker's boss, Horace Greeley.

The first woman thought to have reached the summit of Longs Peak was Addie Alexander in 1871. Little is known of St. Louis–born Alexander, though three separate newspaper accounts from the *Boulder County News* (8/26/1871), *Rocky Mountain News* (8/9/1873), and the *Greeley Colorado Sun* (8/14/1873) give her credit. She was in a party led by Mr. Al Dunbar of Estes Park. The better known Anna Dickinson and Isabella Bird both claimed the peak in 1873 with different groups, but on the same route through the Keyhole. Bird's narrative of her ascent in *A Lady's Life in the Rocky Mountains* is still recognized as classic travel literature today. Dickinson's ascent was also well publicized, as she accompanied the F.W. Hayden Survey to the summit on September 13th.

What is noteworthy about Dickinson, and the unfortunate Carrie Welton and Agnes Vaille, is the character thread common to them and other women of the mountains. They believed they could do anything a man could and deliberately pursued mountain adventures. One reflection of this spirit is the report in the September 6, 1873, *Rocky Mountain News*, which reviewed a speech by Dickinson wherein she stated, "Women are the chief obstacles to themselves. She seldom looks to the future. She lets that take care of itself. But if her determination is different, if she thinks like a man and acts like a man regarding her daily labor, her remuneration and success will be the same as a man's." Kudos to Dickinson, who also wore practical but scandalous trousers on her climb!

In researching this book, I became better acquainted with the Reverend Elkanah J. Lamb, who deserves to be mentioned in the same light as Joel Estes and Enos Mills as influential pioneers. Lamb was foremost a fire breathing preacher, but he also had a passion for nature and the benefits of outdoor experiences. He first climbed Longs Peak via the Keyhole in 1871. While making the first descent of the East Face from the summit, he had a near-death experience. Working his way down the Notch Couloir, then across what is now called Broadway, he faced the 1,000-foot-high ice and snow–covered gash that would soon bear his name. Lamb wrote, "Trying to get a hold of the rock wall with my fingers, just my feet pressing the ice, my grip and foothold failed and down I went with almost an arrow's rapidity. An eternity of thought, of life, death, wife and home concentrated in my mind in those two seconds." Fortunately, he was able to catch himself before gaining too much speed and, using his pocketknife as an ice axe, was able to traverse to safety. For his mishap, the prominent ice chute east of Mills Glacier was later named Lambs Slide. Lamb returned to the area in 1875 and homesteaded in the Tahosa Valley. He called it the Longs Peak House. He supplemented his ranch and his preaching by guiding on the peak. He charged $5, roughly $80 in today's money. Of his budding guide business, he offered, "If they would not pay for spiritual guidance, I compelled them to divide for material elevation." Elkanah Lamb sold the Longs Peak House to Enos Mills in 1902. Lamb then built his final house on the northern edge of Tahosa Valley near today's Wind River Ranch. He died on April 9, 1915, at the age of 83.

Elkanah Lambs' son Carlyle was born October 24, 1862, in Guthrie, Iowa. Carlyle made his first Longs Peak climb in 1879 at the age of sixteen. Over 56 years, Carlyle made it to the top 146 times. He was the guide on the area's first two recorded fatalities. In 1884, Carrie Welton died of exposure, and in 1889 Frank Stryker accidently shot himself. Carlyle deserves recognition as the mountain's first rescue provider. Both Welton and Stryker were still alive when Carlyle was forced to leave them to summon help. In both instances, young Carlyle set the example for today's rescuers with extraordinary feats of physical stamina and strength in trying to assist others. He last made the summit in 1935.

Enos Mills was born in Kansas in 1870 and moved to Colorado for his health in 1884. The next year, while working for his uncle, the Rev. Elkanah Lamb, the fifteen year old made his first ascent of Longs Peak. As noted above, Lamb sold his ranch in 1902 to Mills, who renamed the ranch The Longs Peak Inn. Mills' plan was to improve the guiding business by providing an interpretive focus on features of special interest. He made over forty trips to the summit in various weather and seasons to educate himself about the subtleties of the mountain. Mills ultimately stood atop Longs Peak over three hundred times. In 1906, his last year of guiding, he was believed to have climbed Longs 32 times during the month of August, including six ascents by moonlight.

Remarkable, considering Mills was likely preoccupied with rebuilding his lodge that year after a devastating fire. The main building burned again in 1949. The site and remaining buildings were purchased by the Salvation Army in the early 1990s as a retreat center. Some of the old buildings still stand, including the ten-room Forest Cabin built in 1908, but the grounds are not open to the public. Mills is known as the "Father of Rocky Mountain National Park." His leadership, passion and foresight led to the creation of the national park in 1915.

January 15, 1915 - Rocky Mountain National Park established
July 26, 1915 - Richard "Dixie" MacCracken begins as Rocky Mountain National Park's first national park ranger.
August 25, 1916 - The National Park Service is established as an agency in the Department of Interior.

A side story relating to the establishment of the park was the effort to understand the Native American use of the region. Native Americans used the area for hunting and commerce. There was little evidence of their time here, however, as it was primarily a summer seasonal use. The harsh winter winds and snow discouraged year-round occupation of the area. In 1912, as the battle to create Rocky Mountain National Park was heating up, the newly formed Colorado Mountain Club threw their support behind Mills. It was noticed that the maps used to impress Congress

Ranger Dixie MacCracken of Rocky Mountain National Park. Courtesy of RMNP

were generally devoid of names for topographic features. To remedy this, the club formed a committee to research names connected with early Colorado history. Miss Harriet Vaille and Miss Edna Hendrie were tasked with researching Indian names. Current books were inadequate, so the two women elected to go straight to the source! Through the club, they organized a camping trip and arranged for a small party of elder Arapahoes to come to the park area for a two-week visit. The guests came from the Wind River Reservation in Wyoming and had hunted and lived in the Estes Valley in their youth.

Through an interpreter, Sherman Sage and Gun Griswold offered many stories and names for features. A popular story that Gun shared was of how his father caught eagles for their feathers on the summit of Longs Peak by setting out tallow and hiding in an oval-shaped hole. Guns' father had climbed to the summit from the south side, as Powell's party later did in 1868. Today, over thirty names of Indian origin have been affixed to mountains, trails, lakes, and other landforms in the park.

The 1910s, '20s, and early '30s were the golden era for the mountain guide. Shep Husted guided for Mills for several years. Over his time in the park, he is credited with reaching the summit 350 times. Almost all of the trips were via the Keyhole Route. In response to the Agnes Vaille tragedy, Superintendent Roger Toll had ranger Jack Moomaw put up the Cables Route on the North Face in 1926. This became the preferred ascent route for many years, with the descent by way of the Keyhole Route. The cables were removed in 1973, as a result of the Wilderness Preservation Act of 1964. The Wilderness Act challenged managers to reevaluate man-made objects in wilderness. The cables tended to make it easier to summit Longs Peak and allowed ill-prepared visitors to potentially get in harm's way. Despite some public opposition, the decision to remove the cables has stood the test of time.

Since it was first gazed upon, the East Face of Longs Peak was considered unclimbable. Several Colorado climbers, however, were determined to attempt it in September 1922. Unfortunately, they were scooped by James W. Alexander. The September 8, 1922, front page of the *Rocky Mountain News* declared, "For the first time in history, the sheer precipice which rises 2,200 feet on the east side of Longs Peak from the waters of Chasm Lake has been scaled." The previous day, the mathematics professor from Princeton University had climbed alone. "In crossing the glacier at the foot of the precipice, Professor Alexander was required to cut seventy-six steps in the ice and from then on completed his climb by clinging to the small projections of the rock in constant peril. ... Climbing the face of the precipice is a task which has always been the subject of much discussion among mountaineers in the park, many old-timers and guides claiming that the feat was impossible." Two days later on September 9th, Alexander repeated the perilous climb with park ranger Jack Moomaw.

I would like to draw your attention to a pattern starting to emerge of the "impossible" being subsequently conquered. Parallel to this, the concepts of tourism, adventure, and National Parks began to compliment each other after the turn of the twentieth century. Remember, in 1864 William Byers wrote that Longs Peak would never be climbed. It was a mere four years later that Powell and Byers himself stood on the summit. The East Face of Longs was considered impossible to climb, yet Alexander paved the first of many new routes in 1922. In 1927, German emigrants Joe and Paul Stettner pioneered their Stettner Ledges Route, which was the standard for difficult routes for decades. Their climbing techniques were well beyond most Colorado climbers at the time. The brothers used pitons and carabiners and knew how to belay each other.

Other notable events during this era:

- 1902 - The American Alpine Club is formed.
- 1907 - A 24 horsepower helicopter is first flown in France.
- 1912 - The Colorado Mountain Club is formed.

By the late 1920s, many visitors and climbers were becoming more comfortable with topping the summit of 14,259-foot Longs Peak without a guide. In the 1930s, major events in the park were the construction of the Trail Ridge Road, the drilling of the water diversion tunnel under the park, and the exceptional work done by the Civilian Conservation Corp (CCC) during the Depression.

World War II accelerated the development of mountaineering equipment and techniques through the formation of the Army's legendary Tenth Mountain Division. Dozens of rangers and climbers alike responded. The Stettner brothers joined up. Other noted mountaineers were Brad Washburn, Bill House, Bob Bates, Terris Moore, Dick Leonard, and James Ford. Rangers such as Dick and Doug McLaren, Ernie Fields, Bob Frauson, Bob Weldon, Laury Brown, and Bob Bendt also answered the Army's call for "men able to pass a night in the winter woods without dying of exposure or fright." Ranger "Pat" Patterson became the director of the 87th Mountaineering School at 9,000-foot Camp Hale in Colorado. Classified "secret" by the military when first written, *The Manual of American Mountaineering* by Ken Henderson of the American Alpine Club became the climber's Bible for decades. However, the war's single greatest contribution to mountain rescue was the nylon rope. The halt in Philippine hemp manufacture dictated an emergency substitute for the old Manila line. The Plymouth Cordage Company tested the new synthetic; it stretched 39 percent before breaking. The 7/16-inch diameter, 120-foot length was adopted—and is still the standard today. As author and retired ranger Butch Farabee wrote in his book *Death, Daring and Disaster*, "the 10th Mountain Division members are heroes. Paying the supreme sacrifice, 990 of them never made it home; the legacy they leave, however, endures. Every time a lost child is reunited with a terrified mother or a careless climber is given a second chance, the specter of the legendary Mountain Troops is there."

After the war, Americans rekindled their love affair with their national parks. In 1948, Rocky Mountain National Park exceeded one million visitors for the first time. Unfortunately, this milestone also ushered in more fatalities and injuries in the park. From Carrie Welton's death in 1884 to 1941, a period of 57 years, 50 lives were lost in the park. It took only 17 years for the next 50 to die.

Notable advances in the search and rescue community from this period:

- 1940 - Ranger Ernie Fields established the first mountain rescue cache in Rocky Mountain National Park.

1940s Rocky Mountain National Park rescue cache. Courtesy of RMNP

- 1947 - Boulder (county) Rescue in Colorado was one of the first volunteer mountain rescue teams in the country to organize. This was the nucleus for today's Rocky Mountain Rescue Group.
- 1948 - Mt. Rainier hosts the National Park Service's first mountain rescue training.
- 1959 - The Mountain Rescue Association (MRA) is formed, with Mt. Rainier NP an original member. Rocky Mountain NP joined in 1966 and Yosemite NP in 1967. By 1997, there were thirteen national parks serving as ex-officio members.

Back at Rocky Mountain National Park, the last great "impossible" to be conquered was the sheer, 800-foot over-hanging face of the Diamond on Longs Peak. At a reunion event in 1991, well-known 1930s Longs Peak guide Hull

1964 - Rangers Tom Griffiths and Ernie Kuncl practice litter lowering on Mills Glacier below East Face of Longs Peak. Photo courtesy of Tom Griffiths

Cook shared, "we (the guides) loved the Diamond as beautiful scenery. The idea of climbing it never occurred to us. We wanted to stay alive!" Yet, the Diamond would not be denied. As climbing skills and techniques continued to develop through the 1950s, the pressure mounted on the park to allow a first attempt. For years, the National Park Service refused to permit such a climb, because of the real inability to rescue anyone hurt or stuck. Finally, in July 1960, the park issued a first permit. A critical condition of the permit was that the climbers had to prearrange a support/rescue team on their own. As with many things in life, timing is everything. Californians Bob Kamps and Dave Rearick were in the park climbing when they heard the rumor of the possible permit. They were first in line and, with the help of several locals, set up their support group and received a permit on July 27, 1960. On August 1st, they began a successful 2½-day climb on the Diamond. They called their new route the Ace of Diamonds; it is now commonly known as "D1." Today, there are dozens of established routes on the 800-foot face. Some of the best climbers can now do the route pioneered by Kamps and Rearick in a matter of hours without artificial climbing aids—a measure of the evolution of climbing skills. To many people, this type of climbing activity may seem foolhardy and reckless. However, climbers account for a very small percentage of fatalities and injuries in the park.

Twenty years after the park exceeded one million visitors in 1948, visitation passed two million. The thought that national parks were being "loved to death" started to gain traction, and the old ways of rangering were about to be turned upside down. During the summer of 1970, riots broke out in Yosemite Valley. The violence exposed the need for a professional law enforcement program in the National Park Service.

In 1976, the General Authorities Act was passed by Congress that codified the authority of national park rangers to carry firearms and make arrests, execute warrants, and conduct investigations in order to *"maintain law and order and protect persons and property within areas of the National Park System."* Gone were the days of the service revolver being carried in the glove box or briefcase. Today's new rangers attend a 21-week training course at the Federal Law Enforcement Training Center in Georgia, followed by an 11-week field training assignment, and are required to attend forty hours of law enforcement refresher training each year. This is a good thing.

Similar pressures from escalating visitation were being felt in other parks and in other ranger program areas, most notably in search and rescue (SAR) and emergency medical services (EMS). For example, the evolution of EMS can be traced from the classic story told by ranger Bob Sellers after a body recovery at Mt. Rainier NP in 1961: "Jack Morehead was the smallest among us, so he was unanimously elected to be belayed under the snow to the bottom of the waterfall. ... He found the victim, so we tied him in and we hauled Jack up. He (Morehead) was totally miserable and in the early stages of hypothermia but in those days we didn't know what to call his condition. We did know he needed a hot bath and a stiff drink." It was not until 1968 that rangers started to receive advanced medical training. Coordinated by Mt. Everest climber and former Rocky Mountain NP seasonal ranger Dr. Tom Hornbein, rangers at Mt. Rainier National Park were taught a 110-hour course in "Winter Survival and Medical Emergencies—Advanced Shock Treatment." Similar training was initiated that same year for Rocky Mountain National Park rangers following the epic winter rescue of Dick Kezlan. In 1972, 23 NPS rangers graduated from the agency's first EMT course—a 100-hour program taught by Vietnam-experienced Navy corpsmen at North Carolina's Camp Lejeune. In 1978, the now well-established park medic program was first taught at California's Fresno Valley Medical Center. Sequoia/Kings Canyon ranger John Chew and Yosemite ranger Butch Farabee deserve recognition for nurturing the development of this course. Countless meetings with ranger and hospital staff were necessary to develop protocol and establish a training agenda to address the needs of rangers in the field.

In the search and rescue community, significant strides to improve safety and training were made during the 1970s and '80s. Some examples are:

- 1970 - The National Association of Search and Rescue (NASAR) was formed, with ranger Bill Pierce elected president.

- 1972 - The American Rescue Dog Association was established.
- 1976 - The first SAR management team was used in California's Lassen National Park. Ranger Dick McLaren was SAR Boss.
- 1979 - Larimer County (Colorado) Search and Rescue was incorporated.
- 1979 - A Memorandum of Understanding was signed by the United States, Soviet Union, Canada, and France for the joint formation of a satellite system for locating downed aircraft.
- 1984 - The first North American Technical Rescue Symposium was held at South Lake Tahoe.

Modern technology would soon enter the backcountry.
- 1990s - Visitor reliance on cell phones was noted as one of the most significant technological impacts witnessed by park rangers.
- 2003 - Personal locator beacons, which send distress signals to government satellites, became legal for the public to use. Today, they can be rented or bought for less than $100. The last few years has also seen a marked increase in the use of hand-held Global Positioning System (GPS) units.

In theory, with GPS and cell phone a lost or injured hiker should be able to direct searchers right to their location. Then again, the reliance on technology may contribute to overconfidence and lack of preparedness and cause the problem in the first place.

So where does this leave us? Over the last fifteen years, annual visitation to Rocky Mountain National Park has hovered around three million visitors. It is inevitable that some visitors will get hurt, break a law, or need assistance. As I used to tell rangers new to the park that the mission of the national park ranger hasn't changed in over ninety years. The fundamental responsibility is still to "Protect the park from visitors; protect visitors from the park; and protect visitors from each other."

What has changed is how rangers go about their business. In this chapter, I have touched upon the development of visitor use in the park and

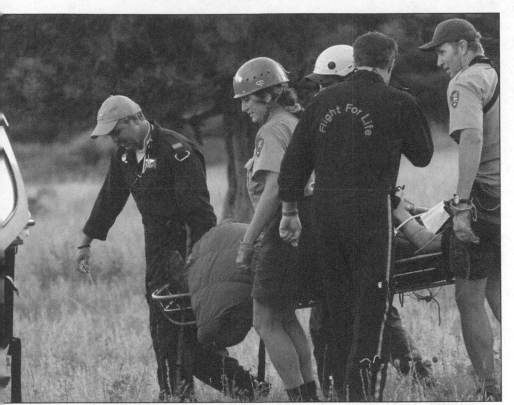

Lumpy Ridge rescue in 2005. Loading victim in helicopter. Photo courtesy of Walt Hester

the parallel developments in emergency services. Over the years, Rocky Mountain National Park has hired and will continue to hire staff with strong law enforcement, search and rescue, and emergency medical services skills. While park rangers are prepared and willing to help those in need, the fundamental responsibility for a safe, enjoyable visit still lies with you, the park visitor.

I recommend you take a moment to turn to the chapter titled "Safety Tips" at the end of this book. This chapter provides some basic concepts to help ensure a safe visit to the park. They have been developed by park staff based on years of experience in analyzing why and how visitors get in trouble. They are relevant for use on all public lands. I believe that reading these recommendations now will make better sense when you begin to read the stories of *Death, Despair, and Second Chances in Rocky Mountain National Park.*

ONE

National Park Service Employees

"You know, if I ever die while at work in the mountains, do not cry for me because you will know that I died doing what I love. But if I die in a car accident on my way to an office job, then cry for me because you will know I was miserable and not doing what I loved."

Ranger Jeff Christensen shared these words with a special friend. Seemingly innocent at the time, Jeff's words were, in turn, graciously passed on to Jeff's parents in their time of need. They, in turn, shared them with the park staff and incident management team during the extensive search effort for Jeff. Jeff Christensen died in the mountains he loved on July 29, 2005, while on backcountry patrol as a Rocky Mountain National Park Ranger. He was 31 years old.

Jeff grew up in Minnesota and graduated from the University of Minnesota in 1998 with a Bachelor of Arts degree in history. Seeking quality of life and with few obligations, he gravitated to Colorado with thoughts of being a ski bum for a while. He wound up at Winter Park Resort where he became a ski patrolman. Like many other young folks, he migrated up the valley to work summers in Rocky Mountain National Park. His first summer, Jeff worked in the maintenance division. During the autumn of 2001, he went to a seasonal law enforcement training school for national park rangers in Santa Rosa, California. He was subsequently hired into a seasonal law enforcement ranger position on the west side of the park for the summers of 2002, 2003, and 2004. Jeff was enjoying a life remarkably similar to that of many park rangers before him. Ski patrol in the winter, park ranger in the summer, with a few weeks off between seasons to play and travel. Jeff was even able to buy a small condo at Winter Park as an investment and winter home. Like many before him, at some point Jeff would have found a way to get hired as a permanent park ranger. There would have been support for such a move.

What set Jeff apart and made him a good candidate for a future permanent ranger position was his humble appreciation of life. Jeff certainly was occasionally overwhelmed with the "wah-hoo!" effect, as when skiing the deep powder at sunrise at Winter Park, but he also appreciated the poetry and rhythm of the experience. Similarly, while working as a ranger, he understood that it was a privilege, not a right, to work in a national park. He understood the importance of assisting visitors and the value of protecting parks for future generations, while appreciating the peace of mountaintops and the effort to get there. Most of all, Jeff enjoyed a good beer, a good joke, and the camaraderie of those working in the service of others.

Ranger Jeff Christensen. Courtesy of RMNP

The summer of 2005 was Jeff's first summer on the east side of the park. A friendly jest in the park is that the Grand Lake or west side is "the wetter, better side." True, but the east side is where a majority of the emergency response incidents occur, and Jeff wanted to sharpen his skills and learn more about the park. On July 29th, Jeff was assigned to do a backcountry patrol in the Chapin Pass area off the Fall River Road. He spent the first couple hours of his shift cleaning up the inevitable paperwork associated with law enforcement responsibilities. By 10:30 a.m., he was being shuttled to the trailhead by ranger Melissa Streator. Jeff was not totally familiar with this particular area and questioned Streator about his proposed route. He had originally intended an ambitious 22-mile route across the Mummy Range to Lost Lake, then down the north fork of the Big Thompson River drainage. Due to the late start, Streator convinced Jeff that a more reasonable route would be over the summits of Mt. Chiquita and Ypsilon Mountain to Lawn Lake, then down to the trailhead. Jeff had recently completed a two-day patrol to the Lawn Lake area, so he was familiar with that part of the proposed route.

Though shorter, this was still an ambitious hike, considering the late start. The route requires hikers to traverse the Mummy Range, including the summits of Chiquita, Ypsilon, and Fairchild. The average height of these peaks is 13,255 feet. Upon parting, Christensen told Streator that he hoped to be out by the end of his shift (4:30 p.m.) for personal business. Streator shared that 5:30 p.m. might be more realistic and she would notify the evening patrol shift about a trailhead pickup for him. By 11:00 a.m., Jeff was on the trail. The weather was clear with light winds.

When Jeff failed to check in for a trailhead pickup that evening, his fellow rangers began a passive search effort at trailheads, his residence and other likely locations. Initial search teams were sent into the field the next day and were unsuccessful in contacting Jeff. Veteran rescuers often get a sense of how an incident may or may not develop. That evening, many on the park staff had an uncomfortable feeling about why Jeff was still missing. With emotions starting to simmer, and it being the height of the summer tourist season, the decision was made to bring in an incident management team headed by Eddie Lopez to manage the search and coordinate with other park operations. This decision was based in part on the lessons learned from the search for ranger Randy Morgenson years earlier in Sequoia National Park. It was thought that managing this search with local ranger staff, who were close to Jeff, could influence objectivity and affect safety. By day two, the search morphed into a massive effort that ultimately involved close to 100 searchers, dog teams, and five helicopters. Despite this effort, Jeff's body was not found until Saturday, August 6th, and that was by three visitors out on a day hike.

In reviewing the available evidence, it appears that Jeff bypassed Mt. Chapin and likely went to the summit of Mt. Chiquita. He then descended one of the north gullies that run east from the saddle between Mt. Chiquita and Ypsilon Mountain. This is an area of relatively easy terrain, but rarely travelled. At some point, he likely slipped, fell, or tumbled and sustained the injury to his head that ultimately led to his death. He also bruised his hip, cut his wrist, tore his clothing and had numerous scrapes and lacerations, indicating a significant fall. The evidence indicated that after his fall he reached into his pack to remove a T-shirt, which he wrapped around his head to stop the bleeding. He then walked to the location where he was discovered. The time window between when he fell and actually lost consciousness could not be determined. According to the Larimer County coroner, in addition to the non-life-threatening injuries, Jeff suffered a left temporal skull fracture that led to a subdural hematoma or significant internal bleeding inside the head. This increased pressure on the brain eventually renders a person unconscious and leads to death. The coroner placed the time of the injury at approximately 4:00 p.m. to 8:00 p.m., with the time of death between 6:00 p.m. and midnight of July 29, 2005, the same day he left the trailhead. As noted, he was not found until August 6th.

Two significant episodes of rain passed through the area during the search and washed away potential evidence, so how far he walked and the exact location of the accident will probably never be known. What is known is that ranger Jeff Christensen was well liked and respected by his peers and supervisors. He died doing what he loved to do.

At Jeff's memorial service following the recovery of his body, Chief Ranger Mark Magnuson offered a fitting tribute to a fallen ranger:

We are rangers. We walk the last of the wild lands, patrolling the interface between man and nature. Ours is the world of the sun and sky, cloud and storm. Ours is the world of flower and tree, rock and mountain. We rest by the waterfall and cool our feet in the deep pools of the glen. The elk and deer, the coyote and fox, our silent companions. The hawk and eagle follow us by day; the owl leads us by night.

We are rangers. We travel alone, silent caretakers of a world fast disappearing. It is not our job; rather it is our honor, to behold that which nature has bestowed upon us. It is not our job; rather it is our privilege, to play some small part in preserving this beauty for our children and their children beyond them. We travel alone, there are few of us, and the task which lies before us is enormous. Some say we face risk, even unnecessary risk, but in our hearts we know that it is nothing compared to the loss of the wilderness. It is nothing compared to the loss of the bear, the cougar, and the wolf. We risk all to protect that which endures beyond our individual selves, that which we love beyond all else.

We are rangers. We treat our fellow man with respect. We understand those who seek solitude in the wild places. We are teachers to those who wish to tread for the first time on ground made of dirt rather than concrete. We watch in delight at the smile of the visitor who first substitutes the canyons of skyscrapers for that of massive cliffs.

We feel the excitement of the family who first hears the bugle of the elk, the child who sees the bighorn ram, and the grandmother who reviews her life while sitting by the flowing stream.

We are rangers. We keep those who would harm the land as well as those who would harm their fellow man at bay. We care for the sick, search for the lost, and assist those who cannot assist themselves. Sometimes we bring home those who would not otherwise return.

Jeff Christensen was a ranger. He was one of us. We could not feel more honored. Jeff knew who he was. "If I ever die while at work in the mountains, do not cry for me because you will know that I died doing what I love." Those were Jeff's precious words, given as a gift to his parents. Those of us who walk the last of the wild lands will not cry for him. We will see him as the sun rises above the peaks. We will hear him as the wind in the trees. We will taste the cold mountain water cascading in the streams and remember him. We will know when the coyote calls that it is Jeff, reminding us all that we are rangers.

John Muir said "Climb the mountains and get their good tidings. Nature's peace will flow into you as sunshine flows into trees. The winds blow their own freshness into you and the storms their energy, while cares will drop off like autumn leaves." We will listen to these words and we will do their bidding. Jeff, we do not say good-bye, for the ranger in you will live forever.

After each fatality or major search or rescue incident, a post incident review is held. The primary purpose is to review the park's response to the incident and to attempt to draw conclusions as to why the accident occurred and critique the response. As Jeff was an on-duty, government employee, his death drew extra scrutiny from a team of experts within the National Park Service. This team found actions and behavior which may have contributed to this accident. Listed below are those relevant to the safety messages provided to the public by the park staff and emphasized in this book:

1. **Let someone know where you are going, what route you are taking, and what you plan to do.** Ranger Christensen changed his intended route, and the park staff did not know this. Why Jeff had not attempted to report by radio his fall and injuries, or even his location, remains uncertain. Radio reception in the area was good and Jeff's park-issued radio, evaluated after the accident by a qualified radio technician from outside the NPS, was found to be in good working condition. It may not have prevented his death, but it could have narrowed the search area. He possibly could have been found sooner and fewer people exposed to dangerous terrain during the search. Many park visitors enjoy hiking alone. This is okay! While cell phones are a good item to have in a pack, the cell coverage in the park is still spotty, and cell phones/GPS units should not be relied upon. Again, let someone know your plans and stick with them.

2. **Understand your route and the conditions you may encounter.** Hikers are often late, as they underestimate their trip. Jeff's original route was overly ambitious, and he got a late start. Ranger Streator wisely convinced him to pick a more modest route. There are several publications providing information on hikes and climbs in the park. The

park's Backcountry Permits Office and visitor centers are open daily and provide excellent information on day hikes, as well as overnight trips. Once you have determined your route and shared it with someone, stick to it. Each year, the ranger staff receives numerous "overdue hiker" calls from concerned friends. More often than not, the tired hiker or climber shows up late. This also is okay. I can assure you that the rangers in Rocky Mountain National Park would rather have someone report an overdue friend than not call and delay the start of a potential search effort.

3. **Consider the risk you may be putting others in by the results of your actions and decisions.** The search for Jeff Christensen also illustrates the difficulty of finding a missing person in the rugged terrain of the park. As noted later in chapter thirteen, there are a handful of lost people who have never been found. In spite of dozens of searchers, five helicopters, search dogs, and modern GPS-based search tools, Jeff was found by three hikers not associated with the search effort. The point is that countless people risked their own lives searching for Jeff in the same rugged terrain. There is a point where one needs to decide that one is indeed lost. The wisest decision is to hunker down, engage in a survival strategy, and wait to be rescued. This has repeatedly proven safer for the lost person, as well as the rescuers.

Ranger Jeff Christensen was the first Rocky Mountain National Park ranger to die while patrolling the backcountry of the park.

The work of park rangers, however, is but one of many park functions and responsibilities, such as campground management, interpretive services, and maintenance responsibilities. Reflecting this diversity are brief narratives of the seven other national park employees that have died in the history of the park.

The first known fatality was that of Kenneth Meenan, a temporary or seasonal ranger. On August 5, 1934, Meenan sustained serious injuries when his motorcycle collided with a car on the Trail Ridge Road north of the Grand Lake entrance. His left foot was crushed and subsequently amputated, but septic poisoning developed. Meenan died in St. Luke's Hospital, in Denver, on August 13, 1934. He was 22 years old and a former gridiron star at Northwestern and Illinois universities. The Superintendent's report dated September 7, 1934, stated, "Meenan was a splendid fellow and a first class ranger."

On October 13, 1939, Raymond A. Johnson, thirty years old, died from injuries sustained in an off-duty motor vehicle accident on the Bear Lake Road. From Grand Junction, Colorado, Johnson had been a popular seasonal ranger for four years. He had returned to the park to work boundary patrol during the hunting season in the Never Summer Range on the west side of the park. He died in a Denver hospital from the injuries (compound fracture of his left leg and skull fracture) sustained in the October 9th accident when his roadster left the Bear Lake Road and crashed into a tree. The *Estes Park Trail* newspaper reported the cause of the accident as "a tire blowout, which threw his car off the road."

Oscar Jacobson was yet another seasonal ranger who died in an off-duty accident. Jacobson was the driver of the vehicle in which Raymond Young from Grand Lake, Colorado was also killed. This accident occurred approximately 4:00 a.m. on August 17, 1947, on the Trail Ridge Road, approximately four miles north of Grand Lake. Two other occupants were seriously injured.

Harold Grey was from Lynn, Massachusetts. In 1954, he was working as a seasonal camp tender at Glacier Basin Campground. Grey suffered a heart attack on June 27, 1954, and died on July 4, 1954. He was 54 years old.

As noted earlier in the chapter "A Bit of History," the late 1960s and early 1970s was a period of fundamental change for the ranger profession. Sadly, the profession lost one of those veteran rangers, who would have been instrumental in bridging that cultural gap between ranger generations. Fall River Subdistrict Ranger Nat Lacy was ranger family. He began his career in Yellowstone. His uncle, Edmond B. Rogers, was a superintendent at Yellowstone National Park. In the early 1960s, Nat was the chief ranger at Virgin Islands National Park. In 1963, because of concern for his family's safety during the Cuban Missile Crisis, he took a downgrade and was given a hardship transfer to Rocky Mountain National Park.

Ranger Tom Griffiths had his first permanent position under Lacy in 1966. In many ways, it was the classic relationship of the veteran ranger showing the young pup the skills and responsibilities of rangering. Tom Griffiths remembered Lacy as a great supervisor, who could even make working in the entrance station fun! One of the first things Lacy did for Griffiths was to give him a copy of the 1936 U.S. Cavalry Horse Manual.

Tom also remembered Lacy as a good family man. In the hours before Nat Lacy's accident on June 24, 1966, Griffiths remembers him walking around with his son on his shoulders at a picnic for new seasonal employees. Never one to mind the clock, Nat Lacy had the habit of checking the campgrounds and park horses each evening. After the picnic, he rode his small motor scooter over to Aspenglen Campground, and then up the road to Endovalley, which at the time was a small campground. He then went up to check on the horses, which were kept in Little Horseshoe Park. He never returned. His wife had gone to bed prior to his coming home, which was not unusual. Awake at 5:00 a.m., Mrs. Lacy thought he may have run out of gas or stayed at the Wrangler quarters at the corral. She later called park headquarters to report him missing. Rangers began looking for him, and Nat Lacy was found off the shoulder of the road around 9:30 a.m., about 300 yards west of the Fall River Entrance Station. The cause of the accident was inconclusive. It appears he may have hit a small rock and lost control of his scooter or perhaps was forced off the road by another vehicle. He left behind a wife and three children.

Initially, I was unable to find much information on Denzel "Denny" Baker. Records indicated that on October 15, 1978, the 58-year-old employee suffered a fatal heart attack in the employee housing area. The rest of the story was later provided by retired Chief Ranger Dave Essex. Baker was single and worked as an electrician. Unfortunately, he had a drinking problem. In the late summer of 1978, he was sent to Grand Lake to work on a wiring job. On the return trip in a government vehicle, Baker and the vehicle disappeared for several days. The demons had caught up with Denzel Baker, and he had gone on a drinking spree. When found, he was terminated and given a few days to vacate his government quarters. After several days, staff noticed his vehicle had not moved. Rangers entered Baker's quarters and found him dead. On the table was his termination letter.

To conclude this chapter on a more positive note, I find myself guilty of contemplating the nature of death, and having dignity in that final event—about how we all wish to die painlessly and at peace with ourselves, preferably surrounded by loved ones and/or in a special place filled with happy memories. For many folks, a national park, such as Rocky Mountain NP, is such a place. Though he was unfortunate to die at such a young age, I am convinced Jeff Christensen died a happy man. I think the same can probably be said for Bob Drury, the last National Park Service employee to die in the park before Jeff.

Bob was a quiet fellow and a bit of a loner. He was fifty years old and a seasonal ranger at the Aspenglen Campground. Bob loved the park and enjoyed long walks alone, so it was not surprising that Bob was out walking along the Trail Ridge Road on May 15, 1996. Each year, the park staff strives to open Trail Ridge Road by Memorial Day weekend for the summer season. This six to eight week plowing operation starts at the Many Parks viewpoint in early April. As the road crew plows out the road, the staff opens sections of the Trail Ridge Road to hikers and bicyclists, but not to cars. This is a wonderful opportunity to enjoy the alpine tundra without traffic as it awakens from winter. For the casual walker, it would be difficult to get any closer to heaven than on a day in May walking along Trail Ridge Road. It is still a long way to summer at 11,000 feet, yet you can often catch a hint of the warming earth from the plains below on the brisk breeze. The piercing blue sky, in contrast to the still majestic snowfields, is razor sharp.

By May 15th, Trail Ridge Road had been opened to Rainbow Curve for vehicles, and then you had to walk. It was one of those priceless spring days, and Bob was approximately .6 miles below Rock Cut when he died alone of an apparent heart attack. He was found by a NPS maintenance person at 2:10 p.m. He had been seen by coworkers the day before, so this unwitnessed death was believed to have occurred earlier that day. The subsequent coroner's report determined Drury's death to have been a natural event due to coronary artery disease. Fifty years of age can probably be considered early in life, but Bob loved the park, and I believe he, too, died a happy man.

National Park Service Employees

August 5, 1934	Kenneth Meenan, 22	**North of Grand Lake Entrance** NPS temporary ranger on motorcycle had *collision with vehicle.*
October 13, 1939	Raymond Johnson, 30	**Along the Bear Lake Road** Popular NPS temporary ranger suffered skull fracture when *tire blew out* causing vehicle to leave the road and strike a tree.
August 17, 1947	Oscar Jacobson, age unknown	**4 miles north of Grand Lake Entrance** Jacobson, off duty NPS temporary ranger, was the driver with 3 occupants in automobile accident. Raymond Young also killed. Vehicle went off road approx. 4 a.m. *Fatigue and excessive speed* likely factors.
June 27, 1954	Harold Grey, 54	**Glacier Basin Campground** Seasonal camp tender. *Suffered a heart attack* on June 27th. Died on July 4, 1954.
June 24, 1966	Nathaniel Lacy, 43	**Just west of the Fall River Entrance Station** Fall River Subdistrict Ranger had a *motor scooter accident* after checking campgrounds just west of Fall River entrance.
October 15, 1978	Denzel Baker, 58	**Beaver Meadows employee housing area** Maintenance electrician. *Suffered a heart attack.*
May 15, 1996	Robert Drury, 55	**Near Rock Cut on Trail Ridge Road** NPS seasonal campground ranger. Off duty, *suffered heart attack* while walking along Trail Ridge Road.
July 29, 2005	Jeff Christensen, 31	**Mummy Range** NPS seasonal ranger on backcountry patrol. *Fell and struck head,* resulting in subdural hematoma.

TWO

Falls While Hiking and Scrambling

Full of energy, bravado, and a generally modest level of wisdom, young males repeatedly put themselves in soon-to-be-fatal situations. Falling is the leading cause of death and injury in the park, with a significant majority being young males in their early twenties. Falls have claimed 85 lives. This chapter focuses on those 59 individuals who died from falls while out hiking or scrambling in the park. The other 26 fatalities occurred during technical climbing activities and are discussed in the next chapter.

As you read the following stories of these park visitors who have slipped, slid, or fallen to their deaths in the park, consider how you can avoid a similar circumstance. Not all the fatalities are discussed. A complete list of those who have fallen and died while hiking is shown in the table at the end of this chapter.

Falls on Rock

Most hiker fatalities involve individuals who fell from a rock surface. The locations of these incidents are primarily on the east side of the park, with only three occurring west of the continental divide.

The first known fatality in the park resulting from a fall took the life of Louis Raymond Levings on August 2, 1905. Levings, age 21, his cousin Dean Babcock, and George Black camped at Lawn Lake the evening of August 1st. The next morning, they hiked to the summit of Mt. Fairchild.

At this point, Dean Babcock returned to Lawn Lake, while Black and Levings decided to climb Ypsilon Mountain. Interested in getting photographs of the snow cornices, Black and Levings tried to descend the east face of Ypsilon by climbing down one of the arms of the "Y." Partway down, Levings was lowering himself from a rock to a foothold below, when the rock he was holding broke off, causing Levings to fall a couple hundred feet to his death. George Black eventually worked his way down the slope and made it to Estes Park that evening. The next day, a hiker was sent to Lawn Lake to notify Babcock of the death. At the same time, a party consisting of Black, Shep Husted, and Johnny Adams returned to the accident scene and lowered Levings' body with ropes to the scree slopes at the foot of the "Y." Judging it too difficult to carry the body all the way out, the group decided to bury the body where it was. They returned the next day with cement carried in on their backs and buried the body in a crypt against a large boulder. Later that summer, Levings' parents were taken to the site and were content to leave the body there.

This story continues 23 years later, in the summer of 1928, when Harold Dunning and Ted Matthews hiked to the burial site out of simple curiosity. They found it disintegrating and in bad shape. Dunning reported this to Levings' father, who contacted his nephew, Dean Babcock, to have a galvanized iron container made for the remains. Time ran out that summer, but over the winter, Dunning and Babcock had the container finished by the McGeorge Tin Shop in Loveland. It was built in pieces in order to be carried in a pack and reassembled at the gravesite. On August 15, 1929, Dunning, Babcock, ranger Walter Finn, and Cyrus Albertson, a Methodist minister from Loveland, made the trip to the site. They transferred all the skeletal parts they could find to the casket, and then reburied it under a ton of rocks. They placed a bronze marker on a large boulder below the grave to mark the site.

In an example of a solo hiker making a poor decision, John Tallmadge, age 21, died near Hallet Peak on July 11, 1952. This Wauwatosa, Wisconsin, native was a summer employee at the Bear Lake Lodge. He told his friends he was going to climb Hallet Peak and Flattop Mountain on

George Ogden, Jr., age 21, fell while solo hiking on Spearhead Mountain. Originally from Duncanville, Texas, Ogden had just completed summer studies at the University of Colorado in Boulder and was staying with family friends in Estes Park. They reported he had gone out for a day hike on August 15, 1988, and did not have any climbing equipment. Rangers Rick Guerrieri and Linda Stuart were on a routine backcountry patrol when they found Ogden's body in the vicinity of Spearhead Mountain just beyond Black Lake. They had noticed a backpack and climbed down to investigate when they discovered Ogden's body. He appeared to have died instantly. Rangers believe he scrambled on steep rocks, lost his footing, and fell. His body was removed by helicopter sling load that evening.

This last year, 2009, was a typical one for search or rescue incidents in the park. There were the usual high number of incidents, including five fatalities. But what set the year apart was the quirkiness of some of the incidents. On the positive side, the ranger staff performed an excellent "save" of a cardiac patient in August. In May, a solo backcountry ice climber fell and was severely injured. The next day, he was saved by two skiers who had made an impulsive, last minute decision to cut a few turns before work one morning. These stories are shared in other chapters in this book.

On the less positive side is the death of Carol Nicolaidis. In this book, I have tried to identify some predictable situations (kids near water, steep snowfields, lightning, etc.) that shout "watch out!" to unsuspecting visitors. On the other hand, the sheer randomness and suddenness of accidents continues to amaze me—just the plain bad luck.

On September 4, 2009, good friends Carol Nicolaidis and Debra Layne were hiking downhill from Bear Lake to the Fern Lake Trailhead. This popular eight-mile hike offers stunning views in the Odessa Gorge. A little north of the Odessa Lake spur trail, Nicolaidis and Layne stopped to put on rain gear. It was approximately 12:30 p.m. when the two started down the trail again with Layne in the lead. Moments later, Layne heard Nicolaidis shout "Debra!" and turned to see her tumbling down a steep slope, then over a short cliff and into Fern Creek, 50 feet below the trail.

A pleasant afternoon hike suddenly became fraught with soon-to-be-fatal problems. Nicolaidis did not lose consciousness and was initially communicating clearly with Layne. She was lying in a supine position and could move her hands and feet, but was certain she had either broken her back or her hip and could not move. Worse, the lower two-thirds of her body was partially submerged in the 50 degree creek water. It would be another 30 to 40 minutes before other hikers came by the accident scene and 60 minutes before the first bystanders were able to reach Nicolaidis. This initial group had limited EMS training, but recognized the dilemma of attempting to move Nicolaidis out of the cold water to prevent hypothermia versus causing more damage to a possible broken spine. Their solution was to build a dam or diversion in the creek to route most, but not all, of the water away from Nicolaidis. They were able to slip a space blanket under her and over her and covered her with other clothing items in an attempt to keep her warm.

Hopefully, the reader remembers my caution about poor cell coverage in certain parts of the park. The Odessa Gorge is one of those areas. The first scratchy cell call came in to the Estes Park Police Department a little after 1:00 p.m. Because of the poor cell phone coverage, several of the 911 calls were dropped before a basic picture of an injured female hiker was put together. Pending further information, an initial rescue team of rangers Michelle Blank and Ethan Baer gathered EMS gear and left the Fern Lake Trailhead around 2:00 p.m. Though a popular trail, the location of the injured hiker was in one of the more isolated areas of the park due to poor communication and lack of a helicopter landing area. It would take the rangers an hour and half to hustle up the four miles, with an elevation gain of 2,000 feet, and be the first at the accident scene. It was not until 2:15 p.m. that a more detailed description of the hiker's severe injuries was received by cell phone.

Rangers Blank and Baer arrived approximately 3:30 p.m. Nicolaidis had been in the water close to three hours. The initial caregivers shared that her level of consciousness had decreased significantly and hypothermia was a major issue. The rangers observed that Nicolaidis was moaning, but unable to speak. Her skin was cold to the touch, her breathing shallow and she was responsive to pain only. Other than a bruise over her left eye, there were no visible bruises, lacerations, or obvious fractures noted. The rangers' first actions were to remove all her wet clothing, replace them with dry gear, and apply heat packs. Additional rangers with advanced EMS training began arriving. A cervical collar was applied and Nicolaidis was moved to a small bench out of the stream bed, but her condition continued to deteriorate. CPR was initiated around 5:00 p.m. and an Automated External Defibrillator (AED) utilized in an unsuccessful attempt to shock the patient. CPR was stopped an hour later after no spontaneous respirations or pulse were found. A technical raising of the body was performed, and it was carried out to the Fern Lake Trailhead, arriving approximately 11:00 p.m. The Larimer County Coroner later reported that Nicolaidis died as a result of blunt force injuries. Hypothermia contributed.

So, what went wrong here? What lesson is to be learned? In a post incident interview, Layne shared that an uphill hiker had passed them shortly before the accident. He had the inside of the trail, and general trail courtesy directed Layne and Nicolaidis to the outside, or cliff side, of the trail. This is common practice on the trails. It was a heavily wooded area and did not appear dangerous. The trail surface was relatively benign, slightly uneven, with a 3–6 inch high wall along the cliff side of the trail. Layne further shared that they had just put on rain jackets, and perhaps Nicolaidis was attempting to adjust her day pack and rain jacket while hiking, thus causing her to be momentarily distracted. I think we are all guilty of doing this at one time or another. As mentioned, the fall was not witnessed.

In the most basic analysis, the lesson from this tragedy is simply to be constantly vigilant of your footing, particularly if moving downhill. Wilderness trails are not flat. Uneven, often wet, or gravelly surfaces demand a hiker's constant attention.

Hiker Fatalities in the Longs Peak Area

From the original Native Americans and the early explorers, to today's hikers or climbers, Longs Peak has captured our imagination and spirit through the decades. Each year, an estimated 15,000 visitors make an attempt for the summit. Most are day hikers. As the northernmost "14'er" in Colorado, it remains a challenge even to the most experienced backcountry user.

Rapidly changing weather, the threat of lightning high above treeline, and the degree of exposure and isolation along the trails make the Longs Peak experience rewarding but dangerous. Because of the uniqueness of Longs Peak and Mt. Meeker, I have grouped the incidents that occurred in this area into this section. There have been 21 hiker fatalities: 2 unwitnessed falls likely from the East Face of the peak, 5 in the Loft area between Mt. Meeker and Longs Peak, and 14 that occurred in the Keyhole/North Face area. For each fatality, there have also been numerous searches or rescues over the decades. The elements that make a hike more dangerous also apply to rescue efforts.

The two unwitnessed falls from the East Face of Longs Peak are found in the Superintendent's monthly reports. In the first case, the reports for July and September 1921 describe the circumstances around the missing Gregory Aubuchon, age 18. The Aubuchon family was from Indiana and had been camping in Glacier Basin Campground. Apparently Gregory's parents had refused him permission to climb Longs Peak, so he snuck away in the middle of the night. He was reported missing the following day on July 21, 1921. A search was started, but suspended after four days, as nothing was discovered to indicate his whereabouts. On September 16, 1921, Aubuchon's body was found on Mills Glacier by rangers Higby and McDaniel. The report stated that the body had been found "about under the Notch," but it was undetermined if he was climbing up or down. He did not sign the summit register, so most likely he was ascending when he fell.

The second unwitnessed incident occurred ten years later, when on September 13, 1931, a body was found by Walter Honacker and his hiking companion on Mills Glacier below the Alexander's Chimney route. The body was identified from a time slip from the Jefferson Coal Company in Piney Fork, Ohio. It was believed to be Mr. R.B. Key. Little is known about Key. He was alone when he fell from somewhere above Mills Glacier. Honacker and his friend initially pulled the body down to the foot of the glacier opposite the lower end of Alexander's Chimney before leaving to notify park authorities. Late that afternoon, Superintendent Edmond Rogers and rangers Jack Moomaw, Walter Finn, Paul Ambrose, Harold Ratcliff, and Howard Baker carried the body down to Chasm Lake before darkness stopped their effort. Monday morning, rangers brought the body down to the Longs Peak Inn, where it was turned over to the Boulder County Coroner.

The Loft Route is not for the fainthearted, though it can normally be done in mid to late summer without technical gear. The most important decision for this trip is proper route selection. The route starts innocently enough by traveling a short distance south from Chasm Meadows, then up and around the obvious Ships Prow formation. A moderately steep ascent up to a permanent snowfield called the Apron leads to a cliff band. It is important to work your way up and to the left along a prominent ramp before working back to the right, then up to the saddle between Meeker and Longs. A key challenge is the extent of the snowfield, which changes seasonally, and the difficulty is finding the ramp to traverse left. The first of five hiker fatalities here was William A. Pistorio, age 19, who fell to his death on October 1, 1975. In this unwitnessed fall, Pistorio fell 150 feet while hiking alone below the Apron.

In 1992, nine people died in the park, six of them within a three-month period during the summer. It was not a pleasant year for the ranger staff. One of those killed was Gary Boyer, age 34. Boyer was the second fatality in the Loft area.

One of the difficult aspects of a fatality in the park is notifying the family. If relatives are in a remote city, this is often arranged through a local police department or member of the clergy. If the victim's family is in the area, a representative of the park is tasked with this responsibility—

usually a member of the Superintendent's staff. As the Chief Ranger, I did this a number of times over the years, yet I remember the Boyer fatality as one of the most difficult notifications. Gary Boyer and his wife and small child from Edmond, Oklahoma, were visiting the area for several days. On July 29, 1992, Gary left around 3:00 a.m. to summit Longs Peak alone via the Loft Route. He was believed to be familiar with the area from having made other ascents of Longs Peak on previous trips. He carried an ice axe, water, lunch, parka, hat, and a poncho, but no overnight gear or crampons. His wife, Melinda, reported him missing early the next morning, when he failed to return Tuesday evening. On Wednesday, rangers Dave Herrick and Andy Brown struggled against fierce winds in the Mt. Meeker area, and were able to find what they presumed to be Boyer's body about 3:00 p.m. Boyer was in the gully on the right side of the East Arete on the north side of Mt. Meeker. He appeared to have fallen a considerable distance. Unfortunately, his pack was not found, nor was there any identification on the body, so for the moment they could do no more than assume that the body was that of Gary Boyer.

In radio contact with the rangers on the scene, I sat in the motel room with Melinda Boyer as the rangers described the clothing and physical features of the body. With each affirmation of a clothing item or physical characteristic, I watched the dreams and life of Melinda slowly seep out of her eyes with the realization that her husband was dead and her child now without a father. It became a question of who would cry first, Melinda or me.

The cause of this fatality was poor route selection leading to a fall from a steep area. For some unknown reason, Boyer was in an area to the left and considerably more vertical than his intended route via the Loft. Recovery efforts included a technical litter lowering and several hundred feet of scree evacuation in poor weather conditions. His body was flown out later in the afternoon.

Following Boyer was Timothy M. Maron, age 26, from Denver, Colorado. Maron signed out at the Longs Peak trailhead register on September 9, 1997, to solo hike up Longs Peak via the Loft Route. He appeared to have fallen from below the cliff band on the upper portion of the route.

On August 4, 1999, James D. Page was hiking with his 28 year-old son, Sam. They were en route to Longs Peak and had previously made the summit through the more common Keyhole Route. They had passed the Apron, but by noon were caught in wet, drizzly weather near Gorrell's Traverse. James Page slipped on the wet rock and tumbled down 90 feet of steep rock, sustaining severe injuries. Sam was able to descend to assist him and spent more than three hours with his father, protecting him with spare clothing and attempting to call for help with the aid of a whistle. When this proved unsuccessful, he left to find help. On his way down, he was contacted by ranger staff, who had been alerted by other hikers that someone possibly needed assistance. Darkness and dense fog hindered the search effort that evening. Visibility was diminished to the point that searchers had difficulty seeing each other's headlamps while only a few

Longs Peak Rescue. Packaged victim in litter prior to hauling to helicopter landing zone.
Courtesy of RMNP

feet apart. The search teams retreated to the Chasm Lake shelter late in the evening in hopes of improved weather. By 3:00 a.m. Thursday, the teams were back in the field working their way up through the saddle area. At 6:30 a.m., James Page's body was found below the Gorrell's Traverse area. He had succumbed to his injuries and likely hypothermia.

On September 3, 2006, Clayton Smith from Louisville, Colorado, and a hiking companion summited Mt. Meeker and were descending near the Loft. Smith, unroped, slipped and fell almost 300 feet, sustaining massive traumatic injuries. Two rangers were on patrol in the area and witnessed the fall. They were able to reach Smith within 30 minutes, but found no pulse. A helicopter was used to recover Smith's body.

The Keyhole and Cables Routes are the most popular routes to the summit of Longs Peak. This is where most of the hiker fatalities and rescues have occurred over the years. Following are a few stories of the 14 hiker fatalities in the Keyhole/North Face area.

Gray Secor, Jr., was the 16 year-old son of a prominent Longmont, Colorado, attorney. On August 29, 1932, around 8:30 a.m., he and his friend Carroll Frantz passed the Boulderfield shelter cabin on the way to the summit of Longs Peak via the North Face cables. They had planned to return by way of the Keyhole Route. At 11:45 a.m., a shaken Carroll Frantz staggered into the Boulderfield cabin and told guide Hull Cook that Secor was unconscious from a fall near the False Keyhole. Cook grabbed some first aid gear and headed up the mountain. He told Frantz to wait at the cabin. Cook found Secor's body at the foot of a deep crack about halfway up to the False Keyhole formation. An examination found that the boy's skull was fractured and he was dead. Hull Cook carried Secor's body down over his shoulder over a quarter mile before Robert Collier, a hiker, brought some canvas and helped carry the body back toward the Boulderfield cabin. In a later interview with rangers, Frantz stated that Secor had told him he was going to take a shortcut, and that Frantz begged him not to. Frantz continued along the main trail for a few feet, when he heard some rock fall. Turning back, he could not find Secor. Frantz scrambled down the main trail and found Secor bloody and moaning, which is when he went for help.

John A. Fuller, age 20, was a student at Iowa State College, where his father was a professor of civil engineering. Fuller was a frequent summer visitor to Estes Park and had been on the Longs Peak summit thirteen times prior to the fatal trip. On August 8, 1938, he was interested in trying out some new mountain climbing shoes and pursued a route to the right of the standard Cables Route. Witnesses reported they heard a small rock avalanche and saw Fuller's tumbling body. He fell over 500 feet to the Left Dovetail, the large snow formation above the Boulderfield. It is not clear whether Fuller had been struck by a rock or lost his grip and fell from the face above the Dove.

On August 27, 1962, YMCA summer employee Ken Murphy, age 19, and two friends left early and used the Cables Route on the North Face to reach the summit of Longs Peak. Murphy was in the best shape of the three hikers and raced ahead to the summit. When the two companions got to the summit, Murphy was not around, and they returned to the YMCA. When they didn't find Murphy at the YMCA, they notified park rangers. A four-person rescue team headed by ranger Vince Hefti left that night and found Murphy's body early Tuesday morning. It appears Murphy fell close to100 feet from the Northwest Ridge above the Keyhole on Longs Peak.

Only a few weeks later on September 30th, Pasadena, California, native James S. O'Toole, age 20, attempted the Longs Peak summit with fellow Denver University student, Eric Brookens. The two separated at the Boulderfield because Brookens wanted to take a picture of the Diamond. Brookens went up and down the Keyhole Route and then, not finding O'Toole, reported him missing at the ranger station around 7:00 p.m. O'Toole's body was found by a rescue team the next morning. Evidence indicated that O'Toole ascended the Keyhole Route, then attempted a shortcut on his descent by traversing over toward Chasm View. It appears that he fell to the west of the cables and landed on the left wing of "The Dove" snowfield above the Boulderfield. Superintendent Allyn Hanks told the *Estes Park Trail* that O'Toole and Brookens "innocently broke an unwritten rule of the mountains when they separated. If climbers will keep their parties together, carry adequate clothing and emergency rations, and stay on recommended routes, such tragedies can be avoided."

Another fatality occurred on June 12, 1972, when Lincoln Park, Michigan, native Paul F. Russell apparently ignored the warnings about icy conditions posted at the Longs Peak Trailhead. Again, the Keyhole Route was still considered "technical" because of the snow and ice on the route. Russell, age 24, hiked to the Keyhole with a friend. His friend stopped there, but Russell pushed on through the snow and ice without any technical equipment. He died when he fell more than 150 feet near the upper end of the Narrows section of the route.

Timothy Fromalt, age 27, was from Longmont, Colorado. On July 29, 1990, he slipped and fell while descending the Homestretch on Longs Peak. He and friends had made it to the summit, but on their way down the group encountered moisture on the rocks. In a tragic sequence of events, one of the friends started sliding on the wet rock. Fromalt stopped his friend's slide, but in doing so lost his balance, slid, and tumbled 50 feet, striking his head. He was breathing but unconscious when his friends and other hikers got to him. He then stopped breathing, and CPR was started, but to no avail. Lightning and heavy rain hindered the body recovery.

In 1995, the only hiker fatality of the year occurred on August 25th, when Jun Kamimura, age 33, died in a 400-foot fall from the Ledges section of the Keyhole Route on Longs Peak. The year witnessed an unusual spring and summer with heavy snowfall and persistent cloud cover slowing the snow melt rate at higher elevations. Normally, the Keyhole Route is declared open by park staff by mid-July. "Open" means that the snow and ice have melted sufficiently that hikers do not need technical gear or expertise to summit Longs via this route. By late August, the route was still considered technical due to conditions on the route, particularly on a 130-foot stretch of snow in the Trough, where ice axes and crampons were highly recommended. The park designation of technical versus non-technical is an advisory to hikers. Many chose to ignore the warnings, including Kamimura. On his descent in the Ledges part of the trail, he encountered two rangers on patrol and told them he was suffering from the altitude. The rangers offered to help him get down to the Boulderfield area, and Kamimura had begun to follow them when the accident occurred. As reported in the *Estes Park Trail-Gazette*, Kamimura twisted a foot or ankle, causing him to fall. The accident occurred around 6:00 p.m. Mike Pratt, one of the rangers, was a paramedic. He was able to get to Kamimura within 30 minutes, but determined him dead due to extensive head injuries. Kamimura was a medical doctor from Japan and worked for a pharmaceutical company in Boston, Massachusetts.

The park staff would be tested with another challenging year in 1999, with seven visitor deaths within a three-month period. In an eleven day period in August, rangers responded to four fatalities, three of which were falls on or near Longs Peak, with the other a lightning death. I previously mentioned the death of James Page on August 4th. On the day before, August 3rd, 75-year-old Raymond Decker of Baton Rouge, Louisiana, died in a 150-foot fall from the precipitous Narrows section of the Keyhole Route. Decker chose a methodical trip. He had a backcountry permit and planned three days to reach the summit. He camped at Goblins Forest the first night out, and camped in the Boulderfield (12,760 feet) the second night, before his summit attempt. It is unknown if Decker made it to the summit, or whether he was heading up or down at the time of his unwitnessed fall.

Because of seemingly good health and sound decision making, the death of 42-year-old Gregory Koczanski on August 14th could be considered unusual, but it is also instructive of the hazards in the park. From Vienna, Virginia, Koczanski and his family had vacationed in Estes Park several times. His father-in-law, J.G. Pinkerton, was a professional storyteller and had presented programs locally at the library and to service organizations. Koczanski had always wanted to climb Longs Peak and had been planning for the hike a good part of the year according to his brother-in-law, Marc Pinkerton. Gregory's wife, Kathy, was with him as they worked their way through the Keyhole in the face of a strong westerly gale. After making their way to the Ledges area, the couple decided to turn back because of the high wind and concern for safety. Kathy was ahead of her husband and did not see the actual fall. Later, rangers on the scene believed the strong, gusty winds might have caused Koczanski to lose his balance and slip off the narrow stretch of trail. The accident occurred around 9:45 a.m., and the park was alerted by a 911 cell phone call. By 10:08 a.m., other hikers were able to reach Koczanski and found him unconscious and with no pulse. Because of the strong winds, Koczanski's body could not be flown out by helicopter until late that afternoon.

In the opening paragraphs of this chapter, I noted there have been 59 hiker fatalities. Of those, 13 individuals were under the age of 17, and most were on some type of organized outing or with parents. Parents, youth leaders, scout leaders, please read through these next two stories carefully.

Aren't kids just full of energy? The Baldeshwiler family, from Lansing, Illinois, arrived in the park on Monday, June 28, 1982. That evening, they attended an interpretive program in the Beaver Meadows Visitor Center. The program was presented by Mike Donahue, the owner of the Colorado Mountain School in Estes Park, in which he talked about rock climbing. Young Robert Baldeshwiler, age 12, enjoyed the program and talked with Donahue about possibly taking climbing lessons.

The following morning, the family drove to Bear Lake with the intention of hiking up the Flattop Mountain Trail. Typical of a summer day, the morning was fair, but began to cloud up in the early afternoon. Robert was reported to be wearing only a pair of blue jeans, a T-shirt, tennis shoes, and a visor. He may have been carrying some Kleenex and taffy. At 5 foot, 7 inches tall and 125 pounds, Robert was young and fit, and he soon hiked out ahead of his parents and sister, who last saw him around 2:00 p.m. Robert's parents continued up the trail and soon realized Robert was missing. They spent several hours looking around the Flattop Mountain summit area and along the trail without success. Around 9:30 p.m., they notified park staff that their son was missing.

Each year, the park receives close to a 100 reports of lost or overdue hikers. Around 99 percent of the time, the "lost" party shows up or the initial response team finds the missing party a little worse for wear, but safe. The rangers were not so lucky this time.

On Wednesday, the initial search effort involved twenty people and a helicopter and focused on the trails and overlooks nearby. During the day, another hiker, Jim Anderson, told rangers he believed he saw Robert Baldeshwiler the previous day at 2:30 p.m. near the Emerald Lake overlook on the Flattop Mountain Trail. Robert was heading up the trail pretty fast, but was hiking into a cell of bad weather. Unfortunately, the weather was poor Tuesday evening and Wednesday, with hail, rain, and lightning in the search area. Being unsuccessful on Wednesday, and knowing that Robert was poorly clothed for the wet weather, the search urgency increased.

On Thursday, over 120 searchers focused on the areas north and south of the Flattop Mountain Trail, Odessa Gorge, Tyndall Glacier, and around

Military helicopter transporting searchers during Baldeshwiler search. Courtesy of RMNP

Chaos Canyon. Rangers called in a Chinook helicopter from Fort Carson to ferry searchers from the Upper Beaver Meadows to the higher slopes of Flattop Mountain, from which the searchers could work their way downhill.

In all, four helicopters were involved with the search—the Chinook from Fort Carson, two contract helicopters, and a news media helicopter. Several trained dog teams joined in the search. Based on previous search strategies and the profile of the missing youth, the search area focused within a square mile of the point where Robert was last seen. The search area was divided into segments and each team in the field was directed to search that segment with a predetermined "Probability of Detection" (POD). For example, if the management team wanted segment A searched with a 50 or 100 percent POD, they would assign enough resources to complete the task within that operational period. This practice allows the search strategy to adjust each day to any clues found or the availability of search resources. On Friday, searchers began to refocus on areas downhill from where Robert was last seen, on the presumption that the storm cell he was seen walking into could have disoriented him and driven him downhill.

On Saturday and Sunday, over 200 searchers were in the field, including technical rock climbers searching the snow slopes in Odessa and Tyndall gorges. Where was Robert Baldeshwiler? Not a clue, not one foot print or bit of evidence was found.

On large searches on public lands, most field teams are volunteers from organized SAR teams associated with a county sheriff's department. This is reflected in the bump in number of searchers over the weekend. By Monday, July 5th, the search effort was reduced to 55 members and focused uphill from Bear Lake and the Mill Creek drainage. That evening, the Incident Management Team met with Robert's parents, Lois and Martin Baldeshwiler, and reviewed each day's effort, the weather, and the absence of clues. The difficult decision was made to terminate the search. It was a painful discussion for all parties. Most rangers and searchers have families and could empathize with the Baldeshwiler's, but a point had been reached where there was little likelihood of Robert being found alive. Rangers would post information on the missing youth at visitor centers and at trailheads in hopes of other hikers finding a clue or any evidence.

As fate would have it, three hikers from Boulder, Colorado, were scrambling around in the Tyndall Gorge area on Sunday, July 11th, when they found a blood-stained visor. The hikers almost tossed the visor away, but remembered the massive search undertaken the previous week. They carried the visor on the remainder of their hike, and then turned it in to park staff at Bear Lake around 4:00 p.m. Later that afternoon, a handful of searchers were back in the field. Known for his patience and knowledge of the terrain, ranger Tom Powers went to the point where the visor was found and lined that location up with the place where Robert was last seen. Methodically searching the fall lines, Powers found Robert's body at approximately 6:00 p.m. about 500 feet below where the visor was found. This was at a point about 800 feet above Emerald Lake. A helicopter was used to lift the body off the steep terrain. The autopsy, performed by Larimer County Coroner Dr. Patrick Allen, confirmed that Robert died of multiple skull fractures. There was no evidence of exposure or dehydration, so it appears that Robert died on June 29th, the day he was last seen. A small relief for his family was that he did not appear to have suffered. Speculation was that Robert had got wet and cold during the storm on the 29th. Seeing Emerald Lake from the Flattop Mountain Trail, he attempted to climb down a steep couloir to get out of the weather or to take a "shortcut" back to Bear Lake.

This incident highlights the difficulty of finding a missing person in the vastness of the park's backcountry. Ironically, the area where the body was found had been identified as a primary search segment. Numerous searchers had swarmed over the area, as well as helicopter overflights. One ranger said he had been within 50 feet of where the body was found, but had not seen anything. Another said he had examined the snowfield on which Robert was discovered, but saw nothing. Possibly, the body had been caught somewhere above and tumbled down later. It is difficult to tell.

In this second story, place yourself in the position of the victim's father and think of his decision to leave his daughter by the side of the trail to be picked up later. In retrospect, it doesn't seem like a good decision, but at the time did it make sense? This is the difficulty of trying to determine the cause of a fatality, particularly that of a child in the care of an adult. These losses are especially tragic, and my intention is not to fix blame, but to try to prevent similar accidents in the future.

It was mid July in Rocky Mountain National Park. The air was cool, and the sky a crisp blue. It was a great time to embrace the splendor of the park. Sarah Wolenetz, age 11, was one of a group of nine hikers from a Ft. Collins church who were hiking to raise money for missionary work. On July 11, 1992, the group intended to hike from Bear Lake on the Fern Lake Trail to its intersection with the Flattop Mountain Trail, and then return on the same trail to Bear Lake. Sarah was nursing a sore heel and fell behind the others. Her father, a member of the group, suggested she wait along the trail until the group doubled back to pick her up in a couple hours. She was left at a bend in the trail, with a view of Bear Lake. The group went up the trail and returned a little more than two hours later, at which time they did not find Sarah. After an unsuccessful search by the church group up and down the trail, park staff was notified around 3:00 p.m. A search effort that quickly grew to sixty people with search dogs worked into the evening and throughout the night, in hopes of establishing

> There are two important **safety lessons** to be learned from these tragic incidents:
> 1. **When hiking with children,** you should always stay together. At the least, split into groups of stronger or weaker hikers. Never leave a child alone in unfamiliar territory, whether you're at a shopping mall or on a backcountry trail.
> 2. **Always check the weather** and be prepared for rapidly changing conditions. Talk with park staff to better understand weather conditions in the Colorado high country.

voice contact with the missing girl. Tragically, the body of Sarah Wolenetz was found by searchers early the next morning below a 40-foot cliff. The cliff was in a line with the point where Sarah was last seen and Bear Lake. Searchers speculated that Sarah grew tired or bored, and, knowing her mother was waiting in the Bear Lake parking lot, she decided to head back alone. With the lake in view, she may have thought she found an easier route down, a decision you would expect an 11-year-old to make.

Looking back at some earlier incidents involving youth, a hiking group from Cheley Camp in Estes Park was out on a day hike from Bear Lake to the relatively easy summit of Little Matterhorn Mountain. The date was July 31, 1953. Both Sandra Miller, age 17, and Kathryn Rees, age 15, were considered "advanced campers" and Miller was also a "counselor's aide." Miller had been to the summit of Little Matterhorn three or four times prior to this trip. The hiking group of nine campers and three counselors had an uneventful hike to Lake Helene and ate lunch above the lake. From there, it is roughly two miles of unmarked terrain up to the summit of Little Matterhorn Mountain. Approaching from the west, the group reached the ridgeline that leads to the summit. The *Estes Park Trail* reported: "As they crossed the sloping ridge, each girl had to reach to her right to grasp a large rock to help keep her feet from slipping on the grassy slope. Apparently, when Rees grasped the rock, it moved slightly and startled her into raising her hands over her head and she lost her balance. She rolled down the slope and cartwheeled out of sight, some fifty feet over a cliff." Rees was killed.

Lead counselor Joan Symon told the other counselor, Gretchen Degroot, to go for help. Symon then worked her way down to Rees. Degroot and Sandy Miller started down the north slope of the untracked mountain toward the Fern Lake Lodge to get ranger assistance. Apparently, Degroot and Miller had a slight disagreement on the best route down and separated, but remained within hailing distance for a while. As noted, Miller had made the summit hike before. Degroot had not. Degroot made it to the Fern Lake Lodge and a rescue party was assembled. Alarmed that Miller had not arrived, Degroot led the rescue party back to where she had last seen Miller. Miller was found dead approximately 4:00 p.m. at the base of a 100-foot cliff.

Jay DuPont, age 14, was with a Boy Scout camping trip from Lincoln, Nebraska. On June 14, 1966, DuPont had gone hiking with two others to Thatchtop Mountain, which is above Mills Lake. Apparently, DuPont had expressed a desire to slide down a rock face because he felt it would be more fun and easier, but was told to stay away from the face because of the danger. He separated himself from the party and his fall was not witnessed. DuPont may indeed have tried to slide down, or he may have gone to the edge to investigate and slipped. In *Accidents in North American Mountaineering*, a clear sense of frustration can be heard in ranger Doug Erskine's incident analysis, "A small amount of good sense would have saved a life. DuPont was notorious for doing just as he felt and would not take advice from other people. He was raised in Nebraska and knew nothing of the mountains."

On another Boy Scout outing, 16-year-old Robert Silver, from Cedar Rapids, Iowa, was on a group outing to the summit of Longs Peak on June 26, 1980. At this time, the Keyhole route was still considered a "technical" climb by park staff due to ice and snow on its upper stretches. Signs were posted at the Longs Peak Trailhead. At the Keyhole, four scouts decided to turn around. At the base of the Homestretch, just below the summit, two other scouts turned around after seeing the difficulty that Silver was having. Because of the amount of snow on the regular route, Silver had moved to the north to dry, but steeper, rock. After moving a short distance, he told a companion he was stuck and could not continue. In the meantime, the group leader had gone on to the summit with four other scouts, but was looking down on the situation and giving instructions to Silver about where to put his hands and feet. Apparently, Silver was afraid to move forward, could not retreat, and panicked. Others tried to comfort him and come to his aid, but Silver got uncomfortable and tried to move, then slipped and fell 300 feet to his death.

In a post incident review, we hear from ranger Larry Van Slyke, who noted, "People seem to have difficulty comprehending that conditions at 14,000 feet in June can and often are much, much different than at lower elevations, including those found at the Longs Peak Ranger Station at 9,500 feet. Many people take a chance on those conditions and survive. Some do not." Numerous warnings about hazards on the route were posted at the Longs Peak Ranger Station where the scouts began their hike. Had they read and given credence to the posted information, they might not have attempted the ascent past the Keyhole.

Falls on Snow

Of the 59 hiker fatalities, 7 occurred on snow or ice. It is interesting that these 7 occurred in the summer months. In summer, snow is probably seen more as a novelty than a danger. This was likely the case on August 2, 1917, when Miss Eula Frost, age 19, was on a sightseeing trip up the Fall River Road with Mr. Homer Thomson. When she attempted to cross a large snowbank near the road, the Sterling, Colorado, resident lost her footing and started to slide down the slope. As she fell, she pulled her companion, Mr. Thomson, off his feet. Frost slid a distance of approximately 500 feet before she struck outcropping rocks with her head, rolled another 100 feet over a ledge, and lodged in a snowbank. She was then crushed by a 400 pound rock that had dislodged and fell on her. Mr. Thomson slid an equal distance, but on a slightly different trajectory. He wound up lodged in the trees at the base of the snowbank and escaped serious injury.

On June 16, 1946, 20-year-old Private Thomas H. Evans, from Akron, Ohio, was on a picnic and outing with 200 other soldiers from Lowry Air Force Base. He was last seen on this date at the beginning of the Flattop Mountain Trail above Bear Lake. He was not reported missing to the National Park Service until the 18th because his buddies had thought he missed the buses returning home and were covering up for him to their superiors. Evans had minimal experience in a mountain environment, and inclement, snowy weather hampered the search effort. For 18 days, an intensive search was carried out by rangers and Army alpine troops before being abandoned on July 3rd. On July 7, 1946, Mr. G. Burton Davy, a Boston tourist, found Evans's body wedged between a snow bank and rock ledge a half mile west of Emerald Lake. The July 12, 1946, edition of the *Estes Park Trail* reported: "According to a reconstruction of the tragedy by Ranger Ernest Field, Evans reached the top of Flattop Mountain and attempted to return to Bear Lake via the short cut through Tyndall Gorge. In coming down a snowbank, Evans probably lost his footing and slid/rolled to the bottom, where he apparently hit his head and died of a fractured neck. His hat and glasses were found about 60 feet from his body." Ranger Field estimated that search parties had passed within 50 feet of the body, but failed to detect it because of poor visibility and the body's location.

On August 21, 1959, Mrs. Jeanne Gillett, age 31, was hiking with her husband. Jeanne was from Wausau, Wisconsin, and was the daughter-in-law of a prominent Estes Park couple, Mr. and Mrs. Clarence H. Gillett of Stanley Heights. She and her husband had two young children. Mr. Phipp Gillett shared that he and his wife had hiked up to Hallett Peak via Chaos Canyon and were descending along the edge of Tyndall Glacier. Their progress was slow due to fatigue and loose rock. As darkness approached, they decided the footing was too rough and elected to hike back up on the glacier and go down the Flattop Trail. A short time later, Mrs. Gillett lost her footing and slid past her husband out of sight. Unable to establish voice contact, Mr. Gillett continued up the glacier, came down the Flattop Mountain Trail, and contacted park staff around 11:00 p.m. Rangers Bob Frauson, Jerry Phillips, and Paul Swearingen left immediately and located the body of Jeanne Gillett at 5:00 a.m. She had died of a broken neck. Assisted by a park field crew, they returned with the body to Bear Lake by 2:00 p.m. Phipp Gillett courageously wrote a summary of the incident for *Accidents in North American Mountaineering*, in which he concluded, "The accident was due to poor judgment on my part, overestimating what my wife could do and not understanding the difficulty of the terrain. I found out later we had come down the wrong side of the glacier (the Hallett side), the other side next to Flattop being considered easier."

An unwitnessed fall occurred on August 13, 1962, when Patricia L. Beatty, age 21, slid down the snowfield at the head of Chaos Canyon. From Greenfield, Ohio, Beatty was a summer employee at the Crags Lodge in Estes Park. She had signed in at the Bear Lake Ranger Station early Monday morning and had hiked up Flattop Mountain, around behind Hallet Peak, and attempted to come down Chaos Canyon. It appeared that she walked out on the snowfield, and then sat down in order to slide down before she lost control and slid into rocks. Her body was discovered approximately 3:30 p.m. by summer residents Walter Newport and Dr. Maurice Albertson. They attempted artificial respiration for four hours before giving up. The body recovery was led by ranger Jerry Phillips on Tuesday, August 14th.

The following day, August 15, 1962, Gerald R. Noland, age 20, slipped and fell on a snowfield below Andrews Glacier Tarn. From Seymour, Iowa, Noland was a summer kitchen helper at the YMCA. He and two fellow YMCA employees had hiked up Flattop Mountain, around Hallett Peak and came down near Andrews Glacier, which is still a popular day hike. The group slid down the small snowfield beneath Andrews Tarn. Noland was the last down and was warned about the rocks at the bottom of the snow. He continued down however, lost his balance and dashed into the rocks below. In the following news release, Superintendent Allyn Hanks warned, "The steep permanent snowfields at high elevations in Rocky Mountain National Park are responsible for more visitor injuries than any other source. What appears to be an inviting shortcut in the form of a pleasant slide down a snow bank often results in a shocking plunge to the rocks below."

Chris Rejeske, age 15, was from Estes Park. On July 18, 1975, he and Mark Renshaw hiked to the summit of Ypsilon Mountain. On the descent, they decided to try to slide down a snowfield between Ypsilon and Mt. Chiquita. Unfortunately, Rejeske lost control and slid more than 500 feet on the snow, struck a rock outcrop, and was killed. Renshaw was able to get some help from climbers in the area, and was escorted to the Willow Park patrol cabin to report the incident.

There is limited information on the death of Coy Conley on September 1, 1979, though it appears he was on a sightseeing visit similar to Miss Eula Frost. Conley was playing on a snowfield near the Ute Trail Crossing on Trail Ridge Road when he, too, lost his footing and slid into rocks at the bottom of the snowfield.

Of course, not everybody who slips and loses control on a snowfield dies. Many survive and get a second chance at life. Following are a few examples of the lucky ones.

Charles Mahan, age 20, slipped on a steep snowfield on Ypsilon Mountain on August 7, 1952, while on a YMCA Conference hike. He slid into a rock pile, fractured his left collar bone, and lacerated his left knee. A number of rangers were required to remove him from the accident scene. Conditions forced the party to wait until the next day to remove Mahan by stretcher.

On July 8, 1953, Paul Conrad, age 17, slipped while climbing a steep snowbank in the Black Lake area. He slid and hit rocks, suffered numerous bruises, and a broken wrist. This inexperienced hiker failed to appreciate the true dangers of steep snow slopes.

Acting Chief Ranger Edward Kurtz gave another example of a second chance. He reported that on August 13, 1954, Mrs. Leahdell Dick, age 21, had climbed to the summit of Hallet Peak and planned to come down Andrews Glacier. She mistook a snowfield between Hallett and Otis Peaks for the glacier. This snowfield was too steep and dangerous to attempt without ice climbing equipment. Mrs. Dick, who was alone and had no equipment, slipped and slid down the steep slope, striking the rocks at the bottom. She was cut and bruised and struck unconscious. Fortunately, she broke no bones. When she regained consciousness, she hiked out to Lake Haiyaha, where a fisherman helped her to the Bear Lake Ranger Station.

> **The safety lesson is simple:** Snowfields on any type of slope should be considered dangerous and approached with a healthy dose of caution.

In another incident on August 21, 1978, Tom Hillmer, age 19, and his brother Tim climbed the Stone Man Pass route towards the summit of McHenry's Peak. As they traversed a snowfield, Tom slipped and slid to the bottom and struck the rocks below. He fractured both arms and splintered the patella of one leg. Tim made his brother comfortable, and then descended from the peak for help. A rescue team carried Tom out that evening. After this incident, Ranger Larry Van Slyke wrote in *Accidents in North American Mountaineering*, "During the late summer months, many of the high altitude snowfields become "ice" hard. Travel on those snowfields dictates the judicious use of axe and crampons at times, to protect against unwanted, high speed rides down the slopes." Thirty years later, Van Slyke's safety message is still appropriate.

I would like to conclude this chapter with two positive stories about rescues on Longs Peak. Hopefully, they will lead you to gain a better understanding of the challenges of helping those in need.

Sheila Townsend, 48 years old, described herself as an outdoorswoman with a passion to make it to the summit of Longs Peak. After two previous unsuccessful attempts, she headed off alone on her third attempt on August 19, 2007. Townsend later reflected, "I like to be outdoors and be with nature, and that was (being on Longs Peak) the closest you could get there to heaven." After a successful hike to the summit, her accident on the descent might have taken her even closer to those pearly gates than she bargained for. Coming down the mountain about 4:00 p.m., Townsend got off the designated Keyhole Route and wound up above the trail in the area called the False Keyhole, near the Ledges. After one misstep, she stumbled, lost her footing, and tumbled 200 feet. She might have lost consciousness for a short period of time. In her location, her cell phone could not get a signal, and she could not stand on a broken ankle. Townsend was pretty confident she was the last hiker off the mountain that afternoon and quickly realized she would be spending the night there. Staying calm, she crawled into a small crevasse to try to get out of the wind. She pulled her sweatshirt over her head for warmth and waited out the night, enduring near freezing temperatures at the 13,000-foot level of her shelter.

Around 7:00 a.m. the following morning, she heard the voices of nearby hikers and shouted for help. They were able to contact park staff at 7:30 a.m. by cell phone from a different location, and a rescue was soon mobilized. The rescue team at the park was familiar with the area from previous incidents and routine patrols on the mountain. The initial rescue team, led by ranger Ryan Schuster, left the Longs Peak Trailhead by 9:00 a.m. and reached Townsend two hours later. The rescuers stabilized her ankle and made a medical assessment. More rescuers arrived, and Townsend was placed in a litter and carried some 200 feet back up the south side of the False Keyhole. Due to the history of incidents in this area, rangers had established a fixed anchor system in the area to aid in technical rescue operations. Townsend's litter was then lowered 400 to

500 feet through this system down the north side of False Keyhole, and it was later carried out to the Boulderfield. By 3:30 p.m., a Flight for Life helicopter lifted off and carried Townsend to the Medical Center of the Rockies in Loveland.

Helicopter evacuation from the summit of Longs Peak. Courtesy of RMNP

Sheila Townsend later mused that she was fortunate to escape with only bruises and a broken ankle. She knew it was a mistake to climb alone and made a promise to herself not to do it again. "God was watching over me. Really good. He must have sent lots of angels," she said. "Lots of angels." And a few good rescuers—there were 25 park staff involved in the rescue. They were assisted by a paramedic from the Estes Park Medical Center and ten rescuers from Larimer County Search and Rescue.

Townsend's could almost be considered a textbook rescue operation. The weather gods cooperated, and the rescue was completed in about eight hours from notification to helicopter liftoff. Now, hold the good feeling for a moment, before I provide a contrast with the Villano rescue, an incident that occurred almost two years earlier on the upper Keyhole Route with the same type of injury, but with an entirely different route to the hospital.

Around 11:00 a.m. on September 8, 2005, park dispatch was notified by cell phone of an injured hiker in the Trough area of the Keyhole Route on Longs Peak. Minutes earlier, Jeff Villano stumbled and fell twenty feet while descending from the summit. Villano fractured the tibia and fibula just above the right ankle. His status was complicated by his Type I diabetes, a condition that was normally managed by an insulin pump and medications. Chief Ranger Mark Magnuson described the area as "a steep gully littered with loose rock. It is an area where there have been accidents in the past," and at an elevation of 13,600 feet.

The initial rescue team made first contact with Villano about 2:30 p.m. Sending a small team on foot is standard practice to ensure good communication is established and an accurate patient assessment. Because of the victim's location, and the potential for a helicopter to evacuate Villano from the summit of Longs Peak, the initial plan was to package him in a litter and raise him to the summit. With the weather cooperating, eight rescuers and 600 pounds of rescue equipment were flown to the summit of Longs Peak. The two rescue groups confirmed the original plan to raise Villano to the top of the peak for a morning helicopter evacuation. The weather forecast was promising and Villano's condition was stable. The optional litter carryout is difficult for the patient and labor intensive for a rescue team. By 10:00 p.m., the 11 person rescue team raised Villano over 700 feet to the summit and prepared to bivouac for the evening.

It was not to be pleasant. Like the public information given to visitors, one of the first rules of rescue work is **always be prepared to spend the night out.** The rescue team was well prepared to bivouac. However, spending a night out, and enjoying a night out, are two different things. The conditions at 14,000 feet in September deteriorated, with a brisk wind blowing sleet across the summit. The greater concern though was that the weather in the morning would not allow a helicopter evacuation. Predicting the weather on the summits of Colorado's 14ers is almost as delicate as flying a helicopter in the rarified air at 14,000 feet. Unfortunately, the positive forecast from the previous afternoon failed to materialize, as the eastern sky grew gray with the new day. By 6:00 a.m., it was clear that a helicopter would not be able to land on the summit, and the team began the laborious task of lowering Villano's litter down the North Face to the Boulderfield.

That morning, a second team of 15 rescuers was mobilized and sent up to the Boulderfield to assist the first team with the carryout, in the event a helicopter would be unable to land in that area. The second team tied in with the first team at Chasm View near the base of the North Face around 5:45 p.m. They took over management of the litter and brought Villano down into the Boulderfield. By 7:00 p.m., the weather gods continued to frown on this incident as high winds prevented the landing of a helicopter ambulance. At this point, the only saving grace for the exhausted rescue team was that the slow technical raising and lowering of Villano in the litter was behind them. Without the helicopter, the only option was to place the litter on a wheel apparatus and carry Villano the six miles to the trailhead. Anticipating this, a third team of 15 rescuers made up of volunteers from Larimer County Search and Rescue and Rocky Mountain Rescue Group from Boulder tied in with the other two teams to help carry the litter out. It was approaching 3:00 a.m. on September 10th when Jeff Villano arrived at the Longs Peak Trailhead.

This rescue took nearly 40 hours from notification to ambulance transport at the trailhead and involved over 50 people. The similar situation that involved injured hiker Sheila Townsend in 2007 required only 8 hours, mostly thanks to good weather.

Obviously, Villano and Townsend did not fall and injure themselves on purpose. The park and volunteer rescue teams train for and are well prepared for these types of incidents, knowing that people get into trouble or get hurt. Nonetheless, rescuers are counting on you to make good decisions. As will be mentioned throughout this book, a primary goal is to reduce the number of search or rescue incidents through good decision making on the part of the user of parks and other public lands. Remember that rescuers are not required to help you. They do so out of the goodness of their hearts and care for their fellow humans. Do them the favor of making good decisions based on common sense and information provided by public land managers.

> **Safety Lessons drawn from these incidents:**
> 1. **Be cautious around snowfields**, particularly in the summer.
> 2. **Always leave a trip plan with friends or family.** Nineteen of the individuals who died were hiking alone. This is good reason to be extra cautious.
> 3. **Keep your groups together!** Parents, youth, or scout leaders—if you need to split up, do so with a responsible person in each group.
> 4. **Stay on established trails or routes.** A significant number of hiker fatalities occurred to those attempting a shortcut.

Falls While Hiking and Scrambling

August 2, 1905	Louis R. Levings, 21	**East Face of Ypsilon Mountain** Attempted to descend to photograph snow cornices. *Fell when rock hold broke off.*
August 2, 1918	Eula Frost, 19	**Snowbank near Fall River Pass** Crossing large *snowfield, lost footing* and slid 500 feet to rocks below.
June 26, 1921	H. F. Targett, 55	**Near Peacock Pool below Chasm Lake** *Disappeared while hiking alone* to Chasm Lake. Skull found 19 years later near Peacock Pool believed to be that of Targett. (Not in text.)
July 20, 1921	Gregory Aubuchon, 18	**Longs Peak, East Face** Attempted summit of Longs Peak alone. *Unwitnessed fall. Inexperienced.* Body found 2 months later on Mills Glacier below the Notch. Likely fell from the East Face.
September 13, 1931	R. B. Key, age unknown	**Longs Peak** *Scrambling/hiking alone. Unwitnessed fall.* Body found on Mills Glacier. Identified by a time slip from a coal company in Ohio.
August 29, 1932	Gary Secor, Jr., 16	**Longs Peak, Keyhole Route** Ascended Cables Route to summit. Descended Keyhole route. Told friend he was *going to take a shortcut. Fell near the False Keyhole.*
September 6, 1936	Forrest Hein, 16	**Dusty Dome on McGregor Mountain** *Fell while scrambling/climbing* the face of Dusty Dome. Unroped. (Not in text.)
August 8, 1938	John A. Fuller, 20	**Longs Peak, west of Cables Route** Fuller had been to the summit 13 times. Was apparently interested in trying out some new climbing shoes. *Scrambling. Unwitnessed fall* on to the left Dovetail snow formation.

September 6, 1940	Hoyt F. White, 33	**Twin Sisters** *Scrambling/hiking* near the fire lookout. Unwitnessed fall. Body found 2 weeks later. (Not in text.)
June 16, 1946	Thomas H. Evans, 20	**Tyndall Gorge snowfield** Evans attempted shortcut from Flattop Mountain to Bear Lake. Lost footing and fell on snowfield. Struck rocks at bottom. Body found 3 weeks later.
July 11, 1952	John H. Tallmadge, 21	**Hallet Peak** *Solo, inexperienced hiker attempted shortcut* down cliff bands on south side of peak. Body found 4 months later.
July 31, 1953	Kathryn Rees, 15 Sandra Miller, 17	**Little Matterhorn Mountain** Both were with a hiking group from Cheley Camp in Estes Park. Rees *panicked* when a rock she was grasping became loose, *lost her balance,* and rolled over cliff. Miller was sent to get help at the Fern Lake Lodge, but *fell* over 100-foot cliff.
June 5, 1954	Earl F. Harvey, 19	**Longs Peak, west of Cables Route** Harvey and friend made a successful ascent of the Cables Route. Because of heavy snow, they decided to descend along the ridge above the Keyhole. *Lost footing and fell.* (Not in text.)
August 15, 1956	George Bloom, 21	**Mt. Craig above Grand Lake** Scrambling on descent from summit in *poor, wet weather.* Became separated, *fell* over 200 foot cliff. First recorded use of a helicopter on SAR in the park.
August 21, 1959	Jeanne Gillett, 31	**Tyndall Glacier** Gillett and her husband were attempting to backtrack up the Tyndall Glacier, when she *lost her footing and slid* to rocks below.
July 13, 1960	Lester Reeble, 45	**Near Chiefs Head** On descent. Unroped. Rock hand hold broke, and he fell. (Not in text.)

August 13, 1962	Patricia L. Beatty, 21	**Chaos Canyon snowfield** *Hiking alone* in Chaos Canyon. *Body found on rocks below snowfield.* Unwitnessed fall.
August 15, 1962	Gerald R. Noland, 20	**Andrews Glacier Tarn** *Lost balance on steep snowfield* and slid into rocks.
August 27, 1962	Ken Murphy, 19	**Longs Peak, ridge above the Keyhole Route** Murphy was a YMCA employee who raced ahead of his two companions on the Cables Route to the summit. *Unwitnessed fall on descent* from the Northwest Ridge above the Keyhole Route.
September 30, 1962	James S. O'Toole, 20	**Longs Peak, North Face** O'Toole successfully made the summit via the Keyhole route. On descent, *attempted a shortcut* from the Keyhole Route to Chasm View. *Unwitnessed fall* on to the left wing of the Dove snowfield.
July 17, 1965	Robert E. Brown, 28	**Loch Vale Trail** *Hiking alone.* Unwitnessed 150-foot fall. Body found 12 days later. (Not in text.)
June 14, 1966	Jay DuPont, 14	**Thatchtop Mountain** On a Boy Scout trip, DuPont *defied instructions, separated from his group, and attempted to slide* down a steep rock face. Lost balance and fell 350 feet.
July 3, 1969	Jerry P. Johnson, 12	**Deer Mountain** Not much is known of this incident. Johnson appears to have been scrambling on the rocks above Baker Curve and taken a fall. (Not in text.)
June 12, 1972	Paul F. Russell, 24	**Longs Peak, Keyhole Route** *Poorly equipped for technical conditions. Unwitnessed fall* of 150 feet near the upper end of the Narrows.

August 15, 1974	John Berger, 11	**Twins Sisters** Few details available on this incident. Fell somewhere on Twin Sisters. (Not in text.)
July 18, 1975	Chris Rejeske, 15	**Ypsilon Mountain** Rejeske and friend had hiked to the summit of Ypsilon. *Attempted to slide down a snowfield* between Ypsilon and Chiquita. *Lost footing and slid 500 feet* to rock outcrop.
August 4, 1975	Allan Jacobs, 21	**Elk Tooth near Ogalalla Peak** Unwitnessed fall while *scrambling/ hiking alone* on the Elk Tooth formation. (Not in text.)
October 1, 1975	William A. Pistorio, 18	**The Apron between Meeker and Longs** Unwitnessed 150-foot fall while *scrambling/hiking alone* in steep terrain. Wearing cowboy boots.
May 12, 1977	Asuncion Navaretti, 27	**MacGregor Slab** Fell while scrambling/climbing. (Not in text.)
May 17, 1977	Harold Holtzendorf, 20	**MacGregor Slab** Fell while scrambling/climbing. (Not in text.)
September 1, 1979	Coy Conley, 30	**Ute Trail Crossing on Trail Ridge Road** *Lost footing. Fell/slid on snowfield* near the Trail Ridge Road.
June 26, 1980	Robert A. Silver, 16	**Longs Peak, Keyhole Route** Silver was on a Boy Scout outing to the summit with a local guide. The Keyhole Route was still considered technical due to ice/snow. In the Homestretch, Silver moved above the route to steeper, but dry rock. *Panicked, lost footing* and fell 300 feet.
August 5, 1980	John Link, 43	**Wild Basin near the Cleaver** During a training run for the Pikes Peak Marathon, Link had an *unwitnessed fall* near the Cleaver on steep terrain.

August 24, 1980	Christine M. Ulbricht, 12	**Twin Sisters** On a family outing, Christine and a friend became *separated from the group* off the main trail. *Slipped on wet rock* and fell over cliff band. (Not in text.)
August 31, 1980	James S. Johnston, 25	**Near Stone Man Pass** *Hiking alone. Unwitnessed* 150-foot fall on east side of ridge below Stone Man Pass. (Not in text.)
June 29, 1982	Robert S. Baldeshwiler, 12	**Flattop Mountain Trail** Energetic youth got out in front of his family on Flattop Trail. *Poorly equipped* for changing weather. Likely *attempted shortcut* near the Emerald Lake overlook and fell on steep terrain. Massive search. Body found 12 days later.
June 12, 1984	David P. Ormsby, 23	**MacGregor Slab** Fell while scrambling unroped. (Not in text.)
September 12, 1986	Lawrence N. Farrell, 33	**Longs Peak** Startled by nearby rock fall. *Lost balance. Unroped fall* while descending from Longs Peak on Upper Clark's Arrow route. (Not in text.)
August 29, 1987	David D. Felts, 21	**MacGregor Slab** Became separated from friend. Unwitnessed, unroped fall while on descent. (Not in text.)
December 16, 1987	John R. Schnakenberg, 22	**Deer Mountain** *Scrambling/hiking alone* on south face of Deer Mountain. Unwitnessed fall. (Not in text.)
August 15, 1988	George C. Ogden, 21	**Spearhead Mountain** Ogden was on a solo day hike. *Unwitnessed fall on steep terrain.* Body found by rangers on backcountry patrol.

June 29, 1990	Andrew Tufly, 15	**South side of Twin Sisters** Technical rock scrambling with youth group. Against advice of group leaders, Tufly attempted a descent down a steeper area. *Pulled rock loose, lost balance, and fell down* scree and over cliff band. (Not in text.)
July 29, 1990	Timothy Fromalt, 27	**Longs Peak, Keyhole Route** Fromalt was descending along the Homestretch. He *encountered wet rock and started sliding, lost his balance* and tumbled into a rock. Unconscious, but initially breathing. Stopped breathing. CPR started, then stopped. Lightning and heavy rain during rescue operation.
July 11, 1992	Sarah Wolenetz, 11	**Bear Lake** Church youth group on day hike. Sarah developed a sore heel and was *told to wait along side of trail* for group to return. Later *attempted short cut* back to Bear Lake. Fell over 40-foot cliff band.
July 29, 1992	Gary Boyer, 34	**Mt. Meeker** Solo hike/scramble with plan to summit Longs Peak via the Loft route. *Off route, unwitnessed fall* from north face of Mt. Meeker.
August 16, 1992	John M. Hofstra, 23	**Little Matterhorn Mountain** After successful summit hike, began descent down popular class 3 route. The three companions took slightly different routes to avoid rock fall. Initial cause of fall unwitnessed, unknown. Companions heard rock fall and turned to see fatal fall. (Not in text.)

August 25, 1995	Jun Kamimura, 33	**Longs Peak, Keyhole Route** 400-foot fall from the Ledges section of the Keyhole Route. Witnessed by visitors and rangers on patrol. Kamimura told Rangers he was having *difficulty with the altitude. Appears to have lost his balance, stumbled.* Paramedic on scene in 30 minutes pronounced him dead due to head injuries.
September 9, 1997	Timothy M. Maron, 26	**The Apron between Meeker and Longs** *Solo hiker fell* 150 feet from a stretch of ledges in the Loft area. Unwitnessed.
June 24, 1999	Charles Harrison, 47	**Windy Gulch Cascades area** Harrison was hiking down the Ute Trail from the Trail Ridge Road with his son. They *lost the trail* and moved south into steep terrain. Attempted to reach the Fern Lake Trail visible below. Son went for help. Harrison had *unwitnessed fall,* suffering head injuries. (Not in text.)
August 3, 1999	Raymond Decker, 75	**Longs Peak, Keyhole Route** *Solo hiker suffered unwitnessed 150-foot fall* in the Narrows section of trail.
August 4, 1999	James D. Page, 56	**The Apron between Meeker and Longs** Ascending through the Loft area to the summit of Longs Peak with his son. In wet, drizzly weather near the Gorrell's Traverse area, Page *slipped on wet rock and tumbled down 90 feet,* sustaining severe injuries. Darkness and fog hindered search effort that evening. Page's body found the next morning.
August 14, 1999	Gregory Koczanski, 42	**Longs Peak, Keyhole Route** With wife, Koczanski made it to the Ledges area of the Keyhole Route, but decided to turn around due to high winds and safety concerns. *Unwitnessed fall. It appears a strong gust of wind may have knocked Koczanski off balance.*

July 23, 2003	Kurt Zollers, 34	**Baker Mountain in Never Summer Range** Zollers was a researcher doing field studies on bighorn sheep. Somewhat familiar with the area. *Unwitnessed fall over cliff band.* (Not in text.)
June 23, 2004	Abigail Walter, 13	**Cascade Falls along North Inlet Trail** Walter was with an outdoor education group. *Slipped on wet rock* and fell, striking head. (Not in text.)
July 29, 2005	Jeff Christensen, 31	**Between Mt. Chiquita and Ypsilon Mountain** NPS ranger on backcountry patrol. *Unwitnessed fall. Struck head.* (See chapter one.)
September 3, 2006	Clayton Smith, 58	**The Apron between Meeker and Longs** Smith and friend had summited Mt. Meeker and were descending in the Loft area when Smith *slipped and tumbled 300 feet*, sustaining massive traumatic injuries.
September 4, 2009	Carol Nicolaidis, 62	**Just north of the Odessa Lake spur on the Bear to Fern Lake Trail** Victim *stumbled or slipped off trail*, down 50-ft. slope, and into creek. Died 3 hours later of blunt force internal injuries complicated by hypothermia.
September 10, 2009	John Bramley, 55	**Longs Peak, North Face below False Keyhole** Solo hiker fell in unwitnessed fall. (Not in text.)

THREE:

Falls
While Climbing

Some people fall while climbing; others trip, stumble, or fall while hiking, as listed in the previous chapter. "Climb," "climbing," and "climber" are generic terms that have evolved over the decades. At the turn of the twentieth century, visitors did not "hike" up Longs Peak, they "climbed" it. Even today, you hear hikers boasting of "climbing" Longs, when they really trudged up the Keyhole route. So what is the difference?

For the purpose of this chapter, a key distinction is that climbers use equipment such as ropes, carabineers, ice axes, and crampons to move safely on rock or ice on a near-vertical surface. The sport takes skill, practice, and mental discipline. The average age of the 26 climber fatalities is 29 years, compared to 25 years for hikers.

The distinction between hiking and climbing gained traction on September 7, 1922, when Professor James W. Alexander of Princeton solo climbed the "unclimbable" East Face of Longs Peak.

Climbing techniques and rope management at the time were primitive at best, but they were evolving.

Professor James Alexander on the East Face of Longs Peak in 1922. Photo by Jack Moomaw. Courtesy of RMNP

In 1927, German emigrants Joe and Paul Stettner rode their motorcycles from Chicago to Colorado, an epic journey in itself considering there was no interstate highway system in 1927, and few paved roads. The brothers made their way to Longs Peak and pioneered their Stettner Ledges Route, which became the standard for difficult routes for decades. Their climbing techniques were well beyond most Colorado climbers at the time. The brothers used pitons and carabineers and knew how to belay one another.

Another climbing first occurred on August 1, 1960, when Bob Kamps and Dave Rearick accomplished a successful two-and-a-half day ascent of the never-before-climbed face of the Diamond on Longs Peak. They called their new route the Ace of Diamonds, now known as "D1." Today, there

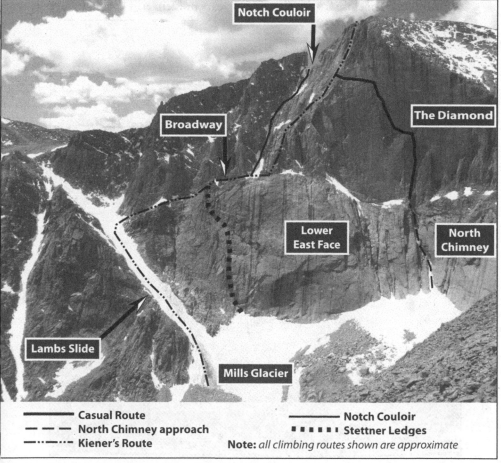

East Face of Longs Peak with climbing routes and features.

are dozens of established routes on the Diamond. Just as the automobile evolved from the Model T to the modern vehicles of today, so has the skill of climbers from Alexander to Kamps and Rearick to today's elite climbers.

Yet, for all the skill and mental discipline required of the sport, climbers do make mistakes, and often in unexpected moments of carelessness. Considering the high angle environment most climbers find themselves in, mistakes are not often forgiving. Here are a few of their stories.

Falls on Rock

Superintendent Roger Toll described one of the earliest climbing fatalities in a letter dated July 24, 1926. Forrest Ketring, age 19, and Reuel James, age 21, had been close friends for several years in Denver. They had done

Newspaper headline article on Ketring fatality. Courtesy of the *Rocky Mountain News*

some mountaineering and James had summited Longs Peak twice via the Keyhole Route. Superintendent Roger Toll reported that the young men "were fairly well dressed for a climb, having high mountain boots with rubber soles. They did not carry a rope or ice axe." On July 22, 1926, they drove to the Longs Peak Trailhead and hiked to the Timberline cabin, where they spent the night with a trail crew. On the 23rd, they woke early, hiked around the north side of Chasm Lake, successfully climbed Alexander's Chimney, traversed to the right, and continued up the steep face toward the Broadway Ledge. Toll wrote, "Apparently they were on the route taken by Professor Alexander of Princeton, when he made the first ascent of the east side of the peak in 1922. A few others have taken this same route during the past few years, but it is recognized as the most dangerous route up Longs Peak."

James later told Toll that Ketring was in the lead and about fifteen feet above him. Ketring said that everything looked all right; the footing was not very good where he was, but it looked better ahead. Remember, they did not have a rope. The boys were feeling well, making fairly good time and confident of success. The weather was clear and sunny and the rock face was dry. James stated that he had glanced back over the route they had come and stole a view of the distant plains on a beautiful day, when suddenly he heard Ketring sliding down the steep rock face. He shot past James without a word or cry, just out of reach to the right of him, and disappeared from sight.

Shaken by the incident, James was able to climb down the route they had come up and found Ketring's body on the snow. He then contacted the trail crew working below Chasm Lake. One of the men, Otho Jones, went with James to the Timberline Cabin, where they phoned park headquarters. Jones then cut two saplings, took blankets, rope, and wire to form a stretcher, and led the crew up to retrieve the body. "Wrapping the body in the blankets, the crew fastened it to the poles and carried it, over very rough and difficult country, to the end of the new trail about a mile distance." Superintendent Toll and ranger Jack Moomaw met the crew below Chasm Lake and carried Ketring's body out on the back of a horse.

Toll concluded his report, "The National Park Service has never recommended the east side route to anyone. It should never be attempted by anyone who is not an unusually competent climber and accompanied by an experienced guide." Unfortunately, Ketring and James did not appear to have the skills recommended by Toll, and Ketring paid the ultimate price. I believe this is the first record of an organized trail crew supporting the ranger staff in a rescue operation in Rocky Mountain National Park. Over the years, park trail crews have been a valuable resource in helping those in need. Young, strong, and knowledgeable about the park, they are often the first called, and the last back. Their support is very much appreciated by the ranger staff.

Author's note: A few publications I researched spelled this young man's name as "Keatring." In Superintendent Roger Toll's report to the National Park Service Director, he spelled the name as "Ketring." I have elected to go with the Superintendent's version.

Overconfidence and a poor attitude likely contributed to the death of Charles W. Thiemeyer in 1928. Thiemeyer was known to have said there were "no mountains in Colorado worth climbing." Originally from Switzerland, the Denver resident was climbing with Mr. and Mrs. Arthur Stacher, all members of the Denver Swiss Alpine Club. The trio summited many Colorado peaks, but this was their first attempt to climb Longs Peak by the East Face. On August 18, 1929, Thiemeyer was in the lead and fell 1,500 feet from the Notch Couloir of Longs Peak. Arthur Stacher sustained deep gashes on his palms from trying to hold the rope during Thiemeyer's fall. Without the rope, the Stachers became marooned for the night. Their cries for help were relayed to the park staff and they were rescued the next day by rangers Jack Moomaw, Walter Finn, and Mark Dings.

The three rangers left the Boulderfield cabin at 3:30 a.m., climbed the Cables Route to the summit, and then descended to a point where they were able to lower a rope to the Stachers and guide them to safety. At that time, the rangers were not aware that there had been a third member of the climbing party with the Stachers. After escorting the Stachers down the North Face to the Boulderfield, the three rangers descended the cliff bands below Mt. Lady Washington to Mills Glacier. The group met up with a party of 12 searchers under the direction of Superintendent E.B. Rogers and proceeded to look for Thiemeyer's body. Because of the constant danger of falling rock, the group spread out and found the remains of Thiemeyer wedged in among the fissures of Mills Glacier. Rangers Moomaw and Dings pulled the body down Mills Glacier, and it was placed in a litter and carried around Chasm Lake to Chasm Meadows, then loaded on a pack horse for the trip to the trailhead.

In the subsequent article in the *Rocky Mountain News*, Stacher recalled, "I was holding the lower end of a 30 yard rope and my friend had succeeded in fastening it, rather insecurely, to a crag, when I saw him slip." "Don't go up there, it's not safe," Stacher had warned Thiemeyer. "Oh, I can make it all right," answered Thiemeyer. A moment later, he fell.

Charles Grant, age 19, from Chicago, Illinois, was reported to have summited Longs Peak 26 times. On September 1, 1946, he was climbing with Estes Park residents Walter Gray and John Purvis on the Stettner Ledges Route. According to Gray and Purvis, Purvis was leading the climb when he fell about 60 feet, but was saved by the rope attached around his waist. During the fall, it was thought that Grant instinctively attempted to catch the rope, but missed, lost his balance and fell 600 feet to his death.

A party of four University of Colorado students—David L. Jones, age 18; Prince D. Willmon, 23; Jane Bendixon, 18; and James Greig, 21—left Monday at midnight on April 19, 1960, to ascend Longs Peak via Alexander's Chimney and the upper Kiener's Route. The weather was fair, and their plan was for a one day climb. Speed was important, and the group packed lightly. Upon reaching the base of Alexander's Chimney, Greig was not feeling well and decided to return to the Longs Peak campground. When the other three failed to return that night, Greig contacted park rangers, as well as the Rocky Mountain Rescue Group (RMR) out of Boulder. Gregg said the three "were well equipped and expert climbers," which was later proven not to be the case, at least in relation to the difficult weather on the summit.

Ranger Bob Frauson and seasonal ranger John Clark, who was also a member of RMR, left Wednesday morning, April 20th, at 4:45 a.m. for the Chasm Lake shelter. Seven other members of RMR left the trailhead at 11:00 a.m. The day's search effort in difficult weather focused on the North and East Faces of Longs Peak. The missing climbers were not found, but tracks believed to belong to them were noted heading south toward Wild Basin from the saddle between Mt. Meeker and Longs Peak. The searchers returned to Longs Peak Ranger Station for the night.

Approximately 7:00 p.m. that same evening, an exhausted and hypothermic Jane Bendixon stumbled into the home of N.L. Sutherland in Allenspark. She was rushed to Estes Park Hospital with severe frostbite. Bendixon told rescuers the climb went well until the sudden storm struck, at which time they were still a few hundred feet below the summit of Longs. They decided to traverse over the slabs to the Notch, then on to the south side of the summit. They had hoped to find the Keyhole Route down, but visibility was near zero and the group was too low for this escape route. They got to a point where they rappelled down a steep slope. In near whiteout conditions, Jones rappelled once more, but told Bendixon and Willmon to stay where they were under a rock overhang with a snowdrift in front. Jones spent the night in a small niche in the rock below them. The group was about "500 feet above timberline," according to Bendixon. She described Willmon's condition as very poor, "his skin had already begun to blister and bleed." She apparently was not as worried about Jones, who was in "the best shape of all of us." The next morning, all were weak and frostbitten. Willmon encouraged Bendixon to rappel down to Jones, which she was able to do. Feeling too faint to rappel farther on her own, Jones was able to belay her below his position. Weakened from the cold, at some point she fell near the end of her rope and lost consciousness. When she came to, she could not hear or see either man. She untied from the belay rope and staggered down the mountain for help, arriving at the Sutherland residence that evening.

The next morning, a search team left Wild Basin to retrace Bendixon's tracks back up Hunter's Creek to the South Face of Longs Peak. Another team left Longs Peak Ranger Station to climb over the col between Longs and Meeker. At about 11:00 a.m., the two parties met in the snow cirque south of Longs Peak. Later that afternoon, they found the bodies of Willmon and Jones. In *Accidents in North American Mountaineering*, rescuer H.F. Walton wrote, "from the position of the bodies, Jones must have fallen from a point close to where Bendixen last saw him. Willmon must have rappelled or climbed down the rope almost to its end before he fell; the marks he made in the snow were close to Bendixon's. Both men died from hitting rocks as they fell. Both were badly frostbitten. Had they not been frostbitten, they probably would not have fallen." This was consistent with the story told by Bendixon. They appeared to have been unable to control their descent because of fatigue and frostbitten hands. A Lowry-based H-21 helicopter removed the bodies.

Willmon was an experienced climber with a strong mountaineering background. Perhaps his enthusiasm for the one day assault was contagious and resulted in the group being overconfident and inadequately prepared for the sudden, bad weather. As one rescuer said, "They were inadequately clothed for Longs Peak at any time of year." In the post incident analysis, Walton offered that, "Willmon was not only a first class rock climber, but a good mountaineer who had had winter experience. It is incredible that he should not have gone prepared to meet bad weather if it came. He and Jones had just been climbing Shiprock and other pinnacles in New Mexico and southern Colorado; perhaps it was hard to adjust psychologically to the fact that they came to a major mountain where it was still winter. Also, had they known the mountain better, they could have saved themselves. A continuous snow couloir leads down from the Notch to the shelter of Wild Basin." This incident is yet another reminder of the importance of being properly prepared for rapid weather changes above timberline in the mountains of Colorado.

Myron M. Fritts, age 19, fell from the north chimney of Hallett Peak on Friday, July 14, 1961. From Detroit, Michigan, Fritts was a student at Notre Dame University and a summer employee of the Colorado Transportation Company working at the Fall River Pass Store. He was climbing alone and left a map of his route with coworkers before signing in at the Glacier Gorge Trailhead with the destination of Hallett Peak. When he failed to show up for work Saturday, company employees notified park rangers. That day, ranger John Mueller checked the summit register and did not find Fritts' name. A military helicopter was used in the unsuccessful search, with ranger Bob Frauson as the spotter. Three climbers from the Denver/Boulder area discovered Fritts' body on Sunday morning, July 16th, around 10:30 a.m. The body had to be carried out after a difficult lowering.

Denver area resident Blake Hiester, Jr., age 48, was a former president of the Colorado Bar Association. On August 27, 1966, while leading a party consisting of his son, Richard, age 18, and two friends up the Kiener's Route, he lost his footing and fell 1,200 feet from the base of the Notch Couloir Chimneys (13,300 ft.) to Mills Glacier. He was not roped in or belayed. The exact cause of the fall is unknown, though it was believed Hiester was on one of the more difficult variations of the regular route. Hiester was familiar with Longs Peak, having made 22 attempts on the peak from different routes. However, it had been six years since he had last climbed this particular route. The group was also behind schedule and was possibly hurrying in the face of an approaching thunderstorm. After the fall, the other three climbers continued on because it was safer going up than down. Ranger Don Bachman was on patrol in the Chasm Lake area and quickly learned of the accident.

This incident is especially tragic in that a son witnessed his father falling to his death. It is also an example of the challenges faced by those in the emergency services community in dealing with death. The body had to be recovered, and the fall resulted in Hiester's body breaking apart into several scattered pieces. The body recovery was conducted by rangers Bachman, Doug Erskine, Jerry Phillips, Tom Griffiths, and Larry Collins, new seasonal employee Larry Van Slyke, and Brian Marts, the chief guide for the climbing concession. When the team got to Mills Glacier, they found the legs on separate parts of the glacier. The upper part of his body was nowhere to be seen, but from the blood and small body parts, it was clear that the rest of the body had dropped into the crevasse between the rock wall and front edge of the glacier.

Brian Marts volunteered to go down and try to find the rest of the body. He followed blood signs almost 200 feet down to where the glacier started to flatten out before he was successful. He tied the end of a rope onto the remains, and then climbed back up the rope hand over hand. Collins, Van Slyke, and Griffiths rappelled about 30 feet to a snow bridge so that they could pull the body up. They got it up to about 20 feet below the belay point when it hung up. Van Slyke went down to boost it up over the projection. The team was able to get the body up to the snow bridge, and the rest of the crew pulled it out. There were various other body parts above and around the team, which also had to be collected.

Years later, Tom Griffiths recalled, "We didn't have all of the debriefing teams to come in after dealing with tragedy back then. We were supposed to be tough. We probably did have some nightmares after some of them." In the early 1990s, the National Park Service implemented a Critical Incident Stress Management (CISM) Program to provide counseling to employees who had been involved with critical or stressful incidents. Most emergency services organizations have similar programs today.

Steve Day, age 22, was well known in the park, as he had volunteered and participated in several rescue operations with the park staff. He was also a member of the Hidden Valley Ski Patrol. On June 18, 1972, he was climbing with friends Dave and Johanna Whitman on Pagoda Mountain. When they encountered steep terrain, they decided to seek an easier route. The Whitman's reported the group had set a piton as a rappel anchor. Day was rappelling, the last to do so, when the piton pulled out and he fell 200 feet to his death down the cirque above Keplinger Lake.

In a winter incident, Eldorado Springs, Colorado, resident Robert Elliott, age 26, was climbing with 24-year-old Michael O'Donnell of Boulder, Colorado, in the upper portion of the North Chimney of Longs Peak on January 10, 1981. At approximately 11:00 a.m., Elliott fell 90 feet during a pendulum swing when a "friend" (mechanical cam anchor) placed by O'Donnell came loose. Rangers, along with personnel from Fantasy Ridge Mountain Guides and Rocky Mountain Rescue, were flown to Chasm Lake, where they began a technical climb toward the victim. They reached him about 5:45 p.m. and confirmed the fatality. Because of darkness and dangerous terrain, rescuers remained on the scene overnight and brought Elliott's body out the next morning.

On July 1, 1984, Lee S. Jamieson, 20 years old and a popular Estes Park climber, fell approximately 300 feet to his death. He was climbing with 19-year-old Charles Sperry of Plano, Texas, a summer employee of the Stanley Hotel. They had successfully completed a roped technical climb of the Spiral Route on Notchtop Mountain. As they prepared to descend on easier terrain, they unroped. Jamieson fell to his death when a large rock he was standing on came loose. Jamieson was an accomplished technical climber and had climbed Notchtop before. He essentially grew up in Rocky Mountain National Park and first climbed Longs Peak when he was eight years old. The family so loved Rocky Mountain National Park that donations in Lee's memory were requested to be sent to the Rocky Mountain Nature Association for the purchase of the Jennings property, a piece of private property in the park they hoped would be returned to its natural condition.

In another father/son bonding incident, Jack L. McConnell, age 59, was having the type of day that most of us could appreciate. He was retired and sharing an afternoon climbing with his son—an activity they both enjoyed. The Albuquerque, New Mexico, lawyer had been raised in Colorado, and his son was attending law school in Denver. His son told rescuers that his father had 15 years of climbing experience and was comfortable leading 5.6/5.7 climbs. On May 23, 1994, the McConnell's intention was to climb the White Whale Route, 5.7, on the Left Book Formation at Lumpy Ridge. Jack McConnell was in the lead when he got off the intended route to a more difficult section of the rock face. He shouted down to his son, who was belaying him, "Hey, it's getting a little thin up here," just before he fell and struck his head, sustaining severe head injuries. Neither was wearing a climbing helmet. The son lowered his father as far as possible, and then left to summon help at approximately 3:00 p.m. Initial responders detected faint vital signs, which ceased partway through the four-hour lowering/rescue operation. Over 30 rescuers were involved in the evacuation. Several were flown over from the ongoing search for Alli Bierma in the Cub Lake area of the park (see chapter seven on suicides). McConnell was pronounced dead at 7:40 p.m.

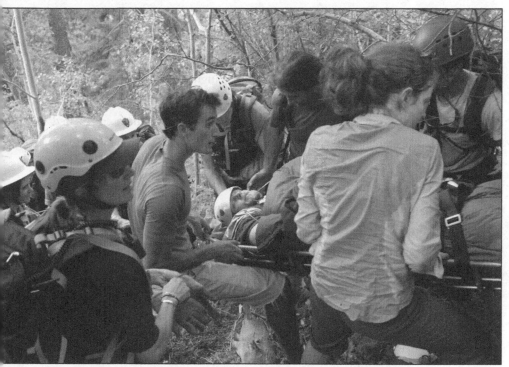

Litter/patient management in 2007 climber rescue in rough terrain below Lumpy Ridge.
Photo courtesy of RMNP.

Estes Park resident Todd Marshall, age 35, fell while climbing on the
Petit Grepon July 2, 1997. This rock spire, one of several collectively known
as the Cathedral Spires, is located immediately to the northwest of Sky Pond.
Marshall was climbing with Mateo Baceda from Italy. As the more experienced climber, Marshall was leading the climb and had just finished the
South Face Route (rated 5.8). In his excitement at having completed the
climb, Marshall was reported to have stood up with his arms upraised and
shouted a "Hurray!" at which moment a strong gust of wind appeared to
have blown him off balance. He fell 70 feet, striking the rock face and sustaining a depressed occipital skull fracture that killed him instantly. He was
not wearing a helmet. Unskilled with self-rescue techniques, Baceda spent
an unpleasant evening stranded on a small ledge, entangled in ropes and
unable to reach Marshall above him or to get off the spire. The accident occurred around 7:00 p.m. Wednesday night. The pair had been expected to

return late that evening. When they did not return by Thursday morning, Marshall's wife, Linda, notified the National Park Service, and a search was initiated. By 9:45 a.m., a resources management employee in the back-country reported seeing the two men, one hanging upside-down. A ranger was able to reach Marshall by mid afternoon and at 3:29 p.m. confirmed the fatality. At about the same time, two other climbers in the area reached Baceda and were helping him down the face of the spire. Baceda was flown out of the Sky Pond area that evening. He was taken to the Estes Park Medical Center for evaluation and released. Marshall's body was flown out Friday morning. Volunteers from Larimer County Search and Rescue and the Colorado Mountain School staff assisted with the incident.

In thinking about those fortunate enough to get a "second chance," it is important to point out that second chances aren't always just good luck. Many times, it is the result of good judgment and/or techniques. Such was the case for climbers Bill Eubank and Brad Van Diver from Boulder. The following narrative was provided by ranger Ernie Field to *Trail and Timberline* magazine, December, 1948:

> *At about noon on July 17, 1948, Eubank and Van Diver had practically finished an uneventful climb of Stettner Ledges on the East Face of Longs Peak. Van Diver was leading the last pitch and Eubank was belaying. When Van Diver was only a few feet from Broadway, he either slipped, or was struck in the head and momentarily stunned by a small rock falling from higher on the peak. In any event, he fell about 40 feet, as he was climbing some 20 feet above his last piton. Eubank fortunately was in an excellent belaying position and was anchored to his position by another piton. As Van Diver fell, Eubank was able to take in a small amount of slack and release sufficient rope to affect a dynamic belay when Van Diver reached the limit of his fall. While Eubank was lifted from his feet by the impact, he was not pulled from the wall since he was held in by his anchor. Van Diver suffered a severe scalp laceration when he scraped his head against the wall as he fell, and was unconscious for three hours while Eubank rendered first aid and signaled for help. A rescue party, led by seasonal ranger George*

Hurt, arrived at the scene several hours later and was able to get the injured climber off the face before dark. Both of these young men are very good climbers, and have studied a number of technical manuals of the subject. It is believed that this accident, although painful for Van Diver, illustrates how a good knowledge of climbing techniques, and a proper application of the same, prevented a tragedy that could well have been fatal to both men.

In addition to good luck and competence in self rescue, the skills of well organized rescue teams have saved many lives over the years. Hats off to a Rocky Mountain National Park rescue team who earned the National Park Service's first ever Valor Award for a rescue in 1956 for demonstrating unusual courage involving a high degree of personal risk in the face of dangers. The citation for Valor Award reads as follows:

On May 30–31, 1956, rangers Robert N. Frauson, Frank J. Betts, Jerry W. Hammond, and Norman L. Nesbit of a Rocky Mountain National Park rescue team participated in an unusually arduous and dangerous rescue operation. On the afternoon of May 30, Patrick Dwyer, a 17 year-old park visitor, fell when his rappel rope slipped as he was descending the rugged sheer face of Hallet Peak. Dwyer fell free for almost 200 feet, landed on a snowfield, and slid about 200 feet farther before he hit a tree on a ledge less than three feet wide, preventing his falling over a precipice to certain death. Ranger Nesbit was in the vicinity with another climbing group, witnessed the accident, and sent a member of his party to Bear Lake to report it. Nesbit then climbed to aid the victim and await the arrival of help. Rangers Frauson, Betts, and Hammond arrived on the scene about three hours later, and rescue operations, requiring ten separate belays, continued for more than four hours in the darkness through the spring snow which made footing difficult. At one point, ranger Betts crashed through a snowbridge covering a crevasse and was saved only by a sling rope tied to the litter. It was after midnight on May 31 when the trailhead was reached and the victim taken to the hospital. As a tribute to the great courage

in assisting in the rescue operation with complete disregard for their
own personal safety, the Department of Interior confers upon rangers
Betts, Frauson, Nesbit, and Hammond its Valor Award.

These four rangers, along with ranger Jack W. Cahoon from Cape Hatteras National Seashore, were recognized on April 23, 1957.

As earlier noted, the main reason the National Park Service refused to allow climbs on the Diamond in the 1950s was concern that the park staff would be unable to effect a rescue on the Diamond wall, and this would put rescuers' lives at risk. After Californians Bob Kamps and Dave Rearick made their historic first ascent of the Diamond in 1960, several more routes were established and the National Park Service began to gain confidence in the climbing community. It was almost ten years before the first major test of rescue techniques on the Diamond were put to use, and it was recognized as an epic event.

In early August 1969, 16-year-old Kordel Kor and 15-year-old Mike Van Loon began a climb on the Diamond. By 11:30 a.m., they were about 125 feet above Broadway when Kor took a leader fall. He only fell about 10 feet, but he fell into Van Loon, which caused him to lose control of the belay rope. Kor fell another 70 feet and was only stopped when his haul rope caught on their gear. His helmet saved his life, but he was now upside down, with a severe concussion, cuts, a broken bone in his face, and his left leg broken in two places. Other climbers in the area heard the fall and calls for help, and responded to the scene. They were able to lower Kor to the Broadway Ledge. At the same time, tourists heard the cries for help and got word to the Longs Peak Ranger Station by 1:00 p.m.

The initial phase of this rescue operation was to get a ranger with a medical pack and a radio to the accident scene. The first hint that this was not going to be a normal rescue operation occurred when the helicopter carrying the ranger with medical gear developed mechanical problems and made an emergency landing. Fortunately, there were no injuries, and the ranger continued toward Chasm Lake on foot. By evening, over 40 rescuers and volunteers were committed to the incident. Throughout the night, hundreds of pounds of equipment were hauled from Chasm Lake to Mills Glacier, then up to the Broadway Ledge. Key items were 700 feet of ³⁄₁₆-inch aircraft cable with a cable-brake system, 600 feet of rope, a litter, and climbing equipment. By sunrise, the rescuers and necessary gear had reached Broadway where Kor lay.

One of the many unsung heroes of that first evening was Dr. Dick Shepard. For many years, Shepard and his family spent summers at the Wind River Ranch, and Shepard liked to hike in the Longs Peak area. When passing by Chasm Lake heading to the rescue, ranger Larry Van Slyke talked with Shepard, whom he had previously met. Shepard volunteered to assist, though he was not a technical climber. Van Slyke and others got him up the North Chimney that evening. He spent the night on Broadway supporting the rangers in the care of Kor. It was now nearly 18 hours after the accident and Kor was lapsing in and out of consciousness. He was quickly strapped into the litter. Ranger Walter Fricke and volunteer Layton Kor,

1969—Kordel Kor Rescue. Rescuers preparing to lower the litter from the Broadway Ledge. Chasm Lake in the background. Photo courtesy of the Don Magnuson Collection

1969 Kordel Kor Rescue, "Longs Peak Navy." Photo courtesy of Don Magnuson Collection

Kordel Kor's uncle, clipped into the lowering cable to guide the litter down the wall as it was lowered over 500 feet of sloping granite. Try to recall the last time you were in the downtown of a major city and bent your neck back to look up at a tall building. This lowering distance was equivalent to a 45 story building!

To complicate matters, Kordel Kor became agitated because of his concussion and tried to climb out of the litter while still hundreds of feet above the ground. "He didn't know what he was doing and he was super strong," recalled ranger Charlie Logan. "Fricke yelled on the radio, 'Down faster, goddammit, down faster!'" Fortunately, Fricke and Layton Kor were able to restrain the young man for the remainder of the 40-minute lowering. Waiting at the base of the wall was Dr. Sam Luce from Estes Park. For several years, Luce was as much a member of the park rescue team as any ranger. Kor's combativeness during the lowering tended to aggravate his weakened state, and he stopped breathing for the first time as Luce evaluated him. While his litter was carried over the boulders to Chasm Lake, Kordel Kor stopped breathing another five or six times. Dr. Luce miraculously revived him each time.

One last challenge lay ahead. Due to the steep, ragged slopes around Chasm Lake, the park rescue staff used an inflatable raft to ferry litters across the lake. This method saved considerable time and energy, but would the young climber stop breathing again? The rescuers chose to use the raft and crossed without incident. They then carried the litter to a safe helicopter landing zone. After twenty-four hours, Kordel Kor was flown to a Denver Hospital, where he made a full recovery.

In a final "second chance" incident for review, on October 21, 2000, the park dispatch office received an overdue climbing party report concerning John McBroom, age 47, and Terrance Ford, 42. They were attempting Kiener's Route on Longs Peak. They were to have returned on October 20th. Searchers hiked up the mountain and located McBroom and Ford exhausted, but uninjured. They were the third party in two weeks to have endured an unplanned bivouac on Kiener's Route.

Rangers Mark Magnuson and Jim Detterline wrote of this incident in *Accidents in North American Mountaineering*:

> Similar incidents have commonly occurred here at this time of the season in other years, resulting in cold injuries and even death … Each overdue party underestimated the increased difficulty of the route caused by early winter conditions. Under summer conditions, Kiener's Route is a mountaineering classic of easy 5th class climbing and 40–50 degree snow and ice. Early winter snows often cover the route with poorly bonded snow, resulting in climbing difficulties well beyond those of summer. Also, many groups experience route-finding difficulties due to winter conditions and inexperience. An off-season Kiener's climb requires a conservative attitude.

Falls on snow/ice

Some of the more spectacular rescues have occurred on the Lambs Slide, which is to the east of Longs Peak. This thousand-foot snow and ice chute is a popular ice climb in its own right. It is also popular as an approach to the Broadway Ledge and entry to climbing routes on the East Face of Longs Peak. Unfortunately, there have been three fatalities on this particular ice formation.

The Lambs Slide is named for the Reverend Elkanah J. Lamb. He first climbed Longs Peak via the Keyhole Route in 1871. At that time, he also made the first documented descent of the East Face. Probing for a way down, he had the first near death experience on the prominent 1,000-foot ice and snow—covered chute to the southeast of Mills Glacier. In the spirit of Elkanah Lamb's miraculous self rescue, I have included three extraordinary tales of rescue and survival on the Lambs Slide. Keep in mind that the Lambs Slide is not vertical, so those participants tumbling down it normally remain conscious and have time to consider their dilemma in their uncontrolled descent. Take for example, a survivor's own story.

On August 19, 2007, Ben Cort was climbing Lambs Slide with two companions. The group was well equipped for the climb with the standard safety equipment, helmets, crampons and ice axes. None had climbed the route before, and all had limited experience climbing routes such as this. Due to excessive amounts of loose, falling rock that day, they decided not to rope up so that they could move faster and improve their chances of not being hit by rocks.

The following account of the accident was found on mountainproject.com by ranger Ryan Schuster and reposted in *Accidents in North American Mountaineering*: When Cort was near the top, he lost his footing and fell more than 800 feet. In his words, "The next you know I was just flying down the mountain without my ice axe. That's when it gets bad." Traveling at speeds witnesses estimated at 40 mph, Cort stayed conscious the entire time. "Total pandemonium," he said. "I was head over heels and I was smacking my face on rocks. Rocks were coming down with me and then this boulder rolled over me a couple times." When Cort reached the bottom, he initially thought he was dead. "There was a very, very distinct feeling that I knew that that's how I was going to die. I was just sure," he said. "My friends were positive I was dead. I had been climbing long enough and have been around this sport long enough that you take something like that and you know that's kind of it." Remarkably, Cort not only survived but sustained only a broken leg and shoulder, and some scrapes and cuts. "I hit the ground and I felt my feet, I felt my fingers and was just so overcome with gratitude because I knew that God had just decided to save me." Several climbers came to Cort's aid, and he was flown off that night by a Flight for Life helicopter.

Ranger Schuster provided the following analysis of this incident:

Lambs Slide has been the scene of numerous accidents during its storied history. It is a high profile couloir on a high profile mountain, and it receives a lot of attention. The couloir itself goes through many "stages" between April and October, and the conditions are HIGHLY variable. This accident happened in late August, a time when Lambs Slide is beginning to enter its last "stage" before winter. This last stage is characterized by a lack of seasonal snowfall cover and an abundance of black alpine ice.

The decision whether or not to rope up for this portion of the climb is worthy of some discussion. The decision by the group not to rope up was a calculated risk based on their belief that the falling rock hazard was a greater risk than an unroped fall down the couloir. While this concept of moving with speed in the high country is a valid one, it needs to be taken into context amongst several factors. A constant reassessment of your situation and the hazards present is a vital part of maximizing safety in the high country. These are difficult decisions to make when confronted with them under stressful circumstances. The best way to make the correct decision is to constantly reevaluate your situation and talk it out with your partners. Ask yourselves, "What is going to get me hurt?" These men made the best decision they could at the time, and I can find no fault in their decision to climb unroped.

Fortunately for Ben Cort, he survived.

The same can be said of Estes Park resident Nate Dick. Ben Cort gave us a sense of what falling down Lambs Slide was like. Close your eyes for a moment and think about Ben Cort and those comic strip characters you see rolling down a hill or snow bank. Artists usually depict the scene as a small cloud with an arm sticking out one side, a leg another, and a sled or glove out another angle. Got the picture? Well, that was Estes Park resident

Nathan "Nate" Dick on July 14, 1996, and one of the loose items in the picture was Nate's ice axe!

Nate Dick was in good physical condition and enjoyed the occasional solo hike or climb to a summit. On the 14th, he was alone and had just completed his ascent of the Lambs Slide. While glissading down the snow/ice formation, Dick lost control and slid, tumbled, and rolled close to 1,000 feet to the base of the formation. He was unsuccessful in his attempt to self arrest, and in the fall he managed to lose control of his ice axe. Flailing freely, he impaled himself in the neck with the ice axe and lacerated his right subclavian artery. Dick also sustained various injuries to his left hip, right clavicle, elbow, neck, and ulnar nerve when he struck the rocks below.

Fortunately, there were several other climbers in the area, who immediately came to Dick's aid and saved his life. A cell phone was used to contact park dispatch at 10:39 a.m., and a rescue was immediately initiated. In the meantime, climber Vladmir Farkash was able to slow the arterial bleeding with direct pressure until relieved by ranger/paramedic Mike Pratt at 12:06 p.m. Due to strong winds, a helicopter was unable to reach Mills Glacier at the foot of Lambs Slide, but the pilot could shuttle rescuers and supplies to the Chasm Meadows area. From that location, ranger Dan Ostrowski led a litter team up to Dick's location. By 1:30 p.m., Dick was stabilized and packaged in the litter. High winds continued to prevent a helicopter landing in the area, so Ostrowski's team and volunteer climbers lowered the litter down 1,000 feet of snow and scree slope to the west side of Chasm Lake. During this time, incident commander Rick Guerrieri had ranger Scott Hall carry a 65-pound raft up to Chasm Lake. Guerrieri's experience told him this backup plan was necessary in case the wind continued to prevent a helicopter landing above Chasm Lake, which proved to be true. Rangers Hall and Frye inflated the raft and rowed across to pick up Nate Dick and the litter. They then floated back across the lake, where another team carried the litter to Chasm Meadows and a waiting helicopter. By 4:23 p.m., Dick was placed in the helicopter and flown to a hospital in Denver. Nate Dick survived and made a full recovery.

Chasm Lake shelter in summer. Built in 1931. Destroyed by a massive avalanche in March 2003.
Photo Courtesy of RMNP

A chronicle of "second chances" on Lambs Slide would not be complete without a nod to the effort to rescue Dick Kezlan in January 1968. This saga began on January 27, when local climbers Dick Kezlan, age 32, Jim Disney, 28, Ken Paine, 29, and Ken Landis, 40, set off to reach the summit of Longs Peak via Kiener's Route. One of their goals was to coordinate a radio broadcast from the summit to radio station KLOV in Loveland. To do this, they carried two National Park Service radios for a radio-telephone relay. Getting an early start from Longs Peak Trailhead, they intended to bivouac on Broadway Ledge for the evening and climb to the summit the next morning. Poor weather, inadequate conditioning, and equipment problems slowed the group's progress so that they were still on Lambs Slide well after dark. Disney and Kezlan made it to the Broadway Ledge and were preparing a bivouac site. Paine and Landis were teamed together and got within about 100 feet of Broadway, but asked to go back down because Ken Landis was not feeling well. Assessing the situation, the group wisely made the decision to retreat to the Chasm Lake shelter.

It had been a long day. They were tired and cold, and the weather was deteriorating with a wind chill factor of twenty below zero. They discussed the possibility of roping up and decided the hard packed snow conditions were favorable for a descent to reach the shelter with ice axe and crampons only. All were skilled at using an ice axe to self arrest.

Each individual made reasonable progress down the slope, but during the descent the hinge on Kezlan's crampon weakened and broke. Unaware of the now broken crampon, Kezlan stepped down on the broken device, causing his foot to twist and pitch him forward. Landing face first likely stunned him and caused enough disorientation to prevent him from self arresting with his ice axe. Disney later recalled that he heard a groan above him, and "suddenly a dark form was sliding past." He instinctively yelled for his friend to dig in his ice axe. "Then there was this indescribable crunching sound … I never heard it before, but I knew what it was." Making their way down to Kezlan, Disney hoped the results were less serious than they sounded. "I turned him over and could hardly believe what I saw … It seemed his head had been laid open. His face was a mass of blood." It was approximately 8:30 p.m.—cold, dark, and windy.

As luck would have it, Disney was able to notify park dispatch on the borrowed radios and report the injury and the weather conditions. Within minutes, rangers were notified, as well as two volunteer rescue groups and Dr. Sam Luce. As is often the case with SAR incidents, Dr. Luce had just returned home from a long day at the office and was looking forward to a hot meal and quiet evening at home when the phone rang. Gauging the initial report, Luce stuffed his pack with 40 pounds of medical gear and was soon picked up by rangers Bob Haines and Tom Griffiths. By 9:30 p.m., they were on the trail, struggling in the face of the 50 mph winds. "The wind was so strong, one had to lean into it in order to stand," recalled Griffiths. Help for Kezlan was still several hours away.

In the meantime, Disney and his companions did what they could to make the unconscious Kezlan warm by putting him in their sleeping bags and trying to break the wind. Disney then crossed the mile of scree slope and frozen Chasm Lake to the Chasm shelter, where he hoped to find more blankets and first aid equipment. Once again, fate shined on this incident as Disney's pounding on the locked door woke Dr. Dee Crouch and Vic Ray from a sound sleep. Crouch, an experienced mountaineer, was interning at Denver's Colorado General Hospital. He and Ray were at the shelter in anticipation of a climb the following morning. They dressed and gathered what they could, and then followed Disney back through the bitter wind to Kezlan. Crouch later described finding "a shambles of equipment, ropes, and blood." Kezlan had lost a dangerous amount of blood, and his forehead was crushed inward. Dr. Crouch knew what had to be done, but he didn't have the tools. All the group could do was keep Kezlan comfortable and wait for additional rescuers.

At approximately 3:30 a.m., Griffiths and Dr. Luce, soaked in sweat from their four hour uphill slog to Kezlan's location, received the depressing description of Kezlan's condition and took over medical care. Exhausted and near hypothermic, Disney, Paine, and Landis retreated to the Chasm shelter. A couple of published accounts of this incident suggest that Dr. Luce was then left alone with Kezlan in the bitter hours of the morning. This was not the case. Ranger Griffiths, Dr. Crouch and Vic Ray stayed with Dr. Luce the whole time. Griffiths helped maintain Kezlan's airway. Crouch assisted with patient management. Kezlan needed intravenous fluid replacement and drugs to reduce swelling on his brain and stop convulsions. Through extraordinary effort, Dr. Luce found a vein for the IV, but temperatures well below zero caused fluids and the IV line to freeze. Luce placed the fluids and medications against his body, inside his coat, which helped. Remember, that was when IV fluids were packaged in glass bottles, not the soft rubberized plastic used today. At one point, Luce had to bypass the intravenous line completely and administer fluids one syringe at a time. Nearly two hours later, at 5:30 a.m., a large litter team composed of volunteers from Rocky Mountain Rescue and Alpine Rescue led by rangers Jerry Phillips and Dave Moore, as well as rescue group coordinator Rod Smith, reached the accident scene. Kezlan was placed in the litter and carried down to the Chasm shelter as dawn approached.

Now, Dr. Sam Luce had one more miracle to perform. The Chasm shelter, at 11,600 feet, was primitive at best. Six or seven people would be considered a crowd, but it was made of stone and effectively got people out of the wind. The small litter, with Kezlan still clinging to life, was balanced on two foot lockers. Disney held a flashlight as Luce and Crouch cleaned away the clotted blood and assessed the damage. Kezlan's head was a mess: a depressed fracture of the right temple, another break from his right ear to right eye, a third crack around the base of the skull, and several bleeding vessels. The first order of business was to stop the bleeding. Next, the doctors knew they must relieve the pressure on Kezlan's brain. Sterilizing his basic instruments, including a camping spoon, over a gas cook stove, Dr. Luce opened Kezlan's skull. A cup of jelly-like blood oozed out of the opening, and thus relieved the pressure on Kezlan's brain. Remarkably, within a few minutes Kezlan opened his eyes and regained a low level of consciousness. He would live. For three more hours that morning, the rescue teams carried and lowered the litter down to the Longs Peak Trailhead and a waiting ambulance. Dr. Sam Luce and Dr. Dee Crouch, along with a well-organized rescue team, saved Kezlan's life. Dr. Luce suffered slight primary frostbite of the toes after staying with Kezlan through the cold night.

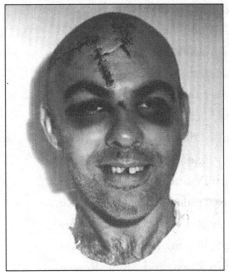

Happy to be alive, Dick Kezlan one week after incident. Photo courtesy of Jim Disney

In writing about this incident in the March 1969 issue of *Trail and Timberline* magazine, Dr. Crouch concluded that "mistakes were made in judgment by this climbing party, but these were mistakes that are made on many climbs without incident. Given a chance, however, the mountain will capitalize on these mistakes as if in violation of its rules. But that is the way it has worked since mountaineering began, and unfortunately that is the way it will always be. The job is to try and prevent at least some of the accidents and to give maximum rescue assistance when they occur. It is said that 'mountains make us try harder,' and that was so true of the 37 people involved in the rescue of Richard Kezlan."

A few months after this incident, rangers Jerry Phillips and Tom Griffiths accompanied Dr. Luce to Denver, where Luce gave a presentation on the medical aspects of the Kezlan rescue. Through the work of Drs. Luce and Crouch, along with the Mountain Rescue Association (MRA), a program was established at Denver General Hospital for rangers and MRA volunteers to attend emergency room training and learn to insert and manage IVs.

Unfortunately, in addition to close calls, there have also been three climber fatalities on Lambs Slide. On September 16, 1978, climber Brant Kauth contacted the park dispatch office from the Longs Peak Ranger Station and reported that his climbing partner, 22-year-old Harvey Schneider of Boulder, Colorado, had fallen on the Lambs Slide. He was unconscious and in serious condition with head injuries. Schneider and Kauth had been near the junction to the Broadway Ledge when Schneider lost his footing. He was not wearing a helmet and was not roped in to Kauth. Schneider died in St. Anthony's Hospital in Denver that afternoon after a helicopter evacuation.

Golden, Colorado, resident Charles O. Nesbit, age 36, was an officer with the Colorado State Patrol. On October 6, 1979, he was part of a three person climbing team working their way up Lambs Slide unroped. At about 10:30 a.m., and approximately two-thirds of the way up the ice chute, Nesbit slipped and immediately went into a feet first, face down, ice axe arrest position. Witnesses said it appeared that the front point of his crampons caught on the hard ice, which caused him to flip over backwards. Out of control, he slid some 700 feet to the talus at the base of the snowfield. One of his partners, William Barber, descended quickly and reached Nesbit at approximately 11:10 a.m. Nesbit was conscious but not coherent, and he later stopped breathing. Barber performed CPR until 12:15 p.m., when he stopped at the recommendation of Dr. Bert Honea. Honea, a Denver physician, had been retreating from the Stettner Ledges Route and stopped to help. Barber then descended to the Chasm Lake shelter, where he contacted ranger Chris Reveley, who coordinated the helicopter evacuation of the body. Nesbit was wearing a helmet, but this did not protect him from sustaining a basal skull fracture when he hit the rocks.

The most recent Lambs Slide fatality occurred on August 10, 1988, when Kevin R. Hardwick, age 31, fell to his death. The Lakewood, Colorado, resident lost his balance when he stopped to tighten his crampons.

Hardwick and his partner had almost reached the Broadway Ledge when he fell. The pair had ice axes and crampons, but were not roped up. Being late in the season, rangers reported the week before that "blue ice" was exposed, meaning it was older and denser and difficult to get a purchase with crampons or an ice axe.

Other snow and ice mishaps

The Lambs Slide is not the only treacherous snow in the national park. Following are five other climber fatalities that occurred on snow or ice.

On April 2, 1973, Jay Van Stavern, a 19-year-old University of Colorado student, took a 1,000-foot fall over the East Face of Longs Peak. He was descending the Cables Route unroped with partner Peter Kopetsky, age 22. While attempting to locate the cable, he fell on the snow and ice, slipped past Kopetsky, and disappeared over the edge of the East Face. His body was found the following evening on Mills Glacier after a difficult approach in three feet of fresh snow.

Another incident is summarized below, as originally reported by ranger Larry Van Slyke in the 1979 issue of *Accidents in North American Mountaineering*. The report is based on the interview with Tom Cunningham, who climbed with Lawrence Berman on July 21, 1978.

Cunningham, 23, and Lawrence Berman, 21, from Louisville, Kentucky, had gotten a technical climbing permit for the Blitzen Ridge on Ypsilon Mountain. They camped below the route the night of the 20th. On the morning of the 21st, the two began their ascent of the intended route via the Blitzen Cutoff. They climbed about 1,200 vertical feet above the Spectacle Lakes via a ramp type ledge. A short distance from the top of the Blitzen Ridge proper, they encountered a section of steep rock that they were either going to ascend or circumvent on a 20 foot–high snow bank. Up to that point, the pair had not been roped up, as the climbing had been very basic in nature. The decision was made to ascend the snow in order to eliminate having to rope up for about 20 feet of climbing. Cunningham started up the snowfield, kicking steps. When he was about 10–15 feet up the snow, Berman started to follow in his steps. Cunningham estimated that Berman had taken only a couple steps up the snow, when for some unknown reason he slipped and fell from the snowbank. The terrain immediately below the snow-field was very high angle and Berman continued his fall for some 1,200 vertical feet.

Cunningham immediately began a descent of the route he and Berman had just climbed. Near the bottom of the route, he began to find equipment that had been carried by Berman. Searching the bergschrund at the top of the snowfield that ran from the westernmost Spectacle Lake, he began finding blood spots on the snow and followed them into a crevasse below the bergschrund. There he found Berman's body with no signs of life. Cunningham left his equipment to mark the body's location and hiked out to notify rangers. The body was re-moved the next day.

According to Cunningham, Berman may have been somewhat in-timidated by the exposure near the top of the route and may have leaned into the snowbank, causing his step to break out under his weight.

Boulder, Colorado, resident William W. Carson, age 42, was at-tempting a solo climb of the 11,800-foot Taylor Glacier when he fell 1,400 feet on August 4, 1990. Another climber witnessed the fall at about 10:00 a.m. and was able to reach Carson on the scree slope at the base of the ice field. Carson was alive but unconscious when the climber first reached him. Carson died before additional help could get to the accident scene. He had a severe head injury and a broken leg. Two rangers were flown to the accident scene by St. Anthony's Flight for Life, and Carson was pronounced dead. Rangers spent the night, and the body was flown out by helicopter the next morning.

On February 3, 1993, Carl E. Siegel, age 30, and his climbing part-ner, Tim Cumbo, both from Boulder, Colorado, finished a successful win-ter ascent of the D-7 route on the Longs Peak Diamond. As they began their descent on the Cables Route, Cumbo reported, Siegel lost his footing near the highest bolt remaining from the old cable system. Siegel swung his ice axe into the rock to arrest his fall, but the momentum of his body and 85-pound pack propelled him downward, and the ice axe was ripped out of his hand. Cumbo and solo climber Derek Hersey made it to Siegel's body and confirmed that he had died. The coroner's report indicated that Siegel died as the results of cerebral contusions caused by blunt trauma to the head. Had Siegel worn a helmet, he might have lived. The body was removed by helicopter on the following day. Fatigue, poor weather, and the weight of the pack were primary contributing factors in the accident.

Sunday, November 15, 1998, was a fine day to be out in the park. The skies were clear with a strong wind and temperatures around 30 degrees. Boulder, Colorado, resident Richard Ladue, age 37, had plans to solo climb the All Mixed Up Route on the northeast side of Thatchtop Mountain about 1,000 feet above Mills Lake. The route is a four pitch mixed ice and rock climb rated as a Winter Ice 4 level of difficulty. Ladue was an experienced climber and had done the route before. He left the Glacier Gorge parking area by 7:00 a.m. and hiked in with two other climbers, who intended to climb the same route.

Ladue made it to the base of the climb before the others and proceeded up the route. By about 9:30 a.m., Ladue was roughly 150 feet up the route. He told the other two climbers he would wait on a flat area to avoid dropping ice on them, but apparently changed his mind and continued climbing to the left of the normal route. Moments later, the two climbers looked up and saw Ladue fall 150 feet to the base of the climb, then tumble down a short snow field and on to a rock scree slope. The climbers found Ladue breathing but unconscious and seriously hurt. One climber left to get help, while the other stayed with Ladue. The first climber made it back to the trailhead around 11:00 a.m., borrowed a cell phone, and spoke with the Rocky Mountain National Park dispatch. Ranger Scott Wanek was the first responder. After a brief interview, Wanek gathered his medical gear and proceeded alone up the trail, arriving at 1:00 p.m. He found the other climber attempting to restrain the unresponsive but combative Ladue. Wanek noted that Ladue was wearing a helmet but had a deep laceration in the left temporal area with bone fragments visible.

There were various large bruises and abrasions about his body. During this time, a field team assembled for a litter carryout, as the wind was too strong for a helicopter and darkness was falling. By 4:15 p.m., Estes Park paramedic Jeff Ofsanko arrived at the accident location and assumed primary medical care. Ofsanko began administering intravenous medications under instructions communicated by radio from an Estes Park Medical Center emergency room physician.

Ladue remained combative, which hindered medical attention. By 4:30 p.m., the litter team arrived and began to prepare a lowering system for the litter. Ladue was still 1,000 feet above Mills Lake, and he would have to be lowered this distance just to get to the lake and then carried another three miles to the trailhead. By 5:30 p.m., now working in the dark, the litter team initiated the lowering to get Ladue over the difficult stretch of loose rock, ice, and snow between the ice route and Mills Lake. While crossing

the lake, Ladue went into cardiac arrest. Wanek and Ofsanko attempted to intubate him, and CPR was initiated but then discontinued at approximately 7:00 p.m. with concurrence of the Estes Park Medical Center staff.

The decision was made to bring the exhausted rescue team out to the trailhead. Two rangers hiked in to stay with Ladue's body throughout the evening. His body was removed

Rescuers Bill Brown and Ryan Schuster guide a litter team during winter rescue. Photo courtesy of John Epperson/ *Denver Post*

by helicopter Monday morning. A subsequent investigation by ranger Rick Guerrieri determined that the ice to the left of the normal route, where Ladue was climbing when he fell, was very thin and had fractured. Guerrieri estimated Ladue fell a total of 279 feet. Fifteen volunteers from Larimer County Search and Rescue and twenty park staff were involved in the rescue effort.

The most recent climber fatality on snow and ice occurred on June 7, 2008. Richard Frisbie, age 66, died while mountaineering on the steep snow slope on the west side of Emerald Lake, which is 1.8 miles west of Bear Lake. The Ft. Collins, Colorado, resident was wearing crampons and a helmet at the time of the accident. Witnesses saw him fall at about 3:00 p.m. and contacted park officials by cell phone. The hikers reached Frisbie about 15 minutes later. He had no pulse and had suffered multiple injuries, including a broken neck, after tumbling over 500 feet down the slope. He appeared to have died during the fall. Rangers arrived two hours later to carry Frisbie's body out to the trailhead.

I'll conclude this chapter with an incident from 2009 that resulted in injuries. It is a unique and instructive tale about a solo park visitor named Sterling Jordan. Jordan, age 57, didn't ask for a "second chance," but random luck or some unexplainable planetary alignment brought Joe Gartner and Scott McCoy into his predicament.

On May 11, 2009, Jordan, a Loveland, Colorado, resident, decided to take a solo day hike/climb in the Flattop Mountain area. Unfortunately, Jordan compounded his eventual problem by violating a primary safety rule—he neglected to tell anyone where he was going or even leave a small note on the dash of his vehicle. May 11th was a Monday, and it being early in the season there were very few people in the backcountry of the park. In fact, his two rescuers later stated they had not seen anybody all day.

That morning, he was climbing up one of the couloirs near Ptarmigan Glacier with ice axe and crampons. For some still-undetermined reason, he fell an estimated 50–100 feet near the upper part of the couloir and fractured his pelvis and several ribs. He was unable to walk, and his pack was 100 feet above him. He knew he was in a bad situation. As mentioned earlier, he did not tell anyone where he was going. His pack was above him, and he could not stand or walk because of his injuries. To his credit, Jordan made the decision to attempt to rescue himself. The first goal was to try and get closer to Lake Helene. He managed to descend over 1,000 feet on his hands and knees using his ice axe. At some point, he collapsed exhausted in the snow and laid there semi-conscious for nearly 24 hours.

The following day, May 12th, Joe Gartner, 31, and Scott McCoy, 27, left the Bear Lake Trailhead around 5:30 a.m. to do some "extreme skiing" down the couloirs around Ptarmigan Glacier. They had stopped for lunch near the Continental Divide on Flattop Mountain and were checking out the different slopes for the next run. At this time they observed what they thought might be a person or a rock on the snow an estimated 1,500 feet below them. Not sensing a problem, they continued to scout a ski run and eventually skied down a route they liked. Fortunately, this brought them closer to the previously noted object, which they were surprised to realize was a person lying prone in the snow. The skiers shouted to the person, and there was no response. As they got closer, Sterling Jordan managed to roll over. He was hypothermic, disoriented, had lost his gloves, and his knees were bloody from crawling over rock and snow. In a classic understatement, Gartner and McCoy later shared that "we were worried we had a situation on our hands."

Rangers package Sterling Jordan in sleeping bag and litter. Photo courtesy of RMNP

Gartner had some first aid training and made a basic assessment of Jordan's condition. Gartner and McCoy also noticed several large chunks of broken cornice around them and felt they were in a dangerous location. Bribing Jordan with homemade cookies, they put his arms around their necks and their arms about his waist, and were able to carry him laboriously out of the main avalanche area.

McCoy was eventually able to make cell phone contact with rangers. Because the wind was gusting to over 70 mph, a helicopter rescue was not possible. It took three hours for a litter team of rangers and medics to cover the

Incident Commander Mark Pita, left, with Joe Gartner, center, and Scott McCoy, right, use Google Earth to find the location of the Jordan rescue. Photo courtesy of John Cordsen, *Estes Park Trail Gazette*

five miles from the trailhead and reach the group. While waiting, McCoy and Gartner piled rocks to make a wind shield for Jordan and make him as comfortable as possible. After Jordan's condition was assessed by the rescue team, he was placed in a sleeping bag on a sled and carried back to the trailhead by a team of twenty rescuers.

In a post incident review, Joe Gartner and Scott McCoy shared that there was a 1-in-100 chance they would have been there that day. "There were a lot of ways we wouldn't have come across him. No one else was out there. Flattop is for backcountry skiing. On a windy weekday, it is not usual for anyone to be out there." Gartner and McCoy were presented with the National Park Service Search and Recovery Award, which is given to citizens who assist with rescue incidents.

Sterling Jordan was moderately experienced in mountaineering. Like many people, he enjoyed being in the backcountry by himself. He had proper equipment and was generally cautious during his solo backcountry trips. When the accident occurred, he was climbing with an ice axe and crampons on roughly a 65 degree slope—challenging, but not beyond his skill level. He made a full recovery.

Falls While Climbing

July 23, 1926	Forrest Ketring, 19	**Longs Peak, Notch Coulior** *Climbing unroped. Lost footing.* Fell 800 feet.
August 18, 1929	Charles W. Thiemeyer, 28	**Longs Peak, Notch Coulior** *Overconfident* Swiss national on first attempt of East Face. Fell and *belay failed.* Fell 1,500 feet with climbing rope. The couple climbing with him had to be rescued the next day by rangers.
September 1, 1946	Charles Grant, 19	**Longs Peak, Stettner Ledges Route** Grant had been to the summit of Longs Peak 26 times. His partner John Purvis fell 60 feet. Grant *instinctually tried to grab the rope, but missed, lost balance, and fell* 600 feet to his death. Purvis was okay.
April 20, 1960	David L. Jones, 18	**Longs Peak** Climbing party of 3 encountered *sudden bad weather below summit on East Face. Inadequate clothing.* Attempted to descend by contouring around summit to find Keyhole Route.
	Prince D. Willmon, 23	Unsuccessful. *Lost. Hypothermic/ Frostbitten.* Jane Bendixon able to rappel off and stagger into Allenspark for help. Jones/Willmon later found dead. It appeared they *fell trying to rappel with frozen/frostbitten hands near Keplinger's Couloir.*
July 14, 1961	Myron Fritts, 19	**Hallet Peak, North Chimney** *Solo climber. Unwitnessed fall.*
August 27, 1966	C. Blake Hiester, 48	**Longs Peak, Kiener's Route** Climbing with his son and 2 friends, Hiester *lost his footing and fell* 1,200 feet from the Notch Chimney. He was *unroped.* Overconfidence and haste with an approaching storm may have been contributing factors.

June 18, 1972	Steve Day, 22	**Pagoda Mountain** Well known local resident fell 200 feet when *rappel anchor piton pulled out.*
April 2, 1973	Jay Van Stavern, 19	**Longs Peak** Van Stavern and his partner had completed an East Face climb. While descending the North Face *unroped,* Van Stavern *slipped on the snow/ice* and slid over the edge of the East Face to Mills Glacier.
August 20, 1973	Joseph Holub, 22	**Ships Prow formation above Chasm Meadows** Holub was *free climbing when he slipped on a short, steep pitch.* He fell about 30 vertical feet, then tumbled another 100 feet down steep scree slope. (Not in text.)
July 2, 1975	Diana Hunter, 26	**Cathedral Wall in Glacier Gorge** Hunter had just completed the climb and was unroped. *Standing on rock which dislodged, lost balance* and fell 800 feet. (Not in text.)
June 1, 1977	Michael Neri, 21	**Longs Peak, Broadway Ledge** Carrying heavy pack. *Slipped on wet tundra grass* while traversing Broadway. Fell to Mills Glacier. (Not in text.)
July 21, 1978	Lawrence Berman, 21	**Ypsilon Mountain, Blitzen Ridge** Berman was *climbing a 20 foot near-vertical snowbank* above a 1,200-foot high angle snowfield. *Unroped fall.* Partner above did not witness what led to fall.
September 16, 1978	Harvey Schneider, 22	**Longs Peak, Lambs Slide** Near Broadway Ledge. Crampons/ice axe. *No helmet. Unroped. Lost footing* and fell/slid 800 feet to bottom.
October 6, 1979	Charles Nesbit, 36	**Longs Peak, Lambs Slide** Crampons/ice axe and helmet, but *unroped. Lost footing* and fell/slid 700 feet. Died of basal skull fracture.
January 10, 1981	Robert Elliott, 26	**Longs Peak, North Chimney** *Mechanical cam anchor set by partner came loose.* Fell 90 feet. Held by rope, but died of spinal injuries.

July 1, 1984	Lee S. Jamieson, 20	**Notchtop Mountain** Unroped. *Standing on large rock, which dislodged, and lost balance.* Fell 300 feet.
August 10, 1988	Kevin R. Hardwick, 31	**Longs Peak, Lambs Slide** Near Broadway Ledge. Crampons/ice axe and helmet, but unroped. Lost footing and fell/slid 800 feet.
August 4, 1990	William W. Carlson, 42	**Taylor Glacier** *Solo snow/ice climb. Lost footing* and fell 1,400 feet.
February 3, 1993	Carl E. Siegel, 30	**Longs Peak, Cables Route** After successful winter ascent of D-7 on the Diamond, Siegel and partner were descending *unroped. Heavy pack. Lost footing* and fell 400 feet.
May 23, 1994	Jack L. McConnell, 59	**Lumpy Ridge, Left Book Formation** Got *off route* on White Whale, 5.7. *Leader fall. No helmet.*
July 2, 1997	Todd Marshall, 35	**Cathedral Spires, Petit Grepon** Marshall was in lead. Finished climb, stood up on small platform, and shouted with joy. *Possible gust of wind knocked him off balance, and he fell 70 feet. Died of skull fracture.* Partner marooned until rescued.
November 15, 1998	Richard Ladue, 37	**Thatchtop Mountain, All Mixed Up Route** *Solo ice climbing. Lost contact and fell 150 feet.* Major rescue effort.
March 3, 2000	Erin C. Sharp, 27	**Longs Peak** Intended *solo climb* of the East Face to summit, then a traverse over to Meeker. Body found below cliff in Loft area. *Unwitnessed.* (Not in text.)
July 6, 2000	Cameron Tague, 32	**Longs Peak, Broadway Ledge** Experienced climber. *Unroped* and approaching the base of the Yellow Wall Route. *Elected to scramble up steep, crumbly rock. Slipped or lost hold* and fell 800 feet to Mills Glacier. (Not in text.)
June 7, 2008	Richard Frisbie, 66	**Snow slope west of Emerald Lake** Solo mountaineering on steep snow slope. Had ice axe, crampons and helmet. *Lost contact and fell/tumbled 500 feet.* Sustained a broken neck. ·

Avalanches

Avalanches are a constant threat in Colorado's steep mountains. Learning to understand the snow conditions that generate avalanches is time well spent for any backcountry user. The Colorado Avalanche Information Center hosts an excellent internet site at which to begin an education. Six climbers have been killed by avalanches in Rocky Mountain National Park. It is important to point out that none of the incidents occurred during what would be considered winter, or December through March.

On October 13, 1973, Boulder residents Robert L. Fritz, age 20, and David Emerick, 24, were climbing a steep couloir above Taylor Glacier near Mount Powell. They were caught in an avalanche, probably on Saturday, and their bodies were found Sunday by other climbers. Fritz had successfully climbed the couloir in recent weeks. However, loose snow had fallen, which broke six to twelve inches deep in the avalanche path. The two Boulder residents were roped together, but it was not determined if they were belaying each other or not.

On July 6, 1976, at 8:43 a.m., Christopher Sommer telephoned Rocky Mountain National Park dispatch to report an overdue friend, Jim Boicourt, 29, from Denver. Boicourt was believed to be in the Ypsilon Lake area. He and Sommer had planned to climb the Blitzen Ridge, a high angle rock ridge on Ypsilon Mountain, that weekend, but Sommer became ill and could not make the trip. Boicourt told Sommer that he would go up on Sunday (July 4) for a day hike to check the conditions in the Ypsilon/Spectacle Lakes area. Sommer believed that Boicourt was competent and would not take unnecessary risks, particularly while climbing alone. A trailhead check by rangers found Boicourt's vehicle parked at the Lawn Lake Trailhead.

Considering the circumstances, an initial team of rescuers was mobilized and left the Lawn Lake Trailhead at 12:30 p.m. on July 6th. About 5:19 p.m., ranger Paul Anderson spotted a red pack on the snowfield immediately below the Y Couloir (the snow-filled gully forming the letter "Y" on the southeast face of Ypsilon Mountain). By 6:00 p.m., a body was found below the pack and confirmed to be that of Jim Boicourt. As Boicourt was alone, ranger Larry Van Slyke deduced the likely cause of this fatality: First, Boicourt was attempting a solo technical climb of the Y Couloir. Second, he fell a great distance over rock and snow, and his body was badly bruised and cut. His clothing was torn, and he had lost his helmet and one crampon during the fall. Third, fresh avalanche debris was noted all around Boicourt's location and in the snow-filled gulley of the Y Couloir. Boicourt was probably the victim of a slab avalanche or cornice fracture. While the potential for avalanches in July is relatively small, the cornice overhanging the Y Couloir was very impressive, according to ranger Anderson, and should have been recognized as a possible hazard.

Climbing solo, Boulder resident Joe Massari, age 45, attempted Kiener's Route on Longs Peak. He was reported missing on April 20, 1991. An unsuccessful four-day search was started by park staff on April 22. The body was not found until June 21, 1991, near Mills Glacier. Because of the weather and snow accumulation at the time of the incident in April, Massari was believed to have had been caught in an avalanche.

What started as a recreational climb on a pleasant autumn day ended in tragedy on Sunday, November 1, 1992, when ice climbers Brad Farnan, 30, and Todd Martin, 24, were swept down an ice couloir on the north side of 12,324-foot Flattop Mountain. Farnan was an experienced guide with the Colorado Mountain School and an Estes Park resident. He and Martin were practicing winter ice climbing skills on the hard ice in the couloir. Two women, with the climbers, were at the base of the climb and reported a big gust of wind and blowing snow around 1:00 p.m. that obscured their view for several minutes. When the sky cleared, they could no longer see the climbers, and they noticed a large buildup of snow at the base of the climb. What was unusual was that it was not a windy day prior to the blinding gust. It was later believed that the wind gust was caused by the avalanche.

The women returned to their base camp at the Sourdough campsite below Two Rivers Lake to wait for the climbers. With darkness approaching, they hiked out to Bear Lake to notify rangers and friends from the Colorado Mountain School. Rangers returned to the campsite that evening and built a fire and burned lanterns throughout the evening in an effort to attract the climbers. The weather deteriorated Monday morning as searchers scoured the area. By Tuesday, wind gusts were reported up to 40 mph along the ridge tops in the area, with snowdrifts up to five feet.

On Tuesday, searchers looking down from the north ridge of Flattop Mountain spotted the men's ice axes and backpacks. They were undamaged and appeared to have been deliberately set down on a small ledge near the top of the couloir. They noticed that a section of cornice above the couloir had recently broken off. It was likely that this led to the avalanche that swept the climbers down the slope. The weather continued to deteriorate as searchers probed the debris field at the bottom of the couloir. As the weather worsened, avalanche conditions increased significantly in the primary search area, and the search was terminated on Thursday. The snowfall for the winter of 1992–93 was significantly above average. Searches by rangers and Colorado Mountain School staff during the summers of 1993 and 1994 were unsuccessful until Martin's body was discovered on August 11, 1994. Farnan's body was finally recovered on August 25, 1994.

FIVE

Heart Attacks
and Other
Medical Deaths

My friend David Adams is a retired Estes Park Middle School science teacher. The kids always loved David because he made science simple, fun, and understandable. David has also worked as a seasonal interpretive ranger for several years at Rocky Mountain National Park, and he was an emergency medical technician. A while back, I went to one of David's interpretive programs titled "Healthy Attitudes at High Altitude." I wanted to learn in a simple, fun, and understandable manner why elevation gain can be potentially hazardous to an individual's health.

As noted in the introduction to this book, the gateway community of Estes Park sits at 7,522 feet (2,293 meters) in elevation. Its counterpart on the west side of the park, Grand Lake, is at 8,437 feet (2,572 meters). Some other key features in the park are Bear Lake at 9,450 feet (2,880 meters), the Alpine Visitor Center at 11,796 feet (3,595 meters), at the high point on Trail Ridge Road at 12,183 feet (3,713 meters). Thirty-six states in our country have high points lower than Estes Park! And **heart attacks are the second leading cause of death in Rocky Mountain National Park.** It bears noting that high elevation and thin air do not cause heart attacks, but they do exacerbate preexisting conditions, which can lead to a heart attack.

David started his program by explaining that "high altitude" is generally defined as starting at 8,000 feet (2,438 meters) and above. What occurs as you gain elevation is a reduction in the atmospheric pressure. There is the same percent of oxygen (O_2) in the air (21 percent), but there are fewer O_2 molecules and less air pressure pushing it into your lungs. For example, if you are visiting the Alpine Visitor Center, there is basically 33 percent less oxygen entering your lungs than at sea level. The elevation of 8,000 feet is the approximate tipping point where most people not acclimated start experiencing some signs and symptoms of altitude sickness, also known as Acute Mountain Sickness (AMS). AMS is a pathological condition that is caused by acute exposure to low air pressure, usually outdoors at high altitudes. A headache is a primary symptom used to diagnose AMS, although a headache is also a symptom of dehydration. A headache occurring at an altitude above 8,000 feet combined with any one or more of the following symptoms can indicate AMS: Lack of appetite, nausea, or vomiting; fatigue or weakness; dizziness or light-headedness; insomnia; feelings of pins and needles; drowsiness; general malaise; peripheral edema (swelling of hands, feet, and face); and shortness of breath upon exertion.

Conversely, an increased pulse rate is one indication that an individual is adapting to high altitude. What is happening is your body is saying "hey, my friend! I am not getting the amount of oxygen I need, so I am going to start to breathe more deeply and faster to compensate." Okay, no big deal yet. However, breathing harder also creates less carbon dioxide (CO_2) in the blood stream, thus raising the PH level in the blood (more alkaline). The kidneys then respond by dumping more bicarbonate ion into the urine, which causes you to urinate more to lower the PH level, etc. Do you see where this is leading? Essentially, there is a feedback of Cause and Effect. So if you have a preexisting medical condition, it can eventually be complicated by the body's effort to adjust to high elevation. Visitors with the following pre-existing conditions should strongly consider not traveling to elevations above 10,000 feet: congestive heart failure, arrhythmias, sickle cell anemia, moderate chronic obstructive pulmonary disease (emphysema, asthma, or chronic bronchitis), sleep apnea, and high risk pregnancies.

By the end of his program, David is faced with a flurry of raised hands and shouts of "What if ___?" or "I have ___!" David, in his best middle school teacher manner, calms the crowd and shares the information listed here.

It is appropriate to support David's plea to enjoy the park. Yes, heart attacks are the second leading cause of death in the park, with 72 fatalities in the park's history—or 24 percent of the total fatalities. Another way to look at this statistic is to realize that there is not quite one heart attack fatality per year. What is more revealing though is that the park staff responds to an average of 190 medical incidents each year. Many are for symptoms of AMS or preexisting conditions complicated by AMS, and over 18 percent, or 34, occur on average at the Alpine Visitor Center. So who wants to ruin a good vacation with an ambulance or helicopter ride to Denver? Pay attention to what your body is telling you. For those that don't, the consequences can be fatal.

Take for example the death of Colorado Congressman William N. Vaile, age 51. Congressman Vaile was a U.S. Representative from Denver, Colorado, and a cousin to Roger W. Toll, Superintendent of Rocky Mountain National Park. He was also related to Agnes Vaille, who died tragically in the park in 1925. (The two branches of the family spelled their names differently.) Born in Kokomo, Indiana, Vaile moved with his parents

1. **Enjoy the park!** Millions of visitors do so each year without catastrophe striking! Just be aware of the signs and symptoms of AMS.

2. **The best prevention** for AMS is to drink large amounts of water and allow adequate time to acclimate. The average person has been tested to be 80 percent acclimated after 10 days at 8,000 feet. Unfortunately, most visitors aren't here that long. See #3 below.

3. **Everyone is affected by altitude,** and an estimated 75 percent of the population will experience some symptoms of AMS if they go higher than 10,000 feet. Obviously, some more than others. The solution is to recognize the initial symptoms listed above and act accordingly. Rest, drink lots of water, pace yourself, or descend, descend, descend! The classic symptom of moderate or escalating AMS is a headache that remains after taking ibuprofen, acetometaphen, or aspirin. This indicates your body is still stressed. Do not deny that you have the symptoms of AMS, particularly in a hiking group where peer pressure may force you to keep going up the trail when you should head down to lower elevation. Note: No one with AMS should be left alone.

4. **If you are elderly** and/or have a preexisting medical condition, as listed above, be sure to consult with your doctor before going to high elevation.

to Denver in 1881. He attended public schools, and later graduated from Yale University in 1898. He studied law at the University of Colorado and Harvard Law School. During the Spanish-American War, he served as a private in the First Regiment of the Connecticut Volunteer Field Artillery from May 19, 1898, to October 25, 1898. Vaile was elected to Congress in 1919 and served four successive terms until his death in Rocky Mountain National Park on July 2, 1927.

It appears that William Vaile lived a full life. Yet Vaile had been in a vehicle accident not too long before his death and had been warned by his physician that "the condition of his heart was not satisfactory and [he] was warned against severe exertion." On July 2nd, he was on an outing with his family to the new national park. They drove up to Fall River Pass, where he and his nine-year-old son tried to walk to a rock cairn at 12,000 feet, near the present day Alpine Visitor Center. Vaile walked approximately 200 yards before collapsing and dying without regaining consciousness.

Another school of thought suggests dying quick and fast from a heart attack in a beautiful place doing what you love ain't all that bad. For those readers over 50 years old, myself included, I bet we have thought a moment or two about how our lives will end. I think most everyone hopes they die quickly, painlessly, and, most important, with dignity.

Take for example Charles Hupp, age 54. Winters in Estes Park can be a bit rough. Cold temperatures and strong winds off the Divide often keep people inside. There are several mornings each winter when residents are a bit grumpy from lack of sleep after a strong wind rattles houses and windows the previous evening. In the 1920s and '30s, the loneliness and isolation was even more pronounced for the few residents and rangers stationed in the park. In those days, people tended to keep an eye out for one another, and there was time to sit and visit. In Horseshoe Park, the wind can be particularly biting as it races down Fall River Canyon from the Divide. Ranger Jack Moomaw lived alone in the Horseshoe Park Ranger Station, about one-half mile from the Horseshoe Inn, where Charlie Hupp had been hired as a caretaker for the winter of 1925–26. The inn was located just south of Fall River and west of today's road. There is an interpretive roadside exhibit with a picture of the inn near the above location. Hupp was a "local" and was getting on in years, so Moomaw checked him every few days and enjoyed a cup of coffee and shared stories. They were the only people for several miles around.

Years later, Jack Moomaw wrote in his book, *Recollections of a Rocky Mountain Ranger*, that he was surprised one day in late March, when he went to visit Hupp, that he was dining on the more expensive tinned food left by the owners. As the caretaker, he was allowed to eat the food stored in the cellar, but normally kept to the basic tins. Moomaw also noted that Charlie Hupp seemed in unusually fine spirits on that March visit, particularly as Hupp had not been well over the winter, and his heart was bothering him.

On March 30, 1926, it had been almost a week since Moomaw last made it back by the Horseshoe Inn, and this time he noticed there was no smoke coming from the chimney. Checking the screen door, he found that it was latched on the inside. Sensing something was wrong, Moomaw looked in a window and saw someone in a bed. Using a wire to unlock the door, Moomaw entered the building and found Charlie Hupp dead.

What is interesting is that Moomaw described the room as "freshly clean and tidied up." Hupp had shaved and taken a bath. His clothes were neatly folded on a chair. Remember that a few days earlier he had eaten a fine meal and was in good spirits. Did Charlie Hupp know his time was up? Did he know to enjoy a couple of good meals, then clean himself up before going to bed one last time, so he wouldn't be a nuisance to his friend Jack Moomaw, who Charlie knew would probably find him dead? Somehow, it seems as though he knew he was going to die before going to bed that last time.

Following are a few additional incidents where the victim seemed to be enjoying himself before tragedy struck:

On July 4, 1937, William S. Moore, age 75, was fishing in the Onahu Creek. The superintendent's report, dated August 6, 1937, stated, "according to the Grand County coroner's investigation, Moore appeared to have fallen in the stream; he was able to climb out of the water, but suffered a heart attack because of the exertion. The cause of death, according to the coroner, was coronary thrombosis."

John E. Barney, age 41, from Friend, Nebraska, was riding horseback with a friend near Calypso Cascades in the Wild Basin area on July 22, 1946. It was not clear if Barney fell or was thrown from his horse, as his companion, D.G. Hayek, only heard the body fall. The *Estes Park Trail* reported on July 26, 1946, that the exact cause of death was not determined, though the Boulder County Coroner thought Barney suffered a heart attack.

Abe Brown, age 57, was from Louisville, Colorado. Late on July 11, 1953, Brown and two friends arrived at the Sand Beach Lake Trailhead in Wild Basin. They rested in their car and left at approximately 2:00 a.m. to fish the lake. The three friends were longtime hiking companions. Some two miles up the trail, at 3:20 a.m., Mr. Brown collapsed. One friend stayed to attempt artificial respiration, while the other went for help. Mr. Brown was a miner and construction worker. Sadly, he left a wife and two children.

On June 12, 2008, 70-year-old Robert Bacon of St. Louis, Missouri, was enjoying a beautiful early summer day by hiking with his wife above Alberta Falls. He collapsed on the trail, and a visitor contacted park dispatch by cell phone at 11:05 a.m. CPR had been started by other visitors and a physician in the area. Ranger staff first arrived at 11:40 a.m. and inserted an airway and administered oxygen. Additional staff arrived and continued CPR until 12:28 p.m., when Bacon was pronounced dead after consultation with the park's medical advisor at Estes Park Medical Center.

Albert Langemann, age 55, was snowshoeing with his family on the Longs Peak Trail on January 10, 2009, when he suffered a fatal heart attack.

On July 20, 2009, Maynard Brandsma, age 62, was 100 yards below the summit of Longs Peak when he suffered a fatal heart attack at approximately 10:30 a.m.

It should be noted that additional fatalities have been averted by proper medical attention. A fine example of a professional emergency response occurred on August 10, 2009. At approximately 11:15 a.m., the park dispatch office received a 911 cell call from a family member reporting that Manfred Neugebauer, age 73, was suffering a possible heart attack two miles up the Flattop Mountain Trail. He had lost consciousness for approximately 30 seconds and suffered chest pain and profuse sweating. He had no cardiac history. An initial team of two rangers made it to Neuge-bauer by 12:13 p.m. and administered oxygen. By 1:06 p.m., a nine person litter team and Estes Park paramedic Joel Bitters arrived at the scene, assessed Neugebauer's condition, and began administering medication. At 1:13 p.m., Neugebauer went into cardiac arrest. The initial respond-ing rangers had brought a defibrillator, and a shock was applied to the victim. His pulse was restored, and he regained consciousness.

Neugebauer was loaded into the wheeled litter and carried back to the Bear Lake Trailhead, then transferred to an ambulance and taken to the Glacier Basin Campground meadow to meet a medivac helicopter. This was truly a lifesaving rescue.

For the record, a simple analysis of the 72 heart-related fatalities shows that 64 were male and 8 were female. The average age for the men was 62, with the oldest being 78 and the youngest 24. For women, the average age was 69, with the oldest being 76 and the youngest 61.

Rescue team carrying Manfred Neugebauer to helicopter in Glacier Basin Campground meadow. Photo courtesy of RMNP

Other Medical Fatalities Not Cardiac Related

Five other visitors have died in the park for medical circumstances not related to a heart problem.

On July 13, 1954, Mrs. Roger G. Van Blarican, age 34, suffered hemorrhagic anemia while parked along the road near Lower Hidden Valley. From Hawthorne, California, Mrs. Van Blarican was with her family,
who had stopped along the road so one of their sons could fish. Mrs. Van
Blarican stayed in the car. When the family returned, they found her unconscious. Artificial respiration was attempted for 25 minutes before rushing to the Estes Park Hospital, where she was pronounced dead. It was
learned that she was subject to low blood pressure and anemia and had become faint on Monday while trying to climb Seven Falls near Colorado
Springs. It is likely that elevation played a role in this fatality.

In another unfortunate case, Robert B. Salt, only 26 years old, died of
acute diabetic shock at his backcountry campsite at Pear Lake in the Wild
Basin area. Salt was a Longmont, Colorado, resident. He had been packed
in to Pear Lake on June 20, 1956, by Kermit Pierce of Allenspark. When
Pierce returned on the 26th to pack him out, he found Salt dead. There
were no witnesses or indication that this was a suicide.

Edith Zockett, age unknown, suffered a stroke on June 18, 1959, while
staying at the Hatchett cabin in Moraine Park. She was transported by ambulance to her home in Amarillo, Texas, where she died two days later of
a heart attack. This is one of those unusual incidents where a serious incident occurred in the park, which led to the eventual death outside the park.

On August 3, 1985, 27-year-old Nancy L. Garbs of Columbia, Missouri, collapsed while visiting the Never Summer Ranch. She later died in
the Granby Clinic. The Grand County coroner's report was undetermined
as to the cause of death. The autopsy found that Garbs had several rup-
tures in her stomach and had peritonitis. She also had aspirated some con-
tents of her stomach.

Lastly, on June 22, 1987, Charles S. Housman, age 77, died of natural causes at his private cabin near Grand Lake.

Heart Attacks and Other Medical Deaths

March 30, 1926	Charles Hupp, 54	**Died in sleep** at old Horseshoe Park Inn.
July 2, 1927	William N. Vaile, 51	**Hiking** near Fall River Pass.
July 1, 1936	A.B. "Ben" Servey, 46	Local resident **fishing** in Horseshoe Park. Did not feel well. Went to car and was later found there dead.
July 4, 1937	William S. Moore, 75	**Fishing** in Onahu Creek
August 1, 1941	Wesley F. Diem, 30	From St. Louis, Missouri. **Camping** in Longs Peak Campground.
July 22, 1946	John E. Barney, 41	**Horseback riding** near Calypso Cascades in Wild Basin
August 16, 1948	Mr. L.C. Ingram, 41	From Terrell, Texas. **Guest** at Fall River Lodge.
September 1, 1948	Edward Schneiderhahn, age unknown	From St. Louis, Missouri. **Guest** at Fall River Lodge.
September 8, 1950	Earl S. Davis, age unknown	From Los Angeles, California. **Guest** at Sprague's Lodge.
June 11, 1952	B.R. Schabarum, age unknown	**Driving** on Trail Ridge Road near Rainbow Curve.
July 17, 1952	J. Wayne Kurtz, 57	**Hiking/Fishing** in Big Meadows
September 26, 1952	Ralph S. Corlew, age unknown	Bureau of Public Roads employee. **Suffered heart attack** at Poudre Lakes while on annual road inspection of Trail Ridge Road with the superintendent.
July 11, 1953	Abe Brown, 57	**Hiking** up the Sand Beach Trail in Wild Basin.
July 30, 1953	Mr. A.J. Canino, 53	**Hiking** between Pear and Finch Lakes.
June 27, 1954	Harold Grey, 54	**Camping** at Glacier Basin Campground.
June 2, 1955	Jack Roberts, 43	Military man staying at the Green Mountain Ranch. Suffered **coronary occlusion.**
July 15, 1957	Cecil F. Hall, 66	From Dove Creek, Colorado. **Camping** in Aspenglen Campground.

July 3, 1958	Mr. O.E. Kinnaman, 71	Visiting family at **Bear Lake.** From Colorado. Was the father of the operator of the Bear Lake Livery.
July 17, 1958	Edwin V. Drake, 68	**Camping** at Glacier Basin Campground.
December 28, 1958	George F. Wellman, 73	From Chicago, Illinois. Died in cafeteria at **Hidden Valley Ski Area.**
June 20, 1959	Raymond Harrington, 67	**Camping** at Glacier Basin Campground.
August 24, 1960	George W. Krah, 65	**Camping** at Glacier Basin Campground.
July 24, 1965	Rev. Alvin Whittemore, 61	**Hiking** on a ranger-led program on the Eugenia Mine Trail.
July 22, 1966	Ms. Xana Schurene, 76	**Camping** at Endovalley Campground.
August 12, 1966	Walter Stentzil, 64	From Ann Arbor, Michigan. **Sightseeing** near the Beaver Meadows Entrance.
August 22, 1966	John Rapchak, age unknown	**Hiking** on North Inlet Trail.
July 21, 1967	James B. Clifford, 66	**Hiking** near Ouzel Lake.
October 26, 1968	Marshall Wrubel, 44	**Hiking** on the Nymph Lake Trail. From Boulder, Colorado.
September 20, 1969	James D. Majors, 50	**Sightseeing** on Trail Ridge Road
August 13, 1971	Walter G. Seabold, 56	**Hiking** on Thatchtop Mountain.
August 31, 1971	Roy C. Handshew, age unknown	**Sightseeing** on Old Fall River Road.
September 11, 1971	Rudolph Postweiler, 48	**Hiking** near timberline on Chasm Lake Trail.
September 13, 1971	William Frechtling, 24	**Camping** at Longs Peak Campground.
August 12, 1972	Gerald F. Murphy, 51	**Hiking** on the Longs Peak Trail.
August 15, 1972	Ms. Lilie E. Brown, age unknown	**Sightseeing** at the Forest Canyon Overlook.
August 22, 1972	John Kruppa, 69	**Sightseeing** near the Big Thompson River Bridge.
September 3, 1972	Harry J. Sears, 79	**Sightseeing** at the Alpine Visitor Center.

July 1, 1975	Richard Ankanbrandt, 47	**Hiking** on the Green Mountain Trail.
August 8, 1975	Domingo Alvarez, 64	**Sightseeing** at the Alpine Visitor Center. From Puerto Rico.
September 5, 1975	Virgil Munsinger, 68	**Hiking** near Sky Pond.
September 16, 1975	Don Mullett, 57	**Sightseeing** in the Hidden Valley parking lot.
July 30, 1977	Sam Friedman, age unknown	**Sightseeing** at Lava Cliffs on Trail Ridge Road.
September 1, 1978	Herman Milner, 58	**Camping** at Moraine Park Campground.
September 6, 1978	Grete E. Wignall, 61	**Hiking** on the Loch Vale Trail.
October 15, 1978	Denzel Baker, 58	NPS Housing area (see chapter one).
September 1, 1979	Dr. Edward Sujansky, 43	Denver, Colorado, resident suffered a heart attack at the Keyhole on Longs Peak. He was **hiking** with his son. He had made the summit and was descending.
July 14, 1980	Bernard F. Conway, 62	From England. **Sightseeing** at Alpine Visitor Center.
August 23, 1982	John W. Daly, 73	**Driving** near Tundra Curves. Suffered heart attack and drove off the road, killing his wife. (See chapter six: Motor Vehicle Accidents.)
March 12, 1984	Cecelea Mulvihill, 71	**Sightseeing** in car on Bear Lake Road.
September 22, 1984	Gilbert Hana, 60	**Camping** at Moraine Park Campground.
October 9, 1984	Ruth L. Bruso, 70	**Sightseeing** at Bear Lake.
August 12, 1985	Alice A. Philbrick, 69	**Sightseeing** at Alpine Visitor Center.
June 8, 1987	Dr. J.D. Burger, 65	**Camping** at Glacier Basin Campground.
August 25, 1989	Albert M. Fincham, 52	**Hiking** alone near Granite Pass on Longs Peak Trail.
September 5, 1991	Lawrence Taylor, 46	**Riding motorcycle** in Moraine Park Campground.

June 14, 1994	Robert B. Baker, 70	**Sightseeing** near Rock Cut on Trail Ridge Road.
July 3, 1994	Noel W. Jarrell, 49	**Hiking** up Huffer's Hill at Alpine Visitor Center.
July 17, 1994	Eugene G. Gomolka, 50	**Hiking** on Toll Memorial Trail near Rock Cut on Trail Ridge Road.
September 1, 1994	Jack E. Keene, 47	**Hiking** on the Sandbeach Lake Trail.
May 15, 1996	Robert C. Drury, 50	**Hiking** on Trail Ridge Road near Rock Cut. (See chapter one on National Park Service employees.)
June 5, 1997	Francis W. Clyde, 63	**Camping** at Moraine Park Campground.
August 12, 1997	Mona Barlow, 65	**Sightseeing** on a tour bus at Alpine Visitor Center.
July 7, 1998	William C. Heflin, 70	Boulder, Colorado, resident died while **bicycling** near Gore Range Overlook.
August 14, 1998	Raymond C. Barbknecht, 47	**Hiking** on the Twin Sisters Trail. This incident is notable, as responding ranger Scott Wanek was struck by lightning and fortunately survived.
June 27, 1999	Michael J. Fritzen, 57	Fritzen, a Catholic Priest from Houston, Texas, died of a heart attack while **hiking alone** along the Cub Lake Trail.
August 26, 2000	Edward Calloway, 53	**Hiking** on the Cow Creek Trail.
August 10, 2002	Robert M. Whiddington, 73	**Hiking** on the Nymph Lake Trail. From Boulder, Colorado.
May 24, 2003	Raymond Chu, 78	Suffered fatal heart attack while in the Fern Lake turnaround restroom.
June 23, 2004	Marilyn Frongillo, 71	**Sightseeing** near Lake Irene on Trail Ridge Road.
June 12, 2008	Robert Bacon, 70	**Hiking** with wife near Alberta Falls.
January 10, 2009	Albert Langemann, 55	**Snowshoeing** on Longs Peak Trail.
July 20, 2009	Maynard Brandsma, 61	**Hiking** on Longs Peak near the Homestretch.

Other Medical Deaths

July 13, 1954	Mrs. Roger G. Van Blarican, 34	Suffered from **hemorrhagic anemia** while parked near Lower Hidden Valley.
June 26, 1956	Robert B Salt, 26	**Acute Diabetic Shock**—Pear Lake.
June 18, 1959	Edith Zockett, age unknown	Suffered a **stroke** while staying at the Hatchett Cabin in Moraine Park. Died two days later in Amarillo, Texas.
August 3, 1985	Nancy Garbs, 27	**Peritonitis**—Never Summer Ranch.
June 22, 1987	Charles Houseman, 77	Died of old age/**natural causes**—Grand Lake.

Motor Vehicle Accidents

Joel Estes and his son first wandered into the Estes Valley in 1859 by bushwhacking up from the Lyons area. During the winter of 1874–75, A.Q. MacGregor followed the same basic route and built the first primitive toll road for wagons through what is now Pinewood Springs. The Colorado Territorial Legislature gave him ten years to collect tolls. When this time period elapsed and after a bit of controversy and lawsuits, the road was opened to the public without a toll. This was the preferred and most direct route from the Boulder and Denver area for decades. About this time, the citizens of Loveland saw they were missing out on the opportunity to capture their own tourist dollars. In 1904, the present route up the Big Thompson River Canyon was laid out. Both roads were upgraded and designated state highways in the 1930s.

In 1903, Freelan O. Stanley came to Estes Park from New England for his health after contracting tuberculosis. Stanley drove his invention, the Stanley Steamer automobile, to Estes Park from Lyons to the astonishment of the locals. The high, dry mountain air restored his health, and like many others, Stanley fell in love with the scenery and small mountain community. Stanley later built the Stanley Hotel in 1909 and brought electricity to the town by installing a small hydroelectric plant on the Fall River.

From Stanley's maiden trip in 1903, the automobile quickly became the preferred mode of travel for visitors to Estes Park and Grand Lake. It is not surprising that the next stage of development was a road across the continental divide to link the two tourist destinations. In 1913, the initial work was started on a road up Fall River Canyon. Convicts worked on the road during 1913 and 1914, but complaints about this practice forced the work to be turned over to a private contractor. A second contractor started on the Grand Lake side of the park. The road was completed across the divide in September 1920. There were 16 switchbacks on the road, and on some sections the grade was close to 16 percent. There was also a 1,200-foot-long snow drift near Fall River Pass that was expensive and dangerous to open each spring. While a positive accomplishment for the communities, the road was not terribly conducive to relaxed tourist travel. In fact, the first automobile accident with fatalities occurred on the Fall River Road in 1918.

It wasn't long before a new route over the Continental Divide, following the old Ute Trail, was proposed. The new road was surveyed in 1926–27 with a maximum grade of 7 percent, but most at only 5 percent. Work on the east side started in the autumn of 1929 and continued for most of the winter due to mild conditions. The east side section to Fall River Pass was open to traffic on July 15, 1932. As before, a separate contract had been awarded for the west side of the road. By August 1932, work had progressed and tourist traffic went down the new west side road. Paving was not completed until 1949. Today, the spectacular Trail Ridge Road is the highest continuous-paved highway in the United States, reaching an elevation of 12,183 feet.

With millions of visitors enjoying the park each year, motor vehicle accidents with fatalities are inevitable. Fortunately, these have been few in number, with only 27 deaths associated with 20 accidents. Over half of the fatalities occurred before 1950, when seatbelts were nonexistent and park roads were not completely paved. There have only been three accidents with four deaths in the last twenty-five years. Four of the fatalities were park rangers. Their stories are found in chapter one, concerning National Park Service employees.

The first motor vehicle accident with fatalities occurred on August 22, 1918, on the Fall River Road. On this day, the Reverend E. F. Kimmelshuhe and his family, from Monmouth, Illinois, along with Mrs. C.W. Woods, were ascending the Fall River Road in a Ford automobile. The Reverend Kimmelshuhe was driving. At approximately 2:30 p.m., their car slipped off the edge of the road between switchbacks nine and ten, rolled over, and landed upside down on the switchback below. The Reverend was uninjured and pulled the bodies of the other four out from under the vehicle. His two boys, ages 17 and 11, died within minutes of the accident. His wife died approximately three hours later, and Mrs. Woods died the following day.

Fourteen years later, a heroic story of survival and love unfolded when Mary S. Day drove off the Fall River Road on Friday evening, August 26, 1932. Day, a 35-year-old teacher from Gainesville, Georgia, was driving her two nieces, Lucille, age 10, and Jean, 12, to Denver from Grand Lake, with Alamosa, where they lived, the ultimate destination. Around 8:00 p.m., darkness and poor visibility evidently caused Day to drive too close to the shoulder and lose control of the car about one-tenth mile east of the top of Fall River Pass (just below the present day Visitor Center). The vehicle plunged and rolled over 400 feet down the slope. Mary Day was killed instantly. Jean had apparently been knocked unconscious in the accident, but was not seriously injured. When she regained consciousness in the dark cold of night, she heard Lucille softly moaning. She tried to keep her warm through the long night as a loving sister would. At first light, Jean was able to walk down the switchbacks for help. She had gone almost one-and-a-half miles down the road before being picked up by a surprised ranger Howard Rowland near the Willow Park cabin. An immediate rescue ensued, but Lucille had been seriously injured and died on Sunday, August 28th.

In 1934, luck finally ran out for Bureau of Public Roads employee C.F. Peyton. On July 3, 1934, Peyton apparently fell asleep and drove off the Trail Ridge Road near Deer Ridge Junction and survived. Barely a month later, on July 30th, he and another employee were riding in the back of a dump truck north of Grand Lake when the tailgate of the truck gave way and they fell out. Peyton died of his injuries.

Alcohol as a factor in an accident first came into play with the death of James Fifer, age 32. Fifer was from Boulder, Colorado, and at the time was a cook at the Plantation Café in Estes Park. He died when the vehicle in which he was riding went off the Bear Lake Road and crashed into a huge rock about 7:45 a.m. on June 30, 1936. Fifer was thrown from the car and sustained a skull fracture. The driver of the vehicle, William Dedrick, was severely injured. The Superintendent's Report from July 6, 1936, indicated that Fifer and Dedrick had been fishing at Bear Lake and were returning to town. Excessive speed and alcohol were determined to be the primary causes of the accident.

Greeley, Colorado, resident Shelley Heimbichner, age 15, was spending the summer working at the Bear Lake Lodge. The *Estes Park Trail* reported that on August 7, 1945, she was in a vehicle with six other Bear Lake Lodge employees heading into Estes Park when the vehicle left the Bear Lake Road on a sharp curve and rolled over. Heimbichner was killed, and all the other occupants sustained serious injuries, including the driver, 17-year-old Dean Miller of Albuquerque, New Mexico.

Five years later, another Bear Lake Lodge employee died in a violent accident. Kenneth Swisher could probably best be described as a questionable character. He was hired through the Citizen's Mission in Denver on August 11th and worked as a cook and baker at the Bear Lake Lodge. His coworkers at Bear Lake described him as a likeable person, very willing to work, quite talkative, and extremely fond of beer and liquor. Swisher had very few personal belongings and no identification other than a copy of his work contract.

On the evening of August 29, 1950, at approximately 8:00 p.m., a visitor stopped at the Mill Creek Ranger Station and reported to ranger Karl Gilbert that there was a car off the road and on fire a half mile below the ranger station. Gilbert responded and found Mr. S.B. Gibbons of Estes Park at the accident scene. Gibbons told him that he had been the first on the scene and had pulled Swisher's body away from the flames. Swisher was obviously dead. The vehicle was a 1937 Ford two-door coupe, and it was upside down and in flames 100 feet from the road. In reconstructing the accident, ranger Gilbert estimated Swisher was coming down the Bear Lake Road at 60 mph and failed to negotiate a curve in the road. There were skid marks on both shoulders of the road as far back as a half mile from the accident. Gilbert later learned that Swisher was on his day off and had been drinking heavily the day of the accident. He borrowed the car he was driving to go to Estes Park earlier in the day. Upon returning to the Bear Lake Lodge, he borrowed $10 against his coming salary and continued to drink. He was also caught burglarizing the room of other employees, where he obtained $15 and some clothing. Swisher then helped himself to the car he had earlier borrowed in an apparent attempt to make an escape, at which point the accident occurred.

On July 6, 1954, Richard Williams, age 43, died in a head-on vehicle accident on Trail Ridge Road, 6.5 miles north of the Grand Lake Entrance. Williams was a Denver resident who was a subscription agent for *The Denver Post*. He was speeding and out of control when he collided with Mr. Harvey Shabushing of Milwaukee, Wisconsin. Shabushing sustained non–life threatening injuries.

Irwin C. Oderkirk, age 22, was a Lowry Air Force Base cadet in Denver. On July 17, 1955, he crashed his motorcycle into rocks on the Bear Lake Road at Prospect Canyon. Witnesses reported that Oderkirk was traveling at a high rate of speed when he failed to negotiate a corner and crashed. He had been camping in Glacier Basin Campground with friends. As he was in the military, he was transferred to Fitzsimmons Hospital in Denver. He died two days later on July 19, 1955.

On September 5, 1975, Laurene S. Nuzzo, age 26, was riding on the back of her husband's motorcycle. The Bristol, Connecticut, resident died in an accident approximately 1 mile east of Upper Hidden Valley on the Trail Ridge Road. Laurene Nuzzo and her husband were westbound when they collided with and sideswiped an eastbound garbage truck owned by A-1 Trash Service and driven by 20-year-old Robert River. Mr. Nuzzo suffered a fractured left ankle and cuts/bruises.

In another tragic accident, both John W. Daly, age 73, and his wife, Audrey, 56, were killed on August 23, 1982. The weather was good, and witnesses stated the Daly vehicle was only traveling 20–30 mph when it went off the road and rolled below the Tundra Curves on Trail Ridge Road. The coroner's report indicated that John Daly may have suffered a mild heart attack while driving, causing him to lose control of the vehicle. The couple was from Midland, Texas.

In reviewing these incidents, I am continually startled at the suddenness of events. How can a pleasant visit to the park instantly change to tragedy and forever affect the lives of the participants? In particular, the victims in these last two narratives were filled with hope and promise before tragedy struck.

On June 8, 1995, 19-year-old Alan B. Farwell of Elkton, Maryland, and Forrest "Woody" Sprague, also 19, from Hockessin, Delaware, died in a motor vehicle accident on Trail Ridge Road at Rock Cut when they either accidentally drove off or slid off the road in foggy, icy conditions. Park staff first learned of the missing boys when contacted by Sprague's grandfather, George Van House of Bountiful, Utah, on Thursday evening, June 8th. According to Van House, the two had spent the previous night, June 7th, in Moraine Park Campground on their way to Utah. Van House called because the boys failed to arrive as planned. Preliminary checks did not reveal any specific information on the boys, as they had already left the area.

In reconstructing the events, it appears the boys left early in the morning before rangers closed the Trail Ridge Road at 7:00 a.m. on the 8th due to icy conditions, drifting snow, and dense fog. The road was reopened at 11:15 a.m. that day, but closed again at 5:15 p.m. due to snow and icy conditions. The road was not reopened to the public until Monday, June 12th, due to eight-foot snow drifts on the road. The boy's vehicle, a 1984 Chevrolet Suburban, was spotted by a park snowplow operator on Saturday, June 10th, probably because of the plow's higher driver cab. The vehicle was approximately 700 feet down a 45–50 degree slope and below the point on Trail Ridge Road where, if westbound, the road makes a fairly sharp turn to the right just before passing through the Rock Cut formation. Responding rangers found both boys dead inside the dangerously unstable vehicle. Ropes and anchors were used to prevent the car from rolling farther down the slope.

Another heart wrenching incident involved the death of John Michael Whatmough on September 12, 2005. Whatmough, his wife, and their two-and-a-half year-old son had flown into Denver International Airport on September 10th and rented a midsize SUV vehicle. On September 12th, they drove up and entered the park at approximately 11:15 a.m. Their son was in a car seat in the back, and they stopped several times to take photographs as they meandered through the park. A little after 1:00 p.m., the family stopped at a small pullout on the left side of the Old Fall River Road in order to take some pictures. This location was approximately four-tenths of a mile above Chasm Falls. John Whatmough was driving, and the child was asleep in his car seat. At this location, the road has a modest grade that would cause a vehicle to roll if not properly parked with the brake set.

As is common in traumatic events, Whatmough's wife, Janet, was uncertain about the following sequence of events. There were no witnesses. In essence, they stopped at the turnout, and John Whatmough said he was going to take some pictures. Janet exited the passenger door and walked a few steps towards the rear of the vehicle. Moments after exiting the vehicle, she noticed the vehicle slowly rolling backward down the incline of the road. She yelled, "Stop it!" and tried to grab the passenger side mirror to stop the vehicle. Janet Whatmough recalled that her husband was at the driver's door and sort of halfway in or out. She could not recall if he was trying to get into the vehicle or still getting out of it. In any case, the vehicle slipped backwards off the side of the road and to the left, pulling John Whatmough with it. The vehicle rolled approximately twenty feet. It did not roll over, and the child was uninjured.

Janet Whatmough went down the slope to her husband. He was unconscious in a prone position. His breathing was labored and he had numerous abrasions and contusions. She checked her child, then went back to her husband and was able to hail passing motorists, who dialed 911. Ranger Tara Vessella was the first on the scene at 1:49 p.m., followed immediately by ranger Jim Sanborn. Vessella and a nurse visiting the park found Whatmough without a pulse and not breathing. With the help of other bystanders, they were able to turn Whatmough onto his back and initiate CPR. A paramedic from the Estes Park Medical Center soon took over medical care, but resuscitation efforts were terminated after consultation with a hospital physician. The coroner's report indicated that John Whatmough died from a traumatic rupture of the subclavian artery, causing massive blood loss into the pleural space of the chest.

In the preliminary investigation of the vehicle, rangers Sanborn and Ivan Kassovic observed the key in the ignition in the "accessory" position with the audible warning sounding (dinging). The engine was off. The hand brake was in the down (released) position. The transmission was in the shiftronic manual "drive" mode, which would allow the vehicle to roll as it did. Perhaps due to being unfamiliar with the vehicle, Whatmough appears to have turned off the engine while it was still in gear and also failed to set the hand brake. As he realized the vehicle was rolling, it appears he tried to stop the vehicle by reaching across for the hand brake or to put the transmission in "park." The weight and momentum of the vehicle threw him off balance and off the roadway and under the vehicle. All in a matter of moments.

Motor Vehicle Accidents

August 22, 1918	Mrs. E. F. Kimmelshuhe, age unknown Kimmelshuhe, 17 (son) Kimmelshuhe, 11 (son) Mrs. C. W. Woods, age unknown	**Between the 9 and 10 switchbacks on Fall River Road** Reverend Kimmelshuhe was driving and survived. The vehicle *went off the edge of the switchback and rolled* upside down on switchback below.
August 26, 1932	Mary Day, 35 Lucille Day, 10	**East of Alpine Visitor Center** Drove off edge of road in *poor weather with low visibility and rolled* vehicle.
July 30, 1934	C. F. Peyton, age unknown	**North of Grand Lake** Fell from back of moving truck.
August 5, 1934	Kenneth Meenan, 22	**North of Grand Lake Entrance** NPS temporary ranger on motorcycle had *collision with vehicle.* (See chapter one on National Park Service employees.)

June 30, 1936	James Fifer, 32	**Along the Bear Lake Road** Fifer was a passenger. Thrown from vehicle when it left the roadway. *Alcohol and speed* were the primary factors in this fatality.
1938	Nola Morris, age unknown	**On Trail Ridge Road** Sustained fractured skull when *vehicle rolled* over. No further details found on this incident. (Not in text.)
October 13, 1939	Raymond Johnson, 30	**Along the Bear Lake Road** Popular NPS temporary ranger suffered skull fracture when *tire blew out* causing vehicle to leave the road and strike a tree. (See chapter one on National Park Service employees.)
August 7, 1945	Shelley Heimbichner, 15	**Along the Bear Lake Road** Heimbichner was a passenger in a vehicle with six other Bear Lake Lodge employees that left the road due to *excessive speed.* Heimbichner was the only fatality.
August 17, 1947	Oscar Jacobson, age unknown Raymond Young, 22	**4 miles north of Grand Lake Entrance** Jacobson, off duty NPS temporary ranger, was the driver, with 3 occupants, including Young. Vehicle went off road approx. 4 a.m. *Fatigue and excessive speed* likely factors. (See chapter one on National Park Service employees.)
July 29, 1950	Kenneth Swisher, 35	**Bear Lake Road below Mill Creek Ranger Station** Swisher was a Bear Lake Lodge employee and had been drinking heavily. *Excessive speed and alcohol.*
July 6, 1954	Richard Williams, 43	**6.5 miles north of Grand Lake Entrance** *Excessive speed* and failure to control vehicle led to head-on collision

July 17, 1955	Irwin C. Oderkirk, 22	**Bear Lake Road near Prospect Canyon** Witnesses reported Oderkirk was traveling at a *high rate of speed* on his motorcycle when he failed to negotiate a corner and crashed.
July 12, 1960	Charles Raidy, 34	**East of Milner Pass on Trail Ridge Road** Raidy drove off the road. Limited information available. (Not in text.)
June 24, 1966	Nathaniel Lacy, 43	**Just west of the Fall River Entrance Station** Fall River subdistrict ranger had a *motor scooter accident* while checking campgrounds just west of Fall River entrance. (See chapter one on National Park Service employees.)
September 5, 1975	Laurene Nuzzo, 26	**Above Many Parks Curve on Trail Ridge Road** Nuzzo was on the back of a motorcycle that *crossed the centerline* and sideswiped a garbage truck going in the opposite direction.
September 5, 1977	Jason E. Quest, 20	**Deer Ridge Junction on Trail Ridge Road** Quest, operating a motorcycle, died in a *collision with another vehicle*. (Not in text.)
June 23, 1978	John White-Lance, 27	**7 miles north of the Grand Lake Entrance** Few details are known of this single vehicle accident. White-Lance was the operator and sole occupant. The vehicle was found off the road. (Not in text.)
August 23, 1982	John W. Daly, 73 Audrey G. Daly, 56	**Below Tundra Curves on Trail Ridge Road** Witnesses said the weather was fine and the Daly vehicle was going approx. 25–30 mph when it went off the road and rolled. John Daly was driving. The coroner's report indicated that Daly had suffered a *heart attack*, which likely caused him to drive off the road.

June 8, 1995	Alan Farwell, 19 Forrest Sprague, 19	**Just east of Rock Cut on Trail Ridge Road** Farwell and Sprague missed the road curve to the right in *foggy conditions*. Drove off the roadway to the left and rolled several times.
September 12, 2005	John Whatmough, 32	**Above Chasm Falls on Old Fall River Road** Whatmough *failed to properly park vehicle on incline*. The vehicle rolled backward off the roadway, rolling over Whatmough.
April 28, 2009	Connie Fanning, 55	**South of Grand Lake Entrance Station.** Vehicle rolled over and caught on fire. (Not in text.)

SEVEN
Suicides

For most people, reading about suicides is not a pleasant activity. Yet for many, there is the morbid curiosity that won't let them pull their eyes from the details in the newspaper. I suspect there is a broad range of emotions that whirl through most minds (coward? selfish? why?), while deep down, I also suspect reading about this final act of desperation may challenge the fragile sense of meaning in existence for many readers.

What seems interesting is that the final act of suicide in a national park is contrary to the purpose of a park. I hope most readers will agree that a national park is a place to relax, reflect, and recharge one's soul in the bosom of nature. Millions of visitors do so each year. Fortunately, in the history of Rocky Mountain National Park, only 25 individuals have elected to take their own lives here. This represents roughly 8.5 percent of all fatalities, comparable to statistics from Grand Canyon and Yosemite National Parks that show approximately 7 percent of all fatalities there are suicides. Similarly, the percentage of females that end their life in Rocky Mountain is 20 percent. This corresponds with 22 percent at the Grand Canyon and 19 percent at Yosemite, as well as with national suicide averages.

Someone had to be the first to take his or her life in Rocky Mountain National Park. This distinction lies with Ms. Lorena Pauley, age 39. From Denver, Colorado, Ms. Pauley had suffered a long period of despondency according to her brother, R.J. Pauley. On July 5, 1950, Lorena Pauley took a bus to Estes Park, then another up to Bear Lake that afternoon. It appears that in the quiet of the evening, after the fishermen and hikers had left, she swam out into the lake, then probably succumbed to hypothermia and drowned. Her body was discovered by fishermen the following morning. R.J. Pauley formally identified the body in Loveland later that evening. He contacted park officials after he read a newspaper account of a body discovered in Bear Lake. Mr. Pauley told the authorities in the coroner's office that his sister had been missing since Wednesday morning.

Statistically in the United States, 57 percent of men use a firearm to end their life. In Rocky Mountain National Park, 11 of the 20 men, or 55 percent, chose this method. The first occurred on May 27, 1954, when Mr. A.J. McPhillips left a suicide note in his family's Big Thompson Canyon cabin about four miles east of Estes Park. McPhillips was a Loveland insurance agent and had financial difficulties at the time. The note indicated that his body would be "underground." The subsequent two-week search centered around the Eugenia mine, as there were several old bore holes in the slopes there, and McPhillips had been seen near the old Hewes-Kirkwood Inn Road in Tahosa Valley. The *Estes Park Trail* reported two years later that on June 12, 1956, hikers found McPhillips' body approximately two miles west of the Columbine Lodge near the Longs Peak Trail, just inside the park boundary. He had shot himself in the right temple with a .38 caliber revolver, which was found near the decomposed body.

In the narrative report written by East District ranger Deane M. Shilts, we find the circumstances of the park's third suicide, that of Mr. Norris C. Livoni, age 50, on May 27, 1964. Livoni was from Littleton, Colorado, and owned a construction company with his brother. On the morning of May 26, 1964, he registered at the old Hi-C Motel along the Fall River Road. It was later discovered that he wrote and mailed a suicide note to his brother that afternoon. According to Shilts' investigation, the last people to see Livoni alive were Mr. and Mrs. Gregory Paglia, who operated Tony's Pizza in Estes Park. Close to the midnight closing time on the 26th, Livoni came in and bought a pizza and a taco, which he ate in the restaurant. He also purchased a *Reader's Digest* magazine and two packs of cigarettes, all of which were found in his vehicle the next morning.

The unfortunate visitors that found Mr. Livoni were Mr. and Mrs. Leslie Jorgensen from Franksville, Wisconsin. The Jorgensen's had actually talked to Livoni around 7:00 p.m. the night before at the Rainbow Curve parking area. Trail Ridge Road was closed at the time, and they discussed the scenery. They told Shilts that Livoni appeared normal at the time. That evening, the Jorgensens slept in their car along the Bear Lake Road. The morning of the 27th, they were back at Rainbow Curve by 5:15 a.m. to see if Trail Ridge Road was open. They had passed Livoni's white Lincoln sedan on the side of the road near Upper Hidden Valley on the way up. Finding Trail Ridge Road still closed, they returned and stopped at the Lincoln to see if help was needed and found Livoni dead. It was obvious that Livoni had been shot in the head with a shotgun.

District Ranger Shilts arrived on the scene at 6:50 a.m., followed by rangers Nat Lacy and Bob Binnewies. The three rangers secured the scene pending the arrival of FBI agents Ken Bridenstine and Roy Mischke at approximately 10:30 a.m. Upon closer inspection, it appeared that Livoni had attempted to set his car on fire from the inside and drive over the cliff. The fire in the rear seat didn't ignite the open gas bottle found there, and the vehicle high centered on the road shoulder. It was at this point that Livoni likely shot himself.

In doing research for this book, I had the pleasure of sharing emails with a good friend, ranger Tom Griffiths, who was stationed in the Fall River Subdistrict in 1964. Tom recalled the saga of "Billy Bones" quite clearly. You see, the skull and bones of an unidentified victim sat in a box on a shelf at the Bighorn Ranger Station for several years before disappearing! This story started on September 15, 1964, when a local hiking club found human remains in a solution pothole on top of a rock on Lumpy Ridge. When the rangers went up to investigate, they found the bones, a .22 caliber revolver with one round expended, a partially full pint of whiskey, and some rotted clothes with a few coins scattered about. None of the coins were older than 1945, thus giving an approximate date of the probable suicide. At one point, ranger Nat Lacy sent the remains to the FBI for assistance in identification. There was never a positive identification made, though there was a possibility they belonged to a missing person named Bill, thus the moniker "Billy Bones." This all occurred, of course, before the days of DNA testing, or proper evidence storage for that matter! The bones have disappeared with no trace of history.

Two separate but similar suicides of young men on the Keyhole Route of Longs Peak are recorded. On November 14, 1979, 20-year-old Kris Gedney was depressed about his inadequate scores on his medical school entrance exam. He had been under extreme pressure from his family to attend medical school. Gedney drove up to the park and hiked up the Longs Peak Trail past the Keyhole. At some point, he consumed six times the fatal dose of antifreeze, and then jumped off the Narrows section of trail on the Keyhole Route, falling 200 feet. The Boulder, Colorado, resident left a suicide note in his pack consisting of two handwritten Psalms from the Bible. His body was found on November 16, 1979.

The other incident occurred almost ten years later on July 21, 1989, when Evan R. Corbett, age 19, either fell or jumped near the Trough section of the Keyhole Route. The despondent young man had ingested an estimated 85 sleeping pills while hiking up through the Boulderfield. He appeared to have wandered approximately 75–100 feet from the main trail in the Trough to a very steep and dangerous area. Hikers discovered his body at approximately 8:40 a.m. He had no climbing gear on his person.

The only suicide victim to hang himself was Sarasota, Florida, resident Roger A. Boyce, age 44. Boyce's family later told park staff that he had been depressed. He had sold all his personal property and left Florida in June, saying only that he was going to Colorado. On October 8, 1988, the badly decomposed body of Boyce was discovered hanging outside a tent by a photographer. A park entrance "walk in" receipt dated June 21st was found at the site. The isolated location was approximately 200 yards south of Trail Ridge Road, below the "Mountains, Meadows, and Moraines" exhibit sign and turnout.

Some individuals that commit suicide go to great lengths in an effort not to inconvenience family members or law enforcement officers. John R. Thomas, age 34, covered his car with a canvas tarp and parked off the road west of Deer Ridge Junction, before he shot himself. Ranger patrol did not see his vehicle Thursday night as of 6:00 p.m. The unusual factors caused a passing ranger to stop and inspect the vehicle Friday morning, January 25, 1991. A handgun and a lengthy suicide note were among the belongings. Thomas had suffered a gunshot wound to the chest. The subsequent investigation revealed that Thomas was from California and had a life-long dream to spend time in the mountains of Colorado. He had spent several days in the Boulder area before driving to the park late Thursday evening or Friday morning.

The steep drop offs on Trail Ridge Road offer a tempting option for those plotting to use their vehicle to end their life. The clearest case of this was Mr. Lon Lee Egbert, age 42, from Lakewood, Colorado. On July 4, 1992, Egbert committed suicide by driving his vehicle over a cliff just west of Rock Cut on Trail Ridge Road at approximately 6:38 p.m. There were no skid marks, and witnesses said there was no obvious reason for the accident. In a suicide note, Egbert had prepared a map indicating where he planned to drive off the road in the park. His 1989 Ford Probe rolled several times to a point estimated at 1,500 feet below the road. Egbert was ejected and found dead. The vehicle was removed by helicopter days later.

Three of the suicides in Rocky Mountain, however, are somewhat unique because of their similar method, which is not chronicled in similar histories for other parks. In separate incidents, Bruce Anderson, John Hodge, and Richard Smith simply laid down, exposed themselves to the weather, and died of hypothermia.

In a fatality eerily similar to that of J.P. Chitwood on Flattop Mountain in 1920, hikers found the partially decomposed body of Bruce Anderson, age 28, also on Flattop Mountain, on July 31, 1992. Judging from the level of decomposition, the body appeared to have been there for a month or more, which is unusual considering the popularity of the area. The body was around 300–400 feet north of the Flattop Mountain Trail overlooking Odessa Gorge. Anderson's remains were found with a small daypack, a light jacket, and a Bible. The Larimer County Coroner listed the cause of death as "undetermined," but it appears the Philadelphia,

Pennsylvania, man died from exposure as an act of suicide. The estimated date of death was late May–early June, when cold, wet weather is more common. He had attempted suicide several months earlier. Because of poor weather preventing the use of a helicopter, rangers used a horse to carry the remains to the Bear Lake Trailhead.

On the morning of October 4, 1994, a park visitor found the body of Richard J. Smith, age 45, facedown in a calm, shallow pool of the Big Thompson River near Moraine Park Campground. Fully clothed, but with no shoes, this Ellisville, Missouri, resident had last been seen alive by neighboring campers around 4:30 p.m. the previous evening at his campsite in the campground. There was no evidence of foul play, nor a suicide note. The subsequent coroner's report indicated Smith died of hypothermia. As noted, the pool he was in was calm and shallow, and a person could easily stand up. It appears that Smith simply immersed himself in the water and ultimately died of hypothermia.

John C. Hodge, age 55, took his own life in a similar fashion. The body of this Superior, Colorado, man was found by park visitors on December 25, 2001, approximately 200 yards south of Lily Lake. Again, the coroner's report indicated the cause of death as hypothermia. Like Anderson and Smith, Hodge simply laid down in the snow on a cold, windy night and died. In the subsequent investigation, it was determined that Hodge had been despondent.

Young love is such a powerful, often illogical emotion. On the morning of May 10, 1994, a National Park Service maintenance worker found Kip Lloyd, age 20, lying on the pavement outside his car in the Bierstadt Lake parking lot along the Bear Lake Road. He had shot himself and was unconscious, but still alive. He died four days later in the Poudre Valley Hospital in Ft. Collins. Kip Lloyd had a history of drug abuse and had been reported to be depressed. The subsequent investigation found that he had recently mentioned suicide and finally acted out his darkest thoughts. But Kip Lloyd had an 18 year-old girlfriend named Allison (Alli) Bierma.

They were both from Greeley, Colorado, and had been together for some time. It was later determined that they enjoyed coming up to the national park to hike off trail. Allison had finished her high school course requirements the previous December and was working full time to earn money for college. She was scheduled to graduate with her classmates the following week. Allison's parents later reported that she had been despondent since Kip Lloyd's death, but they did not think she was suicidal.

Kip Lloyd was buried on May 17th. On May 19th, Allison spent the day with friends, hitting golf balls and later smoking marijuana. She left Greeley about 5:30 p.m. after telling friends she was "going to the mountains," but had promised Kip's mother, Patty Lloyd, that she "would be back by dark." When she failed to return by 11:00 p.m., Lloyd called the Bierma family to express concern. A telephone call from the family was routed through to ranger Scot Bowen, and he was asked to drive up the Bear Lake Road to check for Alli's vehicle at the parking area where Kip Lloyd had shot himself. There was no indication that she had been there, but later on the morning of May 20th her 1984 Chevrolet Cavalier was found parked along the access road to the Fern Lake Trailhead. There was no evidence of foul play or a struggle. The engine was cold.

Considering the circumstances, an immediate search was started in the areas of Cub and Fern Lakes. The next day, the search effort grew to over 80 members, including the use of a helicopter, bloodhounds, and divers searching the run-off swollen waters of the Big Thompson River drainage. For several days, searchers were frustrated at not being able to find any evidence, such as personal items or articles of clothing from Bierma, which would have helped direct the search effort. The only possible clue found for several days was a small pebble formation near the Cub Lake Trail that spelled out "RIP," though it could not be positively linked to Bierma's disappearance. Alerts from the dog teams gave some indication that Bierma was or had been in the search area. As with many extended searches, it was only a matter of time before a smattering of psychics and clairvoyants offered their support. Leaving no stone unturned, they were engaged by the investigative team of Ranger Mary Wilson and Special Agent Pat Buccello without consequence. By the 24th, the search had been scaled back to 25 searchers and dog teams, but with little success.

On the 25th, Alli's parents found several notes of a suicidal nature in Alli's bedroom. The notes were hidden in clothing drawers in her room.

By May 25th, Alli Bierma had been missing for six days. Despite the newly found suicide notes, the search was suspended, and park rangers met with Greeley Police to decide on their next steps. Information on Alli Bierma was entered into the National Criminal Information Center (NCIC) network and a missing person flyer was produced and distributed widely around the park and the Greeley area. There had been no activity on Alli's checking account. It was likely that Alli was dead and in the park, so rangers continued to probe off trail in the search area without success for several days.

On June 4th, some acquaintances of the Bierma family came to the park and requested permission to search themselves with their Australian Shepherd, Riley. The dog had not been trained in search or rescue techniques, but was used to hiking in a mountain setting and responded well to voice commands. Normally pets are not allowed in the backcountry of the park, but considering the circumstances, Supervisor Kurt Oliver agreed to allow the group and dog in the park as long as they were escorted by ranger Karla Sweet. On the morning of June 5th, the group moved up the Cub Lake Trail. Being convinced that Allison was likely suicidal, as opposed to a runaway, the searchers looked for possible areas, such as cliffs, from which she could have jumped. Barely an hour into their trip, they spied a low cliff through the trees about 200 yards from the trail. The area had been searched before, but the men felt drawn to the area and decided to look again. Approaching through thick underbrush, the dog alerted. Within a few minutes, Alison Bierma's body was found in a thick growth of young juniper trees beneath the cliff band. Rangers subsequently found her purse, wallet, and identification. There was a four-page handwritten suicide note in the right rear pocket of her jeans.

While editing this chapter in March of 2009, I came across an article on the internet regarding teen depression. The article referenced the April 2009 issue of the journal *Pediatrics*, which noted that an estimated 6 percent of teenagers are clinically depressed and discussed the importance of teen depression screening. Being close to someone who had recently committed suicide would suggest that Alli Bierma needed close supervision and professional counseling. During the investigative process, it was found that those closest to Alli knew she was depressed and had even discussed suicide, but she seemed to be weathering the crisis. There was no mention of professional counseling. I believe a lesson here is to not underestimate depression in a friend or family member, regardless of age.

Most suicide victims have a history of depression and calculate their eventual demise. Contrary to this, Michael P. Carter, age 26, appears to have shot himself out of an impulsive sense of desperation. On August 26, 2001, near 9:00 p.m., residents in the Upper High Drive area, across from the Beaver Meadows Visitor Center, heard several gun shots and notified the Estes Park Police Department. Responding officers and rangers found Michael Carter dead in the driveway of his residence of an apparent self-inflicted gunshot wound. In an interesting twist of government jurisdictions, Carter's rental home was on Larimer County property. However, the driveway accessing the property was slightly inside the boundary of the national park. Due to the continued cooperative relationship between the Larimer County Sheriff's Office and the park, a joint investigation was conducted for the incident.

Carter was separated from his wife, Amy King. She had gone to Carter's residence earlier that evening to pick up their three children, who ranged in age from 17 months to five years. A lengthy argument ensued, with King eventually locking herself in the bathroom. She escaped out the window and attempted to drive away. Enraged, Carter ran after the car and fired three shots at his estranged wife from close range with a .25 caliber handgun. The first shot went through the windshield, but did not hit King. The next two shots went through the driver side window and struck King in the hand and arm. She was able to drive away and made it to the Estes Park Medical Center with the help of a friend. Now in the driveway, and on park property, Carter ended his life with a single gunshot to his head. Fortunately, the children were in the house and were not harmed.

Most suicides are lonely, private affairs. Perhaps this is what Jonathan J. Rozecki, age 19, was hoping for on the evening of November 16, 2003. Boston, Massachusetts, native Rozecki was depressed. Just prior to the incident, he had telephoned his sister in Massachusetts to tell her that he was in a campground in Rocky Mountain National Park and to say goodbye. Concerned, she contacted the Estes Park Police Department for help. Three Larimer County deputies were dispatched to help rangers locate Rozecki. In mid November, Moraine Park Campground is the only campground open, and it had few occupants. A deputy soon found him sitting in his car in the campground. As the deputy approached the vehicle, Rozecki shot himself with a .45 caliber pistol. Ranger Jan Pauley immediately arrived on the scene and determined Rozecki was still breathing and had a radial pulse. He was taken to the Estes Park Medical Center, and then flown to Poudre Valley Hospital in Ft. Collins, where he was pronounced dead.

Suicides

July 29, 1950	Lorena Pauley, 39	**Bear Lake** In the only recorded death at Bear Lake, Pauley took her own life by *drowning.*
May 27, 1954	A.J. McPhillips, age unknown	**Southeast of the Longs Peak Ranger Station** This despondent insurance salesman from Loveland, Colorado, left a suicide note and *shot himself.*
May 27, 1964	Norris C. Livoni, 50	**Upper Hidden Valley on Trail Ridge Road** From Littleton, Colorado, Livoni *shot himself* with a shotgun while sitting in his vehicle
September 6, 1964	Unknown remains	**Found in a solution pothole on Lumpy Ridge** The unidentified remains of "Billy Bones" were found by hikers. The victim had *shot himself.*

September 19, 1977	Eric Rumsey, 25	**Above Rainbow Curve on Trail Ridge Road** From Pittsford, Michigan, Rumsey took his own life by *asphyxiation* with vehicle exhaust fumes. (Not in text.)
November 14, 1979	Kris Gedney, 22	**Longs Peak, Keyhole Route** Depressed by his medical school exam scores, this Boulder, Colorado, resident *ingested antifreeze and jumped* off the Narrows section of the trail.
September 11, 1985	William R. Becker, 21	**Timber Creek Campground** From Ann Arbor, Michigan. *Shot himself* in his tent in the campground. (Not in text.)
September 21, 1985	Edna M. Digman, 44	**Above Many Parks Curve on Trail Ridge Road** It was believed this Longmont, Colorado, resident *drove her vehicle off the road* to commit suicide. The vehicle rolled and burned. (Not in text.)
March 1, 1987	Francis J. Murray, 36	**Copeland Lake Campground in Wild Basin** From Cherry Hills, New Jersey, Murray took his own life by *asphyxiation* with vehicle exhaust fumes. He had previously attempted suicide. (Not in text.)
October 8, 1988	Roger A. Boyce, 44	**Upper Beaver Meadows area** This Sarasota, Florida, native *hung himself* from a tree. A park entrance receipt was found and dated June 21st.
July 21, 1989	Evan R. Corbett, 19	**Longs Peak, Keyhole Route** Despondent Boulder, Colorado, resident *ingested sleeping pill*s and is believed to have *jumped* to his death in the Trough area of the trail.

January 25, 1991	John R. Thomas, 34	**West of Deer Ridge Junction on Trail Ridge Road** This California resident *shot himself* in the chest while sitting in his vehicle.
June 26, 1991	Wilburn J. Parks, 44	**Below Deer Ridge Junction on Trail Ridge Road** This Denver, Colorado, resident *shot himself* while sitting in his vehicle near the 3m sign turnout. He had attempted suicide earlier. (Not in text.)
February 26, 1992	Kurt J. Witbeck, 22	**East of Horseshoe Park on entrance road** Approximately 9:10 a.m., ranger Mary Wilson found this Greeley, Colorado, resident dead in his vehicle of a *self-inflicted gunshot wound.* (Not in text.)
July 4, 1992	Lon Lee Egbert, 42	**West of Rock Cut on Trail Ridge Road** This Lakewood, Colorado, resident left a suicide note and *drove his vehicle over a cliff* near Rock Cut.
July 31, 1992	Bruce E. Anderson, 28	**Near the top of the Flattop Mountain Trail** Anderson had attempted suicide earlier in Pennsylvania. Appeared to have died of *hypothermia.*
May 10, 1994	Kip N. Lloyd, 20	**Along the Bear Lake Road** This Greeley, Colorado, resident *shot himself* in the Bierstadt Lake parking area on Bear Lake Road. He died 4 days later.
May 19, 1994	Allison D. Bierma, 18	**Along the Cub Lake Trail** Bierma was Kip Lloyd's girlfriend. She killed herself by *jumping off a cliff* along the Cub Lake Trail.
October 4, 1994	Richard J. Smith, 45	**Big Thompson River near Moraine Park Campground** The coroner's report determined that Smith died of *hypothermia* in a shallow pool in the Big Thompson River.

July 17, 1997	Hayes W. Reid, 29	**Alpine Visitor Center parking lot** This Springfield, Massachusetts, man *shot himself* in the chest while sitting in his vehicle in the empty parking lot at night. A suicide note was found. Reid was found by a family of visitors from Iowa. (Not in text.)
April 17, 2001	Melanie E. Wood, 32	**Gem Lake** This Boulder, Colorado, woman took a taxi from Boulder to the Gem Lake Trailhead. She then hiked up to Gem Lake in the early afternoon, sat on the beach, and *shot herself* in the head. (Not in text.)
August 26, 2001	Michael P. Carter, 26	**Upper High Drive area across from visitor center** After a violent domestic fight with his former wife, Carter *shot himself* in the head.
December 25, 2001	John C. Hodge, 55	**Marshy area just south of Lily Lake** In a case similar to that of Richard Smith above, this Superior, Colorado, man died of *hypothermia* while lying in the marshy area just south of Lily Lake. There was no indication of foul play. Hodge was found by park visitors Christmas morning.
November 16, 2003	Jonathan J. Rozecki, 19	**Moraine Park Campground** From Brockton, Massachusetts, Rozecki was sitting in his vehicle in the campground. As he was approached by law enforcement staff, he *shot himself.*
February 22, 2004	Shannon Thomas, 36	Near Kaley Cottages east of Horseshoe Park. Attached hose to vehicle exhaust pipe. Died from *carbon monoxide poisoning.* (Not in text.)

EIGHT

Drownings

Before beginning this chapter, a note of caution to the parents of young children visiting the park. Of the eighteen drownings that occurred in the park, nine, or 50 percent, involved children under thirteen years of age, with an average age of seven-and-a-half years old. Reader, water is a magnet to kids. The rocks and soils along the shoreline of most waterways are slippery due to moss and algae growing in the warmer waters along the shore. The stream flows are fast, especially during the spring runoffs. It is not surprising that six of the eighteen drownings have occurred in the North St. Vrain River drainage. This visitor use area in Wild Basin is very popular with the public, as easy trails run along the river. Four drownings have occurred at the Big Thompson River Bridge at the east end of Moraine Park. This is a popular viewing spot, as the Big Thompson River thunders down through the boulders. Please use caution, especially with children, when enjoying the many streams, waterfalls, and rivers in the park.

Warning sign in Rocky Mountain National Park.
Photo by author

The first recorded drowning in the park occurred July 3, 1938. This tragedy unfolded when a group of Denver residents established a camp about a quarter mile west of the Fall River Lodge for the July 4th week-

The Beilhartz family—1938. Courtesy of RMNP

end. Back then, the Fall River Lodge was located just south of the west exit of the present Lawn Lake Trailhead parking lot. A quarter mile west of this location would have put the camping party near the confluence of the Roaring and Fall Rivers below Horseshoe Falls. Alfred Beilhartz, five years old, was the son of Mr. and Mrs. William F. Beilhartz.

After waking that morning, William Beilhartz went to the nearby stream to wash, and Alfred set out with him. Oran Bronson and Walter Hansen, both members of the Beilhartz party, also went to wash about 500 feet up stream. Alfred followed them after his father headed back to camp. When the two men returned to camp, they realized that Alfred was missing and they immediately began searching. The search proved unsuccessful, so the family contacted ranger Moomaw at the Fall River Ranger Station. Moomaw immediately enlisted the aid of the Civilian Conservation Corps (CCC), and within 45 minutes a search effort by over 100 CCC enrollees began under the leadership of Chief Ranger Barton Herschler and Moomaw.

W. C. Hilgedick, chief radio engineer for the National Park Service, who happened to be in the park, established contact between the search parties by means of shortwave radio. A recent innovation in communications, the "portables" were so large, they had to be carried on a searcher's back. Bloodhounds from the Colorado State Penitentiary joined the search on July 4th, and 50 fresh CCC enrollees were brought in from Grand Lake. On July 5th, the Roaring River below Horseshoe Falls was diverted and every inch of the river bed was scoured to the river junction with pikes and grappling hooks, as were the woods and brush for ten miles around the camp from which the boy wandered. By July 11th, only twelve of the original 100 CCC men were kept on the search, since no trace of Alfred Beilhartz could be found. The next day Cascade Dam reservoir, two miles below the confluence of the Roaring and Fall Rivers, was drained, but to no avail.

The ten-day search gained national attention. The FBI entered the case when a threat of kidnapping was seriously considered. Later, a Denver couple reported seeing a boy fitting the missing child's description sitting on a boulder in the Devil's Nest region near where young Beilhartz disappeared. In November 1938, the parents received a hoax ransom note, again hinting at the possibility of kidnapping because the boy was said to still be alive. But the investigation of the ransom note likewise proved fruitless and it was concluded that the boy drowned in the Fall or Roaring Rivers. Sadly, Alfred's body was never recovered.

Ranger Moomaw tried an experiment that pointed out the hopelessness of ever finding the boy if he had fallen into the water. Moomaw later wrote in his book, *Recollections of a Rocky Mountain Ranger*, "one morning before the crews arrived, I filled a gunny-sack with rags and enough stones to give it about the weight of a small body and tossed it into the stream where the boy was last seen. I had to run fast to keep it in sight until it reached Fall River, and there it promptly disappeared under an overhanging bank. I had some boys work that section for days, but they found nothing, not even the sack."

The next tragedy concerning a child occurred on July 7, 1947, when six-year-old Robert Briggs of Wichita, Kansas, drowned in North St. Vrain River near Copeland Falls in Wild Basin. The *Estes Park Trail* reported, "the drowned lad was standing behind his father, Albert W. Briggs, who was taking a picture. The youngster slipped on the steep bank and knocked his father into the swift stream, and [then] rolled into the water himself and was swept downstream." Robert Briggs' body was not recovered for almost an hour. "Ranger Karl Gilbert aided in the search and administrated artificial respiration for an hour in a vain effort to revive the boy."

On August 8, 1953, Robin A. Howarth, age five, drowned in Glacier Creek while fishing with his father. Young Robin was the grandson of A.A. Hyde, one of the benefactors of the YMCA of the Rockies. His family was from Ft. Collins, Colorado. According to information gathered by Deputy Coroner Eddie Banks, the boy and his father, Wilfred H. Howarth, had hiked over to Glacier Creek from their summer cottage about 9:00 a.m. Wilfred Howarth baited young Robin's hook, placed him at a quiet hole on the rushing mountain stream, and cautioned him to stay there. He then walked a short distance upstream and remained only about two minutes before he returned to where he had left Robin. But Robin wasn't there. First, he called the boy, and then ran up the trail, thinking Robin had tried to return home. He then went downstream and discovered his son's body lodged against a small tree 200 yards below where he was last seen. He tried to revive his son, but his efforts were futile.

The next incident involved Danny Saucier, age twelve. On July 21, 1972, Danny was fishing with his father in the Wild Basin area. They were from Boulder, Colorado. When the father and son reached the junction of Cony Creek and the North St. Vrain River, they apparently decided to split up. This was the last time Danny was seen alive. The ensuing search involved over 100 people from the park and the Rocky Mountain Rescue Group from Boulder. Ranger Kurt Oliver found Danny's body on August 1st. It was located in 10 feet of water in the North St. Vrain River, approximately 1.5 miles west of the Wild Basin Ranger Station.

On July 6th of the following year, five-year-old Kurt Primosch of Wichita Falls, Texas, wandered away from his parents and drowned in the North St. Vrain River below the Wild Basin Ranger Station. The missing child was reported to ranger Max Miller at 4:14 p.m. Miller organized an immediate hasty search, but the body was not found until about 6:45 p.m.

This sad saga of innocent neglect continues with six-year-old Christopher Ermijo. On May 14, 1978, Christopher stopped with his family to enjoy the cascades near the Big Thompson River Bridge. The water was high on this beautiful mid-May day. Christopher was a short distance from his family when he slipped on the water-polished rocks, fell into the river, and drowned. He was reported missing at 1:43 p.m., but his body was not recovered until 4:27 p.m.

The scene shifts back to Wild Basin for the next fatality. On July 13, 1986, thirteen-year-old Ellen Marx was walking upstream near the Wild Basin parking area with her eighteen-year-old brother. While horsing around like brothers and sister do, Ellen fell into the North St. Vrain River and was washed downstream. This Minneapolis, Minnesota, girl was rescued by rangers and bystanders after approximately 50 minutes in the cold water. CPR was initiated immediately and a faint pulse was detected by the ambulance crew en route to the Estes Park Medical Center. Ellen Marx was helicoptered to St. Luke's Hospital in Denver, but was pronounced dead at that location.

In yet another painful incident, seven-year-old Rey Dermody of Baton Rouge, Louisiana, drowned on July 3, 1987. At about 1:30 p.m., Rey was with his parents on the trail above the alluvial fan and below Horseshoe Falls on the Roaring River. They were beyond the signs warning visitors of unstable rocks, steep banks, and swift white water when Rey fell in the river. His parents were on the trail above him and did not see him fall in, but other hikers did and immediately called for assistance. He was found about 40 minutes later in a pool, and CPR was started. He was transported to the Estes Park Medical Center, and then airlifted to St. Anthony's Hospital by Flight for Life. About 6:45 p.m., an emergency room nurse reported that Rey Dermody was doing better, with his core temperature up to 85 degrees, and had some purposeful body movements. But by 10:00 p.m., his condition started to deteriorate and he was pronounced dead at 1:31 a.m.

The last and perhaps most heart wrenching drowning involving a child occurred on May 12, 2001. It was yet another beautiful spring day in the park—crisp, clear blue skies, the aspens brilliant with new green foliage, and the streams and rivers putting on a fine display of freshness and gaiety as they reached their peak runoff flow. This was a wonderful place for loving parents and their young son to spend some quality time together.

Mr. Johnson was a retired FBI agent. Through a second marriage, he was blessed with his nine-year-old son, Scott Johnson. The father and son did everything together. On this day, the family had come up to the park from Windsor, Colorado. They stopped at the turnout just north of the bridge that crosses the Big Thompson River on the Bear Lake Road in order to enjoy the cascades just upstream from the bridge. As noted, this is a popular viewing area, as the Big Thompson River leaves the laziness of Moraine Park and begins a quick descent through a large boulder field. It is common for visitors to sit or picnic here by the river. The more adventurous step out onto some of the boulders along the river's edge to enjoy the sensation of the rushing river or capture photographs.

To the unsuspecting, there is no hint of potential danger, as the boulders are generally large and easily negotiated. What is rarely noticed is that they are also quite smooth from being scoured for decades by sand and water. Some are at odd angles or may be damp with spray or have a micro layer of algae. The large boulders also hide deep, turbulent pools as the river rushes around them. But the sun is out and the sky is blue. What could be more innocent for a father with his son?

Tragedy struck quickly and without a sound as Scott and his father stepped out on some boulders not far from shore. Mrs. Johnson was watching from the rivers edge. Mr. Johnson later recalled that he and Scott were standing next to each other on a rock in the river. He had turned around to look in another direction for a couple seconds. When he turned again, Scott was gone. No sound. Just gone.

At 1:50 p.m., park dispatch received a call about a child in the river near the Big Thompson River Bridge. A hasty search of the area downstream revealed nothing and the search quickly expanded to include the Estes Park Volunteer Fire Department and Dive Team, the Larimer County Sheriff Dive Team, and scent dogs. Within an hour, over 50 people were involved in the search, walking the sides of the river and probing the pools and eddies near where Scott was last seen. After nearly three hours of searching, the boy's body was recovered from a deep pool in the river just a few feet downstream from where he had slipped or fallen. It appeared that the strong current pulled him under and wedged or pinned him beneath the rocks.

These tragedies raise the decades old question—where does the responsibility for such terrible accidents lie? The pain and suffering of losing a child in an instant cannot be comprehended. And there is not a rescuer who does not grieve for the families in these situations. While sympathetic to the loss, the courts have consistently sided with the government (National Park Service, Department of Interior), finding them not liable, when a good faith effort to inform visitors of the dangers in a national park has been made. National parks are wild places. To guard, sign, fence, or barricade every potential danger in a park would be impossible, and worse, would detract from the very essence of what a national park is about. Take the time to read and ponder the visitor safety information provided in a park's newspaper, at the trailheads, or in the visitor centers. **Your safety, and that of your family, is your responsibility.**

The following cases show that simple mistakes around water are not the sole province of children. On September 14, 1947, Denver resident Wilmer S. Holley, 30 years old, drowned in the North St. Vrain River while fishing about two miles above the Wild Basin Ranger Station. Holley was fishing with two friends, although his fall into the stream was not witnessed.

On June 19, 1964, 43-year-old James L. Keller of Corpus Christi, Texas, drowned at Chasm Falls on the Fall River Road. Keller was sightseeing with his wife and three children when he slipped on wet rocks fifty feet above the falls. He appeared to have been knocked unconscious when his head struck a rock. He was carried over the falls and was caught in a pocket under the falls. His body was recovered five hours later.

Tragedy struck twice in 1973 at the same location in incidents separated by only four weeks. These are the first two of four drownings that occurred at the Big Thompson River Bridge. On May 27th, Lois L. Matthews, 19, of Orlando, Florida, slipped on the rocks while taking pictures. Her body was found only 20 yards downstream. A month later, on

June 27th, 23-year-old Sherran Haley of Canyon, Texas, also slipped on the rocks and drowned.

Perhaps the sense of invincibility often found in youth led to the next two fatalities. On August 1, 1973, 20-year-old Michael Egan of Bayonne Hudson, New Jersey, was visiting Adams Falls on the west side of the park. Egan was jumping from rock to rock above the falls when he slipped and was swept over the falls and drowned.

Twenty years later, Loveland, Colorado, resident Glen M. Hayes, age 17, died in a similar fashion. Hayes was an honor student and Eagle Scout. At the time of the accident, he was with a group of 24 students participating in a four week science studies program for gifted students offered through Colorado State University. Glen Hayes died when he attempted to jump across the narrow section of rock at the top of Ouzel Falls in Wild Basin. Witnesses stated that he had successfully cleared the water and fell against the rock surface on the opposite side, but slipped down into the water and went over the falls. His body was recovered in the pool at the base of the falls, 50 feet below the attempted jump.

The town of Estes Park has endured two extraordinary disasters in the last 50 years. In 1976, the Big Thompson Canyon flood killed 145 people just east of the town. On July 15, 1982, the Lawn Lake Dam in Rocky Mountain National Park burst, resulting in millions of dollars in damage to the town and three deaths in the national park.

At 6:00 a.m., the sunlight streamed brightly into the Estes Valley, promising of the type of day that has made generations of families fall in love with the area. Few people were moving around downtown. The town water truck was washing down the dust on Elkhorn Avenue.

At about this same time, Stephen Cashman slipped out of his tent in the Roaring River drainage to catch some sunrise photographs. His tent mate, Steven See, elected to sleep in. Farther down the drainage, Stephen Gillette, of the A-1 Trash Company, was making the early morning trash pickup along the Endovalley Road picnic areas.

Nobody knew it, but at this time irreversible erosion of the earthen material around the outlet pipe casing of the Lawn Lake Dam was rapidly accelerating. Lawn Lake was dammed in 1903 (12 years before the park was established in 1915) to increase storage capacity for downstream irrigation. Storage rights were officially granted in 1912. It was estimated that the pre-dam surface area of Lawn Lake was 16.4 acres. By 1931, after the dam was raised five feet, the surface area was more than 48 acres. What is astonishing is that the day before, July 14th, the spillway had been cleaned out by a crew, and a fisherman walked along the dam that evening, and nobody noticed anything unusual.

A little after 6:00 a.m., Cashman recalled, "I heard a terrific commotion that at first sounded like a fighter plane breaking the sound barrier." As the water rounded the last bend before their campsite, Cashman said, "It was a great big wall of water, 15 to 20 feet high … with huge boulders floating before it in the white water! I started to run to higher ground and within seconds everything was covered with water!" As for his friend, "He never knew what happened! He wasn't out of the tent!" Stephen See, 21, from Hilbert, Wisconsin, was swept away by the raging flood. His body was found July 16, 1982, in Horseshoe Park, five miles downstream.

Farther down the canyon, Gillette "heard what [he] thought was a jet crashing." Gillette recalled, "I didn't know what was happening! I really thought at first it was an airplane coming in there. Then I knew it was water and I thought 'Oh, Lawn Lake broke!' It was coming down the drainage. There was so much!" Fortunately, Gillette had the presence of mind to go to the emergency phone at the Lawn Lake Trailhead and call the park dispatch. It was 6:23 a.m.

Within minutes, the serene meadows of Horseshoe Park were "filling with water almost like a bathtub, and the plug in the bathtub was the Cascade Dam," as Chief Ranger Dave Essex recalled. The immediate question was whether the modest Cascade Dam on the east end of the park would hold the water or if Horseshoe Park itself could absorb the water. The Cascade Dam was originally built in 1908 by F.O. Stanley to impound water for hydroelectric generation. The dam was enlarged to its pre-flood level in 1923 and later bought by the town of Estes Park in 1945. It was seventeen feet high, but only had a storage depth of twelve feet due to sediment build up.

Devastation in downtown Estes Park. Photo courtesy of Estes Park Museum.

The Estes Park Police Department was notified at 6:30 a.m. They were contacted again at 6:43 a.m. about the potential of Cascade Dam failing. At risk were the people and structures along the Fall River below the park boundary. More immediate for the park staff were the 250-plus campers in Aspenglen Campground barely a third of a mile below Cascade Dam.

Fortunately, the breadth of Horseshoe Park absorbed and slowed the charge of the water as it spread across the valley, thus buying precious minutes for rangers and the Estes Park police to notify residents and guests along the river. The first warning to visitors in the campground was given at 6:50 a.m. and again at 7:13 a.m. Ten minutes later, as water began lapping over Cascade Dam, the campground was evacuated. Gravity would not be denied. The Cascade Dam collapsed at 7:42 a.m., sending a torrent of water down the 9 percent slope toward the campground and still lazy town of Estes Park. Terry Coates, 36, from Peoria, Illinois, and Bridget Dorris, 20, from Arlington, Texas, had initially left the campground, but apparently attempted to return to retrieve some possessions. They were never seen alive again. Coates' body was found near the Fawn Valley

Inn on July 20th. Dorris' body was not found until August 14th near the fish hatchery. Coates, Dorris, and See were the only fatalities associated with this disaster.

By the time Cascade Dam collapsed, Estes Park police officers and the local radio station had warned the community along the river and in town. Though the flood lost most of its fury again in the flats below the dam and near the Elkhorn Lodge, the surge flowed through Estes Park's downtown around 8:15 a.m. causing millions of dollars in damage. Barely two hours after the flood hit downtown, shop owners and emergency services staff returned to witness the devastation and begin the clean up. Fortunately, the Olympus Dam, east of the town, absorbed the two-foot rise in the lake level.

Drownings

July 3, 1938	Alfred Beilhartz, 5	**Camping near Roaring River** Early morning, the youth followed adults to the river to wash. The *adults lost track of him*. Presumed to have drowned in the Roaring River. Body never recovered despite massive search.
July 17, 1947	Robert Briggs, 6	**North St. Vrain River near Copeland Falls** Youngster was with his father taking pictures when he *slipped on the steep bank* into the river.
September 14, 1947	Wilmer S. Holley, 30	**North St. Vrain River 2 miles above Ranger Station** Holley was fishing with two friends, but the incident was not witnessed. Body recovered.
August 16, 1953	Robin A. Howarth, 5	**Glacier Creek area near the YMCA** Youngster was fishing with his father, who baited his hook and *placed him alone* by a quiet hole. The father then went upstream a short distance and soon returned to find the boy missing. Unwitnessed. Body recovered.

June 19, 1964	James L. Keller, 43	**Chasm Falls along the Fall River Road** Keller *slipped on rocks* above the falls and was carried over the falls.
July 21, 1972	Danny Saucier, 12	**North St. Vrain River near Cony Creek** Danny was fishing with his father when they *apparently decided to split up*. Unwitnessed. Body recovered from the river 11 days later after massive search.
May 27, 1973	Lois L. Matthews, 19	**Big Thompson River Bridge** *Slipped on rocks* while taking pictures.
June 27, 1973	Sherran Haley, 23	**Big Thompson River Bridge** *Slipped on rocks* and drowned.
July 6, 1973	Kurt Primosch, 5	**North St. Vrain River near Ranger Station** Youngster wandered from *inattentive parents* during picnic. Unwitnessed. Body recovered from river two hours later.
August 1, 1973	Michael Egan, 20	**Adams Falls** New Jersey resident *slipped while jumping on rocks*. Fell in river and drowned.
May 14, 1978	Christopher Ermijo, 6	**Big Thompson River Bridge** Youngster *slipped on rocks* into the river and drowned. Body recovered three hours later.
July 15, 1982	Steven See, 21 Terry W. Coates, 36 Bridget Dorris, 20	**Lawn Lake Flood Disaster** These three individuals were camping in the park and drowned during this incident.
July 13, 1986	Ellen Marx, 13	**North St. Vrain River near Copland Falls** Walking upstream with her 18-year-old brother when she *slipped and fell* into the river. Body recovered 50 minutes later. CPR initiated, but died later.

July 3, 1987	Rey Dermody, 7	**Above the alluvial fan on Roaring River** Youngster was exploring above warning signs and became separated from *inattentive parents*. Other visitors saw the child fall in. Body recovered 40 minutes later. CPR started. Child airlifted to Denver, but died 12 hours later.
July 3, 1993	Glenn M. Hayes, 17	**North St. Vrain River at Ouzel Falls** Hayes was fooling around and successfully jumped over lip of falls to other side, but *slipped backwards into the river* and went over the falls.
May 12, 2001	Scott D. Johnson, 9	**Big Thompson River Bridge** Youngster was standing next to his father on a rock on the river's edge. He *slipped* into the river without a sound. Body recovered 3 hours later.

NINE

Hypothermia (Exposure)

Nineteen people are believed to have died of hypothermia in Rocky Mountain National Park's history. Three of them were apparent suicides and are listed in chapter seven. This chapter focuses on the other sixteen people, most of whom were experiencing the park's rugged backcountry when they were overcome by the elements and perished. The term "exposure" was commonly used 100 years ago. The modern term is "hypothermia," defined as abnormally low body temperature.

Caroline J. Welton's place in local history is that of the first known fatality in what later became Rocky Mountain National Park. She died of hypothermia while descending from Longs Peak on September 23, 1884.

Caroline, or Carrie, was born into a wealthy New England family on June 7, 1842. An only child, she was pampered with fine schools in Connecticut and in New York City. Carrie loved animals, especially her horse, named Knight, a gift from her father. She was a fearless rider, and like her mother, Carrie was headstrong. Tragedy struck the family in 1874, when Carrie's horse kicked and killed her father. Since money was not a problem, mother and daughter traveled extensively together, but by 1880 the relationship deteriorated and they went separate ways.

In 1883 and 1884, Carrie visited friends in Colorado Springs and used travel and physical activity as a way to tame her restless spirit. She ultimately arrived in Estes Park the week of September 14, 1884. The preceding winter was a particularly long one, and locals considered the

Keyhole Route dangerous and unclimbable into late August. Apparently, Carrie Welton was discouraged from the attempt by knowledgeable locals citing mountain conditions and unpredictable September weather. Nonetheless, Welton secured the guide service of 22-year-old Carlyle Lamb for the ascent. They left the Lamb ranch on horseback at 5:00 a.m. and were encouraged by a warm and pleasant morning, but by the time they reached the Keyhole the weather had turned for the worse. Carlyle later told his father there was a "strong, chilling wind" and growing clouds. Experience led Carlyle to believe worse weather was coming, and he wisely tried to discourage Welton. Perhaps encouraged by her successful ascent of Pikes Peak in difficult conditions in 1883, Welton could not be persuaded to turn around. Carlyle later noted that "she had never undertaken anything and given it up," so on they went.

Carlyle Lamb and Carrie ultimately made it to the summit in late afternoon, far later than the noontime summit of generally accepted practice. In deteriorating weather, they retreated after a short rest, only to be caught in the snowstorm while in the Trough section of the route. At this point, Welton was showing obvious signs of exhaustion, and Lamb both led and carried Welton. Near 10:00 p.m., they made it back to the Keyhole, and Welton was "so utterly exhausted and chilled that she could not stand alone." After making their way farther into the Boulderfield, Lamb discussed the severity of their situation with Welton. He thought their only chance for survival was for him to return to his father's ranch for help. He gave some of his clothing to Welton and positioned her out of the wind as well as he could before leaving.

By intermittent moonlight, he made it back to the tethered horses and rode to the ranch and woke his father. When they reached timberline on the return trip, "the wind was blowing a gale," but they slowly worked their way toward the Boulderfield. Years later, the elder Lamb wrote that near daybreak, "almost a mile across the boulder field, I came in sight of the tragic spot where Carrie J. Welton lay at rest, having died alone amid the wind's mad revelry and dismal dirge, and which was yet holding high carnival over her body by blowing every section of her garments in unrelenting fury, seemingly sporting with its victim in demoniacal triumph. I remember, with clear distinctness, my involuntary expression as I approached the body: I fear, my young lady, that you are past saving." The Reverend Elkanah and Carlyle Lamb carried Welton's body back across the Boulderfield and down to their horses. They rode back to their ranch around 10:30 that morning.

In the days that followed, newspapers up and down the front range of Colorado sensationalized Welton's death, with many casting unsupported suspicion on Carlyle's conduct. Fortunately, those with a greater understanding of the volatile mountain environment and the Lamb family's reputation rose to the defense of Carlyle, and he was soon found innocent in the court of public opinion. In the larger context of life, a final editorial in the *Denver Daily Times* dated September 27, 1884, summed up:

> *Miss Welton seems to have been unusually romantic, or peculiarly persistent in her desire to behold the glories of the mountain world. Yet, after all, hers was something of the same spirit which in a man carries one off in search of the North Pole and the open seas of the Arctics; and, as so many of the men who have fallen under this influence have done, she surrendered her life in—shall we call it the satisfaction of her curiosity, the gratification of a whim?—or shall we say it was all an accident, and that it could not have been avoided?*

Considering Welton's personality and drive, perhaps this fatality was unavoidable. From a more objective perspective though, it is clear this death did not have to occur. Carlyle Lamb clearly understood mountain weather and had the good sense to try and dissuade Welton from continuing the climb.

As suggested in the introduction to this book, there are those who died in the park who appeared to have lived full lives and probably died at peace with themselves. Dr. Thornton Rogers Sampson appears to have been such a person. Born in Virginia on October 9, 1852, he and his three siblings spent most of their childhood during the Civil War on the substantial estate of their grandfather. At 19, he entered the University of

Virginia to study Greek and moral philosophy. Seeking a greater intellectual challenge, Sampson sailed for Europe in 1874 to study in Edinburgh, Leipzig, and Beirut. He returned to the United States to marry Ella Royster of Memphis, Tennessee, in 1878 and was ordained into the Presbyterian ministry at Charlottesville, Virginia. That same year, the couple departed for Athens, Greece, to pursue Presbyterian missionary work. Before returning to the United States in 1892, Sampson spent five months observing mission stations in India, Ceylon, Japan, Korea, and China.

In 1894, Dr. Sampson entered the world of higher education and became the president of Fredericksburg College. After three years and good progress in freeing the college from a substantial debt, he moved to Sherman, Texas, to become president of Austin College. In 1900, he became the founding president of a new Presbyterian theological seminary in Austin. Dr. Sampson retired from the presidency in 1905, but stayed on as Luther Professor of Church History and Polity. He was revered as a remarkable teacher and known for his wit as well as for the acrid criticism he occasionally delivered to student preachers. He once told a student, "The sermon was both good and original, but the good portion was not original and the original portion was not good!"

As he aged, Dr. Sampson found rest and inspiration in the mountains of Colorado. He first visited Colorado in 1912. His wife, Ella Sampson, later told the *Dallas Evening Journal* of September 20, 1915, "My husband loved the mountains. He said he communed with the wild things while alone in the depths."

Dr. Sampson and Ella arrived in Denver in August 7, 1915. He secured a room for her at the YMCA and departed on August 11th for a three-week fishing and camping trip through the Estes Park region, with plans to return by September 5th. The trip was generally uneventful. Within a week, Sampson had made his way to Rand, a small ranching community at the southern end of North Park, south of Walden, and mailed a postcard to Ella on the 19th. In another postcard from Rand on the 21st, Sampson said he was headed to see friends near what is today

Cameron Pass. In what was his last correspondence to his wife, posted August 28th from Cameron Pass, Sampson stated "he had never felt better in his life and was gaining in strength and health."

Sampson then made his way to Squeaky Bob Wheeler's tent resort camp. An entry later found in his diary indicated he was at Grand Lake on September 1st. All accounts agree that by September 2nd, Dr. Sampson was heading east up the North Inlet Trail to Estes Park, where he possibly intended to attend the dedication ceremonies of the new Rocky Mountain National Park on the 4th. He planned to spend the night of the 2nd at Fern Lake Lodge. It was a not too difficult one-day trip. A couple miles east of Grand Lake, Dr. Sampson was overtaken by Clifford Higby, who was riding to Estes Park on horseback. Higby was a part owner of the Fern Lake Lodge. In subsequent interviews, Higby said he gave Sampson directions to Fern Lake Lodge and told him he would leave a bandana on a rock cairn to mark the point where Sampson should head north into Odessa Gorge. The bandana was later found by searchers on September 13th, east of Flattop Mountain, as Higby claimed.

Later that day, Dr. Sampson was last seen around 2:00 p.m. by a small westbound hiking party. He was resting about six miles from the cutoff through the Odessa Gorge to Fern Lake Lodge. Though the day had started bright and fair, by 4:00 p.m., dense clouds settled on Flattop Mountain, followed by heavy snow and high wind. If you have been on Flattop, you can recall the broad, open sweep of the terrain. Even with today's trail markings, it is easy to get disoriented during foggy or whiteout conditions. In 1915, the trail certainly wasn't as defined as it is today. In fact, there wasn't even a trail from Flattop Mountain to Odessa and Fern Lakes in 1915. It was more of a scramble. The main Flattop Trail descended to Mill Creek Basin, completely bypassing Bear Lake and Bierstadt Lake. The United States Forest Service planned a trail from Odessa Lake to the Flattop Trail during the summer of 1914 and had begun some preliminary work that autumn. That trail was never completed, as the National Park Service took over management of the area in 1915. Perhaps the suggestion of a trail contributed to Sampson's intended route.

In the afternoon, Sampson likely faced not only dense fog, but blowing snow. To give an indication of the conditions likely faced by Sampson, Superintendent Roger Toll later referenced a report provided him by a Mr. Arnold Emch, who wrote about his unsettling encounter with similar weather on Flattop Mountain:

> Heavy masses of fog began to envelop the surrounding rocks and crags, so that we decided to give up the attempt to go down to the North Inlet from this side. At 3:30 p.m., we started on our return trip. The fog was so dense that it was impossible to correctly locate directions. We tried to retrace our route, and after climbing constantly for a seemingly unreasonable length of time we suddenly discovered by reaching a cairn that we were on the top of some peak. We had lost all sense of direction, and decided that it would be best to wait until there should be a break in the fog to get an orientation by studying the geography of the neighboring peaks. Fortunately the masses of fog cleared enough for a moment so that we were able to recognize Hallett Peak in the distance and to make out that we were on top of Taylor Peak.

The Fern Lake Lodge was established in 1911. It remained popular through the 1920s and '30s. A popular activity was to ski or snowshoe into the inn during the winter for races and recreation. The Fern Lake Lodge began to deteriorate during World War II from lack of use. After the war, new ski areas in Colorado accessible by car became popular. On March 31, 1976, rangers burned the buildings and began the process of reclaiming the grounds. The site of the lodge was on the small, open bench northeast of the lake. The current Ranger Station seen today at Fern Lake was built in 1924. The existing trail between Bear Lake and Odessa Lake was completed in 1933. The current Flattop Mountain Trail was competed in 1940.

So, what happened to Sampson? Remember that Sampson last wrote to his wife on August 28th. A large crowd gathered at the Rocky Mountain National Park dedication on September 4th, and Sampson was neither missed nor expected. When he failed to arrive in Denver as intended on September 5th, his wife and friends were not alarmed because he was often delayed during his excursions. It was not until September 13th that the first search effort was mobilized, when Shep Husted, Carl Piltz, and Ira Coleman left Estes Park to search around Hagues Peak, Specimen

Mountain, and Odessa Gorge. Though a late mobilization by today's standards, the search effort quickly gained momentum, but was hampered by poor weather. On the night of the 16th, one element of the search party slept in a foot of snow at Bear Lake.

By the 18th, more than 50 people joined the search, many likely encouraged by the $500 reward offered by Mrs. Sampson for finding her husband dead or alive. By the 18th, the story of the missing reverend began to make the national papers, including the *New York Times*, and there were murmurs that Sampson was a friend of President Woodrow Wilson. Also on September 18th, twenty United States forest rangers were ordered into the field and spent five days searching unsuccessfully along the continental divide. By this time, the Sampson family seemed resigned to the fact that Dr. Thornton Sampson was dead.

Reconciled to her husband's probable fate, a pious Mrs. Sampson declared that, "If God willed it was his time to go, there could have been no more fitting setting." Their son Frank echoed this resignation in a *Rocky Mountain News* article on September 19th: "Father loved the mountains. He said he communed with the highest things while alone in the depths of wild, rugged country. And if father's time had been allotted, what more could he have asked than to have stood alone with his Maker on the top of the peak and [to] give his tired spirit to Him whose hand alone guided him in the night of snow, cold, and peril?"

Seventeen years passed before the mystery surrounding Dr. Sampson's disappearance was finally solved. On July 8, 1932, Mr. Meldrum Loucks, a member of a park trail crew surveying for a new trail between Fern and Bear Lakes, found skeletal remains about one-half mile southeast of Odessa Lake. The left leg showed a fracture of the tibia or shinbone. Under a nearby overhanging rock was a knapsack containing a pipe, tobacco, matches, and a fly box. Frank Sampson identified the pipe as the one he had carved for his father. He also identified his mother's faded handwriting in a letter found with the body. From where the remains were found, it appears Sampson had reached the summit of Flattop Mountain and moved east, or downhill, then turned north at Higby's bandana.

Temporary ranger Fred Binnewies with Sampson bones.
Courtesy of RMNP

While undoubtedly cold and wet, I don't think the good Reverend was lost. If you hike the Bear Lake to Fern Lake trail today, the route heads west before it cuts back on itself just past Sourdough campsite and heads north downhill into Odessa Gorge. At the point where the trail cuts back, you can look to the south and have a fine view of the north facing shoulder of Flattop Mountain. Looking at the rough terrain to the west, it is most likely that Sampson came down the gentler slope to the east of the rugged pinnacles in your view. Crossing the shallow valley before you, he likely passed close to where you are standing and proceeded north to the scree slope where he perished. If you move down the trail, you soon come to the same jumbled rock scree field where Dr. Sampson died. Take a moment to visualize yourself making your way across this slope without benefit of the modern trail. For Dr. Sampson, with the storm now likely engulfing the area, and darkness falling, travel was undoubtedly treacherous over the steep, wet rocks, but he was in the right area. At some point, he fell and broke his lower leg. Though his mobility was restricted, he was able to find some shelter and even built a fire. Alas, it was not enough. Injured, tired, and in wet clothes, he was no match for the cold September storm. He appears to have gone to sleep and died of hypothermia.

This conclusion was also made by Frank Sampson, who wrote to the park superintendent in 1932 after the remains were found: "My conclusions are positive that the one mistake father made, a danger he knew well enough to avoid, was that he built a fire and then lay down at that extremely high altitude in damp clothes on a cold September night. He fell asleep, from which sweet sleep his Maker never aroused him. But for the anxiety his tragic death caused his loved ones, I cannot imagine father wishing for a more peaceful passing—high in the mountains from which all his life he drew his inspiration." Amen. It was the wish of the family that he be buried in the mountains near where he died. On July 17, 1932, his remains were interned in a tomb carved out of rock about 200 yards west of the present day Fern Lake Trailhead, on the north side of the trail.

One of the more intriguing and hotly debated deaths at the time was that of Agnes W. Vaille of Denver, Colorado. Vaille was from one of Denver's leading families. Her social standing and the circumstances of her death resulted in front page newspaper coverage on a national level. Vaille graduated from Smith College in Massachusetts in 1912, and then volunteered with the American Red Cross in Europe during World War I. She was first cousin to Roger Toll, a founding member of the Colorado Mountain Club and Superintendent of Rocky Mountain National Park at the time of the tragedy. By all accounts, Agnes Vaille was a remarkable woman. She was known for her determination and toughness, as reflected in a *Rocky Mountain News* article dated January 13, 1925, reporting her death: "Miss Vaille believed that a woman could do anything that a man could and never for a moment hesitated to undertake tasks that would make many a man quail ... She gloried in competing with men and attaining those things which men said were impossible."

As an active member of the Colorado Mountain Club, she became acquainted with the younger Walter Kiener (1894–1959) on club outings. While Vaille came from lofty social echelons, Kiener had a more humble background. The son of a butcher and sausage maker in Switzerland, Kiener became an expert mountaineer in the Alps. Seeking adventure and escape from a difficult home environment, Kiener sailed for America and ultimately wound up in Denver in 1923. While he studied citizenship and English, he supported himself by working in a small sausage factory, and he climbed mountains on weekends.

According to a narrative given by Kiener to Charles Hewes in 1931, the idea to attempt the first winter ascent of the East Face of Longs Peak came to Kiener and Vaille while resting on the summit of Mt. Evans in the late summer of 1924. It bears repeating that the first ascent ever on this face of Longs had only been made two years earlier, on September 7, 1922, by James Alexander. Perhaps encouraging to Vaille was Elmira Buhl, a companion on Mt. Evans who three days after Alexander's triumph had become the first female to climb the East Face. The less technical Cables and Keyhole Routes to the summit were commonplace as early as the 1870s.

Within weeks, Vaille and Kiener made the first of three unsuccessful attempts on the mountain, one each in October, November, and December. Each was unsuccessful due some combination of poor weather, poor route selection, and limited daylight. According to Kiener's account, escalating opposition to this winter attempt came from family and Colorado Mountain Club members with each failed attempt on account of the potential danger from the harsh winter environment and climbing conditions. From what we know of Agnes Vaille's temperament, this opposition probably only intensified her desire to achieve their goal. Vaille and Kiener returned to their quest on January 10, 1925, accompanied by Vaille's friend, Elinor Eppich. This last attempt had an inauspicious beginning, as drifting snow on the road required them to ski several extra miles to get to Timberline cabin, not arriving until well after midnight the morning of the January 11, 1925.

After a few hours of uncomfortable sleep, dawn initially brought unfavorable weather, so the threesome enjoyed a casual breakfast and conversation, as it did not appear an attempt would be possible that day. However, the wind soon diminished and the sun came out, thus raising their enthusiasm for the assault. Eppich returned to the Longs Peak Inn, and Vaille and Kiener began their journey up to Chasm Lake and the Broadway Ledge. Kiener initially felt confident about the climb, but after traversing Broadway and struggling up the Notch Couloir he noted that Vaille was exhausted and nowhere near the form and level of endurance she was noted for.

At this point, the weather was still fair, but darkness had fallen, indicating a timeframe of around 4:00 or 5:00 p.m. In Kiener's words, as recorded by Hewes, "it was soon evident that she was helpless to proceed, and for close to twelve hours I had to cut the steps alone, handle the rope, and pull, lift, and assist her, until we finally reached the summit at 4:00 a.m." On the summit, Kiener noted his thermometer indicated 14 degrees below zero.

Clearly concerned about the deteriorating state of Vaille, Kiener led her down the Cables Route in the early dawn light toward the Boulderfield. At a point on the lower section of the descent, Vaille slipped and skidded a considerable way down the smooth slope and fortunately was not injured.

Desperate now, Kiener moved Vaille to a small sheltered area with some protection against the rising winds and decided to seek help for a rescue. Kiener crossed the Boulderfield and made it to the Timberline cabin about 1:00 p.m., where to his surprise

Featured story on Agnes Vaille in *Rocky Mountain News.* Courtesy *Rocky Mountain News*

he encountered a rescue party organized by Elinor Eppich. This group consisted of Hugh Brown and his son Oscar, Herbert Sortland, and Jacob Christen. In an extraordinary feat of endurance and sheer will, Kiener led Hugh Brown, Sortland, and Christen back towards the Boulderfield in the face of a strong gale. Being poorly equipped, first Brown, and then Sortland, left the rescue party and headed back down. To compound the tragedy, Sortland was never seen alive again by his friends. Kiener and Christen found Vaille dead and frozen in the same location where Kiener had left her. Exhausted and unable to move Vaille, they left her on the mountain and struggled back to the cabin. Vaille's body was carried off the mountain on January 15th by a group of rangers and friends, including Superintendent Roger Toll.

The Timberline cabin. The cabin collapsed in disrepair in 1929. Courtesy of RMNP

As with the Welton fatality, controversy soon arose as to who was responsible for Vaille's death. Other climbers of the day, along with Elinor Eppich, felt Kiener made several mistakes or pushed Vaille beyond her limits. Unlike Carrie Welton, however, both Vaille and Kiener were accomplished climbers known for their skill and drive. At what point could they or should they have turned around?

Walter Kiener spent four months in a Denver Hospital recuperating from frostbite and subsequent amputations of one or more joints of all his fingers but one and a majority of his toes. In a reflection of their compassion for Kiener, most of his medical expenses were paid by the Vaille family. No longer able to work as a butcher, Kiener was hired by Superintendent Toll to work as a fire lookout on Twin Sisters for several summers. He eventually enrolled at the University of Nebraska to study biology and chose the alpine vegetation on Longs Peak as his specialty. Once again, the Vaille family helped finance his education. He eventually died of cancer on August 24, 1959. Still standing today near the Keyhole on Longs Peak is the Vaille Memorial, constructed and paid for by the Vaille family in 1926–27. At 13,200 feet, it is believed to be the highest structure in the National Park Service.

Let's not forget about young Herbert Sortland. Not much is known about Sortland. His family had a farm in Litchville, North Dakota, and he worked as the caretaker at the Longs Peak Inn. As noted, he was part of the rescue party mobilized by Elinor Eppich and was at the Timberline cabin when Walter Kiener made it there that afternoon. After a brief rest, Kiener, Jacob Christen, Hugh Brown, and Sortland headed back up the mountain in the face of a terrible gale. Being poorly prepared, first Brown and then Sortland were forced to turn back by the high winds and low temperatures. In Kiener's recollections to Charlie Hewes in 1931, he stated about Sortland "the Timberline Cabin was still in view, and both Christen and I thought he could make it, never dreaming that it was the last time that anyone would see him alive."

Once they realized Sortland was missing, an extensive search ensued, but was without success. His body was found six weeks later on February 25, 1925, at the edge of a frozen swamp 300 yards south and east of the Longs Peak Inn. He was found by Oscar Brown, who was carrying garbage out to the Inn's dumping ground. Evidently, Sortland had fallen at some point and dislocated his right hip, thus significantly reducing his mobility. Exhausted, wet, and injured, Sortland undoubtedly died of hypothermia.

The next victim of this silent killer was Denver resident Gerald J. Clark, age 37. He was attempting a new route on the East Face of Longs Peak with two companions, Ed Cooper and Ed Watson. The three were experienced climbers who had each made five previous successful ascents on Longs Peak. On August 7, 1939, Clark was in the lead and successfully made a move over an overhead ledge in Fields Chimney that Cooper and Watson couldn't follow. Watson later explained that Clark had lost the head on his hammer and couldn't secure protection. Safe but wet, Clark lowered their rope to Cooper and Watson, so they could go for help. Dressed in a light flannel shirt and denim trousers, Clark was unprepared for the unforeseen overnight with water and spray running around him and temperatures below 30 degrees as a storm system came through the area.

Ranger Ernie Field, one of the more experienced mountain rescue men in the country, was on a Colorado Mountain Club (CMC) day trip nearby. Leading four other CMC climbers, he responded quickly to the cries for help. "The elements seemed to be against all of us that night, however, and our climbing was retarded by darkness, rain and fog." Like Clark, the rescue party spent a long, cold night out. At first light, three men lowered themselves over the edge of the precipice. "Mr. Clark was so hidden by the storm and trough that the rescuers could not find him when they started down at dawn."

Clark was conscious when they finally reached him, but "he passed out the first time we lowered him out on a rope." For five hours, in snow and sleet, ranger Field and his team "worked down the cliff, lowering the dying man from ledge to ledge on the rope. The descent by each rope maneuver averaged only about 40 feet." Despite the heroic labors of the rescue team, risking death themselves from falling rock and freezing snows, Clark died just after being lowered to the base of the East Face.

In recognition of the extraordinary efforts to save Clark, ranger Ernest Field and Colorado Mountain Club members Robert Boyd and Robert C. Lewis Jr. were named to the Denver Post Gallery of Fame on August 12, 1939.

On Friday evening, August 15, 1958, ten-year-old Bobby Bizup was last seen by his parents near Camp St. Malo on Highway 7. Through Tuesday, August 19th, over 300 searchers were involved with this massive search. Many were from Lowry Air Force Base, where Bobby's father was a Master Sergeant. The weather was wet and drizzly. In the initial period of the search, roadblocks were set up to check vehicles and seek information. Several people thought they had seen the boy at different locations around the Tahosa Valley. Bloodhounds gave strong indications the boy had moved north toward Estes Park. Remains, including Bobby's hearing aid, were found on the east face of Mt. Meeker near Cabin Creek on July

3, 1959, by three Camp St. Malo counselors. The ravine he was found in had been searched three times by different groups, indicating he may have wandered a great deal.

Fifteen years later, Chief Ranger Jim Randall coordinated the search for the next victims of hypothermia in the park. With many rangers, a particular tragedy sticks with them over the years. Such was the case for retired Chief Ranger Jim Randall in recalling the deaths of Fred Stone, age 20, and Joan Jardine, age 21. Stone and Jardine were Colorado State University students in Ft. Collins, Colorado. They intended to ski to the Chasm Lake shelter cabin on Friday, January 21, 1972, and return the next day. When they failed to return, rangers organized a search Monday morning, January 24th.

In those days, the Chasm Lake shelter was kept open for public use, and Stone had apparently been to the shelter the previous summer. With the recent heavy snowfall, it was hoped that the two overdue skiers were stuck in the shelter. Rangers Jim Randall, Bob Dunnagan, and Steve Hickman had prepared to ski to the Fern Lake cabin, but elected to go up to the Chasm Lake shelter to look for the overdue skiers. Ranger Bob Haines joined them. Because of the heavy snowfall, they put tire chains on their vehicle to make it to the Longs Peak parking area. Fred Stone's was the only vehicle in the parking lot. The rangers skied toward the Chasm Lake shelter through high winds and blowing snow. Darkness comes early in January and caught the group just starting the dangerous traverse across the steep face above Peacock Pool. After successfully navigating the traverse, the group made it to the shelter. The door was part way open, with snow blown in, and the inside of the shelter was frosted like the inside of a freezer. There was no trace of the missing couple.

Later that evening, off duty seasonal ranger Walter Fricke arrived at the shelter with a radio from the Rocky Mountain Rescue Group. He and Randall began coordinating other rescuers arriving from the Arapahoe Rescue Patrol, Larimer County Sheriff's officers, volunteers, and the Alpine Rescue Group. It was a cold, bitter night in the shelter. Randall later reminisced that Dunnagan had poor quality ski boots and his feet were near frozen. He kept his feet on Bob Haines' stomach most of the evening to keep them warm.

The following morning, the five rangers carefully skied down the steep slope into the Roaring Fork drainage and failed to find evidence of the missing skiers. Randall and his staff called in a helicopter on Wednesday, when the winds died down, but the spotters on board failed to see any evidence. Ultimately, up to 100 searchers participated, including members of the University of Denver Alpine Club, 65 Green Berets from the Colorado Army National Guard, and search dogs from the SAR Dog Association in Redmond, Washington. A pair of skis were found at Jim's Grove on Thursday, January 27th, and appeared to have been intentionally left there. Later that day, Joan Jardine's body was found in the Roaring Fork drainage below Peacock Pool and about 1.5 miles west of Highway 7. The autopsy indicated Jardine died of hypothermia on Sunday, the 23rd, before the search even started. Her body was found lying on its back with her day pack under her head. On her right side, she had built a small pile of twigs to start a fire and she held a lighter in her ungloved right hand. She was clothed in light gear and in her pack were hair curlers and a flannel night gown. She apparently had been led to believe they were skiing to a warm mountain cabin.

The theory was that Stone may have fallen and was injured and had sent Jardine for help. Searchers found Stone's Kelty A-4 backpack with a broken strap along with his down sleeping bag on Saturday the 29th at the bottom of an icy slope near Peacock Pool. By February 1st, the search had been reduced to about 10 people, and then suspended. On August 4th, ranger Paul Anderson, assisted by two police search dogs from the Denver Police Department, located Stone's body. It was in the Roaring Fork drainage below Peacock Pool about three-quarters of a mile upstream from where Jardine was found.

In another case, 22-year-old Gregory Holzer of St. Louis Park, Minnesota, disappeared while hiking from Grand Lake to Wild Basin on June 18, 1972. His body was found on July 21, 1973, between the North St. Vrain River and Thunder Lake Trail. The coroner's report was inconclusive, but it was believed he died of hypothermia. At the time, there had been no reason to assume that Holzer was in the park. Chief Ranger Randall recalled that Holzer had told his father that he was going to the "Gathering of Peace" near Grand Lake, which was organized by the Rainbow Family. This was the last anyone heard of him until his body was found the following year.

In a fatality similar to that of Dr. Sampson, 10-year-old Jonathan Williams and his father, Ernest, were caught in an early season snowstorm on Flattop Mountain on September 2, 1973. In a father/son bonding trip, the pair camped in Tonahutu Meadows the previous night and headed over Flattop Mountain Sunday morning, the 2nd, en route to Bear Lake. They were caught by a heavy snowstorm with low visibility and lost their way. While trying to descend a snowfield, they both lost control and were injured, probably by hitting rocks at the bottom. Ernest Williams later told rangers they had kept each other warm in one sleeping bag Sunday night because one bag had been lost in their fall. Jonathan was in a "dazed condition" with an injured leg when Ernest left him Monday morning to look for help. Three hikers found Ernest about 10:00 p.m. Monday evening, on the trail between Odessa and Fern Lakes, and escorted him to the trailhead to get help. Due to the urgency, rangers started searching Tuesday morning at 2:00 a.m. As Ernest Williams was not sure where he had been, all snowfields north of Flattop Mountain were searched. Sadly, around 10:00 a.m., Jonathan was found dead south of Odessa Lake.

The death of Bill Gizzie, age 45, is one of those head scratchers that just make you wonder what happened. From Littleton, Colorado, Gizzie may have had a heart attack, which possibly led to death by hypothermia in Chasm Meadow. Gizzie left the Longs Peak parking lot on Saturday afternoon, August 24, 1975, to meet up with three friends who had left earlier. A fifth friend left after Gizzie, and when he met with the first three they realized Gizzie was missing. They unsuccessfully looked for him before contacting rangers. Searchers found Gizzie in a sleeping bag Sunday evening near Chasm Meadows. He was out of sight of the main trail. It was believed he had a nonfatal heart attack which weakened him and led to his eventual death by hypothermia.

A 24-hour search ended Monday afternoon, March 10, 1980, when searchers found the body of Ruth Magnuson, age 29, near the summit of Mt. Alice. The Boulder, Colorado, resident died of hypothermia. Magnuson was a member of an eight person party skiing from Grand Lake to climb the 13,310-foot peak. The group spent Friday night, the 6th, in snow caves near Lone Pine Lake, and then skied up to Boulder–Grand Pass (12,061 ft.). Just short of the pass, the group cached their skies, as the remainder of the route was blown free of snow. Because of poor weather and visibility, two members returned to camp amidst 70 mph gusts of blowing snow and almost zero visibility along the Continental Divide. The remaining six members decided to attempt the summit in spite of the poor weather, and they discussed the importance of keeping each other in sight. About 15 minutes from the pass, the group gathered together for a break, and all were accounted for. When they departed, Ruth Magnuson was the second from the rear. A short distance from the summit, group leader Franz Mohling again stopped to rest and regroup and noticed Magnuson was missing. John Tuckey and Ted Dortignac said they had seen her barely eight minutes earlier. Assuming she would show up soon, Mohling led two others toward the summit, while Tuckey and Dortignac remained behind. When Mohling returned, Magnuson still had not shown up. When the group returned to where their skis were cached, Magnuson was not there either, but her skis were.

According to her companions, Magnuson had fairly good mountain gear, a small transmitter, a compass, and a day pack. At this point, the group split up. Three returned to Grand Lake to report her missing. One remained in the base camp, and the other three returned to the Boulder–Grand Pass to search for her, but retreated due to the poor weather.

Rangers initiated a search Sunday afternoon, March 9th. They were unable to use helicopters because of the weather, so rangers Bob Seibert and Tom Watters led a group of searchers to Thunder Lake cabin in winds that created a 40 below wind chill factor. The next morning, March 10th, Seibert and Watters climbed Boulder–Grand Pass from the Thunder Lake side. When the winds subsided, rangers used helicopters to ferry an additional 14 searchers to the area, including ranger Bob Haines from Grand Lake. Knowing that Magnuson had an avalanche beacon on her person in the transmit mode, the searchers all carried beacons in the receive mode. Approximately 2:15 p.m., Magnuson's boyfriend, John Tuckey, heard her beacon and discovered her body about 400 yards from the summit.

In reviewing this incident, Incident Commander Larry Van Slyke noted that all members of the group were experienced in winter mountaineering and were well equipped for foul weather. Mohling shared that because the group members were so experienced, they did not consider anything amiss until it was too late. Ruth Magnuson died of hypothermia about seven hours after last being seen. Van Slyke noted that "whether she was first hypothermic, and then became separated from the group, or vice versa, it seems to be a classic case of how insidious and speedy hypothermia can be, even with experienced mountaineers."

Being inadequately prepared for the changing weather likely led to the hypothermic death of Marshall, Colorado, resident James P. Duffy, age 24, on December 14, 1981. Duffy was climbing with Michael O'Donnell, who was the climber with Robert Elliott when Elliott fell to his death almost a year earlier on January 10, 1981.

Duffy and O'Donnell left the Longs Peak Trailhead at 4:30 a.m. with plans for a one day trip. They did not carry a tent or sleeping bags and did not register. They successfully made an ascent of the East Face and had planned to descend either the Cables or Keyhole Route by the light of the full moon. Unfortunately, blizzard conditions greeted them on the summit and they were forced to spend the night there. Without a tent or sleeping bags, they broke into a small box housing weather equipment in an attempt to get out of the weather. The next morning, suffering from the initial stages of hypothermia, the two climbers headed down the Keyhole Route in blizzard conditions. O'Donnell later told rangers he last saw Duffy around 8:00 a.m. near the Trough and that Duffy was not doing well. O'Donnell thought he had to keep moving to survive and get help. Often crawling on his knees because of the wind, O'Donnell made it down and contacted ranger staff. Unfortunately, the storm kept rescuers off the upper route for two days. Searchers from the Fantasy Ridge Mountain Guides found Duffy's body 200 feet above the Keyhole on December 17th.

Boulder, Colorado, resident Mark Frevert, age 28, and 19-year-old Colorado State University student Samuel Mitchell, a native of Lafayette, Louisiana, were reported missing Sunday evening, February 6, 1983. They had failed to return from a Saturday climb of the Spiral Route on Notchtop Mountain. Mitchell died of exposure after both climbers were struck by rock fall. The falling rocks killed Frevert. The full story of this dual fatality is found in chapter fifteen.

Thomas Kelly, age 27, and his climbing partner, Bo Judd, attempted the Kiener's Route on the East Face of Longs Peak on September 14, 1993. Both were known as strong rock climbers, but had limited alpine climbing experience. They got a late start and were caught by nightfall some 500 feet below the summit, as they were unable to finish the climb when a strong autumn storm moved over the mountain. That Sunday night, they huddled together for warmth as temperatures dropped and up to 18 inches of snow fell. With morning, the exhausted climbers began to down climb their route. Ranger staff was aware that they were overdue, but were unable to reach them because of the weather.

According to a subsequent reconstruction of the incident with Judd, the two climbers narrowly escaped disaster a couple times on the descent— once when a rappel anchor failed as they approached the Broadway Ledge, and again when Thomas lost a crampon as they descended Lambs Slide. Nonetheless, they made it safely to Mills Glacier only to be faced with thigh deep snow as they struggled toward their gear cache at Chasm Lake while darkness fell again on Monday evening. Exhausted and hypothermic, the climbers repeatedly got separated, but were able to maintain voice contact in the darkness through most of the trip. When Judd reached the gear cache, he immediately fell asleep in his sleeping bag. Thomas never made it. He appears to have tried to take shelter in the boulders only to die that night, a mere 300 yards from camp. Both Judd and Thomas Kelly were found Tuesday morning. Thomas Kelly was survived by his wife, Diane, and two young children, the oldest two years old.

On September 5, 2004, Sudheer Averineni, age 26, was the most recent victim of hypothermia on Longs Peak. Averineni, from India, had recently lived in Ft. Collins. He was last seen by his two hiking companions near the Keyhole formation (13,100 ft.) on Saturday, September 4th, around 10:30 a.m. The other two hikers turned around due to the poor weather. Park staff was notified at 4:30 p.m. Saturday when Averineni failed to reconnect with his friends. Winter weather conditions, including snow, high winds, and below freezing temperatures, rocked the Longs Peak area late Saturday evening and into Sunday. Rangers found his body on the summit at approximately 1:00 p.m. on Sunday. Averineni was wearing tennis shoes, jeans, and a hooded sweatshirt. He had no extra clothing, winter gear, or food. It is not known for certain why he did not try to get off the summit. One theory was that he was unable to find the route due to poor visibility. Due to extreme weather conditions, his body was not flown off the mountain until Monday, September 6th.

Based on subsequent interviews with friends, it appears that Averineni was very goal oriented. Though inexperienced, he attempted the same route unsuccessfully twice that summer, so he was vaguely familiar with the area and perhaps overconfident. This is yet another unfortunate fatality where the victim failed to heed the advice and warnings of literature and posted bulletins at the trailhead.

Safety Lessons from these incidents:

1. **Listen to and pay heed to those who are most familiar with the climb or trail** you are contemplating. Know what you are getting into and be courageous enough to stop and retreat.

2. **Be prepared for changing weather.** Notice that one-third of these incidents occurred in September and October. In this season, the thinking of a great number of visitors hasn't shifted yet from summer warmth to possible winter conditions. Early season snowstorms are common in the Rockies in September and October. These preventable deaths are yet more examples of the importance of proper trip planning.

3. **Manage your risk.** There is a fine balance between moving fast and light for a long and difficult alpine ascent versus a slower trip due to carrying extra gear. See #1 and #2 above.

4. **Know the signs and symptoms of hypothermia.** Early signs are not easily observed or noticed. By the time a victim becomes lethargic, the consequences may be irreversible.

Hypothermia—Death by Exposure

September 23, 1884	Caroline J. Welton, 42	**Longs Peak, Keyhole Route** *Strong willed hiker advanced in poor weather against advice of guide.* Died of exposure near the Keyhole while on descent from summit of Longs Peak.
September 2, 1915	Dr. Thornton Sampson, 63	**Odessa Gorge** En route from Grand Lake area, over Flattop Mountain to Fern Lake Lodge. Caught in early season storm. Broke leg and died of exposure.
January 12, 1925	Agnes W. Vaile, 31	**Longs Peak, North Face** Made the first winter ascent of the East Face of Longs Peak with Walter Kiener. *Late start. Adverse weather. No escape option.* Died of exposure while on descent below the North Face.
January 12, 1925	Herbert Sortland, 22	**Longs Peak** Part of rescue party for Agnes Vaile. *Poorly equipped,* so turned back. *Became disoriented/lost.* Fell and broke hip near Longs Peak Inn and died of exposure.
August 7, 1939	Gerald J. Clark, 37	**Longs Peak, East Face** Experienced climber became stuck on East Face Route. Spent night in drizzle, wet storm. *Poorly equipped.*
August 15, 1958	Bobby Bizup, 10	**Near Camp St. Malo** Became *separated from family* near Camp St. Malo. Massive search in *poor weather.* Remains found a year later.
January 23, 1972	Fred Stone, 20 Joan Jardine, 21	**Lower Longs Peak Trail** Young couple got *disoriented/lost in poor weather* while en route to Chasm Lake shelter. *Poorly equipped.*
June 18, 1972	Gregory Holzer, 22	**Wild Basin** *Disappeared/lost* while hiking from Grand Lake to Wild Basin. Body found a year later. Hypothermia likely cause of death.

September 2, 1973	Jonathan Williams, 10	**Odessa Gorge** Father/son bonding hike from Grand Lake to Bear Lake. *Disoriented/lost in poor weather* on Flattop Mountain.
August 24, 1975	William Gizzie, 45	**Chasm Meadow** Separated from party near Chasm Meadow. *Possibly weakened by heart attack,* led to death by hypothermia. (Not in text.)
March 8, 1980	Ruth Magnuson, 29	**Mt. Alice** Experienced group summiting Mt. Alice from Grand Lake. Victim became *separated from group in poor weather/low visibility.*
December 14, 1981	James P. Duffy, 24	**Longs Peak, Keyhole Route** Completed East Face climb. Forced to bivouac on summit due to poor weather. *Poorly equipped.* Became separated when partner left for help. *Storm* kept rescuers off mountain for 2 days. Body found above Keyhole.
February 6, 1983	Samuel H. Mitchell, III, 19	**Notchtop Mountain** *Injured by rock fall near Notchtop Mountain.* Partner killed. Victim attempted to hike out. *Poor weather.*
September 14, 1993	Thomas Kelly, 27	**Longs Peak, Chasm Lake** *Caught by strong early winter storm* while on Kiener's Route, 500 feet below summit of Longs Peak. *Unplanned bivouac.* Descended following day into night. Became separated from partner during storm/darkness.
September 5, 2004	Sudheer Averineni, 26	**Longs Peak Summit** Goal oriented victim caught on summit of Longs Peak *poorly equipped.*

TEN

Aircraft Accidents

Whether in a helicopter or fixed wing aircraft, flying in the mountains of Colorado is simply more dangerous. The weather is unpredictable, and there is less air pressure at the higher elevations, thus the air is "thinner." The higher in elevation the aircraft goes, the harder the aircraft has to work to stay aloft. This also means there is a narrower window for safe operation for the pilot. Of course, these conditions are not insurmountable with proper planning and a healthy respect for the flight environment. The staff at Rocky Mountain National Park routinely use helicopters for a variety of functions in resources management, maintenance, and emergency rescue operations. Proper planning, training, and knowledge of the effects of elevation have resulted in a good, if not unblemished, safety record.

The fatal fixed winged aircraft accidents in the park are described below, as well as a few miracle misses, where survivors have been given a second chance.

The first aircraft accident in Rocky Mountain National Park, and perhaps the most benign, occurred on August 12, 1945. Lt. Andrew Herczeg, a member of the Denver Civil Air Patrol, was on a routine flight from Craig to Denver when a developing storm forced him north. His single engine aircraft soon ran out of fuel. Herczeg initiated an emergency landing on Trail Ridge Road near Milner Pass. The aircraft was slightly damaged when a gust of wind pushed it into a meadow alongside the highway just as the light plane was touching down. Herczeg suffered only minor injuries, and later the plane was disassembled and removed on a flatbed truck.

Herczeg emergency landing near Milner Pass in 1945. Courtesy of RMNP

In the next crash in the park, three people miraculously escaped death Monday afternoon, November 10, 1947, when their Piper Supercub crashed into the trees above Lulu City at 11,000 feet. The plane was destroyed, but the occupants suffered only minor injuries.

The pilot, Ollie O. Smith, with his brother and sister-in-law, Mr. and Mrs. Foster Smith of Eagle, Colorado, were en route to Bonita, Oklahoma. Unable to make enough altitude and hindered by high winds at Tennessee Pass, Smith flew north to attempt to get across the Divide at Poudre Pass. Again finding it impossible to gain sufficient altitude, the pilot attempted to turn back when the crash occurred. The accident was reported to district ranger Fred McLaren by local resident John Holzwarth. McLaren and ranger Hugh Ebert hiked to the scene of the accident and helped the group reach Granby, where they continued their trip by train.

The first aircraft accident resulting in a fatality occurred on August 29, 1948. Lt. Cranston H. Dodd, 23, of Dallas, Texas, was a Marine air reservist with eleven months combat experience in the Pacific Theater during World War II. At the time of the accident, he was a student at Denver University. He was reported to be on a routine orientation mission from Buckley Naval Air Station in Denver. He crashed his F4U

(FG1) Corsair fighter plane around noon, just north of the ridge top known as the Tundra Curves Saddle, or Iceberg Pass, on Trail Ridge Road. The crash site was 400 vertical feet below the top of the ridge, at an elevation of 11,400 feet.

The Corsair was one of the best fighting aircraft during World War II. This type of plane was flown by undoubtedly the most colorful and well-known Marine Corps ace, Gregory "Pappy" Boyington, in the Pacific Theater during that war. His squadron was immortalized by the television show *Baa Baa Black Sheep* in the 1970s. It was powered by an 18-cylinder radial engine.

Several witnesses to Dodd's crash were·on a guided photographic tour led by ranger naturalist J. Herbert Heger. They said the plane appeared to be working perfectly, and they saw it circling overhead before the fatal

Lt. Dodd's crash site below Iceberg Pass. Courtesy of RMNP

crash. Minutes later, the witnesses watched the plane "roar up Fall River Canyon at treetop height," then turn left or south in an uphill climb towards the saddle where Trail Ridge Road enters the Tundra Curves section of the road. Apparently, the pilot realized he could not make it over the ridge and banked hard to the left in an attempt to turn back down the canyon before crashing. Well-known downdrafts from along the Continental Divide were believed to contribute to the accident. First on the scene of the crash were several members of an NPS road crew who had been eating lunch on Trail Ridge Road just above the site of the accident. Dodd had been thrown from the aircraft and killed instantly.

The subsequent military investigation concluded that Dodd was in an unauthorized area at the time of the crash, that he was conducting unauthorized low flying in mountainous terrain, and that he failed to observe ordinary precautions for flying in mountainous terrain.

Years later, local historian Duke Sumonia discussed the incident with Foster "Frosty" Freeman, who was a seasonal ranger in 1948. Freeman worked for North District Ranger Loren E. Lane, and they had investigated the crash in conjunction with the Navy. Freeman recalled that the Superintendent would not let the Navy take heavy equipment across the tundra to recover the aircraft, and in those days helicopters weren't powerful enough to lift the heavy load. The Navy loaded up the smaller parts they could carry, and then blew up the wreck, causing the engine to roll down the hill.

For years, the wreck remained an object of curiosity for park visitors. In 1997, district ranger Doug Ridley approached the park management team with the idea that it was time to remove the wreckage, particularly as it was in recommended wilderness. Ridley was given approval, but faced two challenges. The easiest was coordinating with the park maintenance division for the use of a powerful enough helicopter to lift the engine and other parts. Surprisingly, the larger hurdle was getting approval from the military to remove and dispose of the 50-year-old wreck. Ridley found that the Corsair was still a commissioned aircraft on the United States Navy inventory. Apparently, the Navy never decommissions a plane, unlike the

Air Force. Persistence paid off, and Ridley helped the Navy put the wrecked Corsair on permanent loan to Bootstrap Aircraft, a non-profit group dedicated to reproducing a complete F4U Corsair aircraft from salvaged parts.

In October 1997, Ridley and other park staff used an Alouette III helicopter piloted by Paul Calloway of Geo-Seis Helicopters in Ft. Collins to remove eight sling loads of aircraft material to a flatbed trailer near Willow Park cabin on Fall River Road. The powerful radial engine was the most difficult, weighing approximately 1,100 lbs. Calloway burned off fuel moving the smaller loads, but still had to bounce the engine down the slope before gaining enough lift to haul it to Willow Park. He had only 23 gallons of fuel left when he returned to Upper Beaver Meadows.

Almost twenty years later, the next crash occurred. On April 9, 1967, six friends were aboard a plane piloted by Jack Henander, age 28. They were returning to Colorado from a fishing trip in Wyoming's Flaming Gorge area. The single engine Piper aircraft left Rock Springs, Wyoming, at 2:31 p.m. and was due to be at Jefferson County Airport by 4:30 p.m. Henander's last radio communication at 3:38 p.m. indicated he was over Laramie and on course with no problems. However, he was flying into an area experiencing snow squalls in the mountains west of Ft. Collins. They never made it.

The following morning, April 10th, crews in 25 Civil Air Patrol planes and helicopters began searching for the plane. Poor weather and severe wind turbulence hampered the initial search effort, which focused in the Red Feather Lakes and Livermore areas. Flying conditions were so difficult that two planes involved with the search effort crash landed. Fortunately, there was only one serious injury. A single engine plane, piloted by Boulder County Deputy Sheriff Dennis Hammond, crashed southeast of Poudre Canyon when it failed to clear a ridge. Hammond and two spotters were uninjured and were flown from the scene by helicopter. Later that afternoon, a second plane with three people crashed in the Poudre Canyon about five miles south of the Ft. Collins Mountain Recreation area. The pilot, Bill Mitchell of Golden, sustained a skull fracture and was flown out by helicopter that evening.

Luck changed for the search effort on Wednesday, April 12th, when smoke drew the attention of pilot Wayne Russell, who along with two passengers was conducting an antelope survey for the Colorado State Game and Fish Department. They spotted three men on the ground and circled over them. With the plane's loudspeaker, Russell confirmed that the three were from the missing plane and directed them to a location where a helicopter was able to land and fly the survivors out.

The three were Charles Grosso, 35, Jack DiGiacomo, 27, and Albert Romano, 52, all of Louisville, Colorado. Grosso and DiGiacomo were treated and released from Poudre Valley Hospital that evening, but Romano was hospitalized for head and back injuries sustained in the crash. The three survivors had sufficient warm clothing but little food and had built a fire for warmth and signal. Being unfamiliar with the area and disoriented, they were able to offer a general distance of about five miles that they had struggled from the plane in the deep snow. The survivors reported that the other three passengers were killed in the crash. The wings had iced up, forcing the plane down on Sunday afternoon. The wings tore off the plane during the crash, and the fuselage plowed into a snowdrift in a narrow canyon. Based on the interview with the survivors, Larimer County Sheriff Ray Scheerer believed the crash site was between Stormy Peak and Signal Mountain in the northeast corner of the Rocky Mountain National Park.

With the crash site likely in the park, Sheriff Scheerer coordinated with Chief Ranger Jim Randall to form ground search parties composed of experienced rangers and volunteer rescue staff. On Monday, the 17th, searchers located one of the sites where the three survivors spent a night, which helped reduce the search area. On Tuesday, April 18th, the wreckage was finally spotted from the air at the 10,300-foot level of South Signal Mountain. Rangers Jerry Phillips, Doug Erskine, and Henry Jones were among those who made it to the crash site on the 19th and retrieved the bodies of Jack D. Henander, 28, William P Elrod, 55, and Charles DeNovellis, 54.

The next fatal plane crash occurred August 16, 1977. Two Vancouver, Washington, residents, pilot Martin Ryan, age 23, and Janet Bonneville,

19, died in a crash approximately one mile southwest of Willow Park on the Fall River Road. In newspaper accounts, Chief Ranger Dave Essex stated that the couple had been visiting friends in the Denver area and left Jefferson County Airport at 5:30 p.m. on Saturday. The plane was a Maule, a two-seat, single engine aircraft. Several climbers directly across the drainage, along with ranger Milton Madden, witnessed the crash. They stated that the plane flew westbound toward Fall River Pass. It did not circle to gain altitude, but flew directly toward the pass. As it approached the higher altitudes, it seemed to slow considerably. Several witnesses thought the pilot attempted to land on the Fall River Road. Unfortunately, a wing clipped a tree, forcing it hard to the left and the plane crashed into a rock and caught fire on impact. The likely factors contributing to the accident were the fact that the plane was flying too low and had insufficient power to lift it over the ridge and unfamiliarity with the terrain by the pilot. The plane may have been overloaded. Investigators noted several cases of Coors Beer with the luggage. Aging baby boomers probably remember the novelty of Coors Beer outside the state of Colorado. Maybe Ryan planned to surprise his friends with a gift, which unfortunately may have contributed to the fatal crash.

A Christmas holiday trip turned into tragedy on December 23, 1979, when pilot Barry L. Krieger made an emergency landing at 12,000 feet in the Never Summer Range between Mount Cumulus and Mount Nimbus. Krieger's mother, 62-year-old Virginia Krieger of John Day, Oregon, died almost instantly when careening pieces of luggage struck her head.

Krieger, his mother, and his three daughters, Claire, 10, Connie, 15, and Cathy, 17, left the Longmont airport about 1:00 p.m. on the 23rd bound first for Las Vegas, then Oregon. The twin engine Piper Apache made it over the Continental Divide, but didn't gain sufficient elevation to climb over the Never Summer Range, forcing Krieger to make his emergency landing in soft snow. Emergency locator transmitter signals were picked up by commercial airline pilots flying in and out of Denver that afternoon. The plane was believed to be in the upper Forest Canyon area of the park.

On Tuesday, December 24th, Chief Ranger Dave Essex positioned rescuers on Trail Ridge Road and near Milner Pass in an attempt to triangulate the source of the transmitter signals. Over twenty rescuers from the U.S. Army at Fort Carson, Rocky Mountain Rescue from Boulder, the Alpine Rescue Team, and park rangers stood by throughout the night in sub-zero weather. On Wednesday, Christmas day, a Civil Air Patrol plane spotted the downed aircraft. The Channel 9 helicopter out of Denver flew ranger Darrell Grossman and several members from Rocky Mountain Rescue near the crash scene, but they were required to hike a quarter mile uphill to the site in 70–80 mph wind gusts. The four survivors were carried down to the helicopter landing zone on litters, then flown to the Longmont Hospital by the Channel 7 and 9 helicopters, as well as a Denver Flight for Life helicopter. All rescuers were off the mountain by 2:00 p.m. Christmas day. Barry Krieger lost both feet to frostbite.

En route from Steamboat Springs to Ft. Collins, Colorado, on April 4, 1989, pilot Jerome Bentley's single engine Cessna Skylane airplane was believed to be somewhere east of Cameron Pass in the Routt National Forest when reported missing the following day. This was ten miles west of the actual crash site on Hague's Peak. An unsuccessful search was conducted for several days before being terminated. It was not until June 30, 1989, that the wreckage and body were found by park researcher Richard Scott. Scott had hiked into the north central part of the park to sample and measure melt water from the rarely visited Rowe Glacier. The glacier is between 13,560-foot Hague's Peak and 13,400-foot Rowe Peak. Scott found pieces of beige plastic and insulation embedded in the ice of the 13,200-foot glacier. In the Estes Park *Trail Gazette*, Chief Ranger Dave Essex reported, "Bentley flew right into the wall up there." It was believed that Bentley flew into a snowstorm and was off course when the accident occurred. The snow buried most of the plane, making it next to impossible to locate during the air search, especially since the primary search area was north of the accident scene.

In another incident, the park staff was notified by the Civil Air Patrol Thursday morning, February 1, 1996, of a possible plane crash in the park. Peter Smith of Littleton was an experienced pilot in a private twin engine Piper Seneca. The evening before, around 7:15 p.m., he filed an IFR (instrument flight rules) flight plan by phone, and indicated his route would be from Erie, Colorado, direct to Laramie, then to Rock Springs, Wyoming, and on to Boise, Idaho, where he would stop for fuel. His final destination was Payne Field in Everett, Washington, where he would report for his U.S. Army Reserve duty.

At 9:20 p.m., Smith contacted air traffic control, said he was airborne, and requested his IFR clearance to Boise. Minutes later, his aircraft was identified on radar and he was issued the IFR clearance. At 9:35 p.m., Smith requested and was cleared to maintain VFR (visual flight rules) on top, meaning at his top cruising elevation of 14,500 feet. Moments later, Smith contacted the Denver Center and asked, "could you give me a radar vector heading just to check that ... We're going up to fourteen five, but if need be we'll climb higher to get over the divide there." The sector controller advised that he "had marginal radar coverage out there at that altitude ... You're going to need a little more altitude before you make that turn." At 9:48 p.m., Smith was contacted by the next sector controller and confirmed he was heading directly to Rock Springs and stated "I'm having a little heading problem here, but switching to the compass nav, but we're VFR on top. In fact, it's pretty much VFR below us now." At 9:57 p.m., the controller tried to advise Smith that radar contact had been lost. There was no reply.

The search began on February 1st, with the Civil Air Patrol coordinating the air search and the National Park Service coordinating the ground effort. High winds and winter weather with limited visibility hampered the search effort and prevented the use of helicopters at higher elevations. For several days, ground teams based out of the Willow Park and Lawn Lake patrol cabins hiked, skied, and snowshoed in the Ypsilon/Fairchild area, but were unsuccessful in finding the missing plane. Also participating were military and privately chartered aircraft. This unsuccessful search effort was suspended on February 13th. On March 3rd, veteran Rocky Mountain Rescue searcher Chuck Demerest spotted the wreckage approximately 200 feet below the summit of Ypsilon Mountain (13,514 ft.). On March 9th, rangers arrived at the accident site and confirmed the identification of the plane and the dead pilot. As there was a fifteen-foot snow cornice above the site, conditions were not safe to conduct an on-scene investigation. On July 19th, a second expedition was made to the wreck and approximately thirty pounds of human remains were removed. The wreckage was removed by helicopter on August 5, 1996.

In the final report, the National Transportation Safety Board (NTSB) stated that "radar data indicated the airplane descended from an encoded altitude of 15,100 feet to 13,900 feet in 1 minute, 31 seconds, or about 800 feet per minute. No distress call was received. Wreckage examination failed to explain why the airplane descended or anything causal to the accident." The NTSB report determined that "the probable cause(s) of this accident was "descent into mountainous terrain for reasons undetermined." Peter Smith was survived by his wife and four children.

The most recent fixed wing crash occurred in April 2000. Rob Donoho, age 52, and his wife, Terri, age 47, enjoyed flying to Page, Arizona, in the summer to visit friends and spend time on Lake Powell. The Ft. Collins couple made the same trip countless times over the previous few years. Rob held a private pilot license since 1982 and had over 4,000 hours of flight experience. He did not possess an instrument rating. Records indicated he had flown over 50 hours in the preceding six months, mostly to Page. These trips were in a Smith Aerostar 601 twin engine aircraft, which Donoho had purchased in April 1999.

On Sunday, April 30, 2000, the couple left Page at around 10:30 a.m., with an expected arrival time at the Ft. Collins Downtown Airport of mid afternoon. They never made it, and their family reported them overdue the next morning. The Donohos had not filed a flight plan, but the known route they frequented and technical data narrowed the primary search area from the northern part of Rocky Mountain National Park north to Cheyenne, Wyoming. Donoho had contacted the Denver Flight Service Station in Grand Junction, Colorado, at 11:15 a.m. He received a weather update for the intended route. This briefing provided information that there were mid- to high-level clouds with some icing along the route and that the Ft. Collins area was experiencing visual meteorological conditions. Initial radar data showed that the last normal transponder-generated altitude of the aircraft was 13,300 feet at a point approximately 40 miles southwest of the eventual crash site. Subsequent "maintenance dump" radar data indicated the aircraft descended to 12,900 feet approximately 20 miles from the crash site and continued the descent to 12,600 feet between that point and the crash site. Another pilot who had been in the same area 15 minutes behind the Donohos' plane described the weather as being overcast skies, with the base of the clouds at about 12,500 feet. He had diverted to the north up over the Wyoming border to stay in visual conditions.

Once again, the initial search was hindered by high winds and low visibility at the higher elevations. Finally on May 4th, a Colorado National Guard helicopter crew spotted the wreckage. The crash site was at the 12,600-foot level on the west side of Comanche Peak, elevation 12,702 feet. This placed it just inside the park boundary. The plane had disintegrated on impact, and the wreckage scatter pattern was over an estimated two acre area. Some of the wreckage had even gone over the ridgeline of the peak and was technically outside the park. The following day, May 5th, rangers Doug Ridley, Mark Magnuson, and Carl Cordova, a Larimer County coroner, and a National Transportation Safety Board investigator flew to the site and began the grim task of collecting the few identifiable body parts and investigating the accident.

This accident was the result of pilot error in descending too soon in poor visibility. Just another 100 feet higher, and he would have made it. The wreckage was removed from the accident site on August 8, 2000. Due to snow and the low angle of the impact, there was minimal damage to park resources. As with many incidents, there was an odd twist in the formality of the investigation. Years later, Ridley retold the story of $100 bills floating in the air! They discovered later that the Donoho's had sold their houseboat in Page and were paid in cash. The investigators returned to the family over $7,000 in $100 bills.

The helicopter is a valuable tool in the management of the park. In searches or rescues, a helicopter evacuation of an injured visitor saves dozens of hours of backbreaking work carrying a litter out of the mountains. While utilization of a helicopter is a necessary component of park management, it is not without risks.

On March 1, 1967, a helicopter was used to herd elk into a trap at Little Horseshoe Park. On board were pilot Virgil Jones of Durango, student pilot Earl Palmer from Montana, and Ted Bucknell, the park wildlife biologist. At the last moment, one of the passengers spotted a telephone line in the path of the helicopter and shouted a warning. Barely twenty feet in the air, the pilot instinctively pulled back on the control stick, which caused the helicopter to fall and the tail rotor to strike the ground, and the helicopter crashed. Fortunately, there were no serious injuries. The helicopter was a total loss. The elk escaped.

In another accident, which happened on Friday, August 11, 1978, four rangers crashed in a helicopter on Grants Pass below the Boulderfield. Rangers Bob Seibert, Chuck Harris, Penny Knuckles, and Jim Bredar were

1978 helicopter crash near Grants Pass below the Boulderfield. Courtesy of RMNP

being shuttled up to the Longs Peak Trail as part of a trails maintenance project. The four were to spread out along the trail to receive sling loads of treated logs that would be used as water bars and log steps during upcoming trail work. Several witnesses reported that it appeared the helicopter was forced into the ground by the wind as the pilot turned the helicopter to land. Incredibly, there were no major injuries, and the five walked out to the Longs Peak Ranger Station. It was also fortunate that no hikers were injured from flying debris.

The crash occurred barely twenty yards from the heavily used Longs Peak Trail, and several hikers had to dive for cover. The aircraft, a Llama on contract to the United States Forest Service and piloted by Mike Staggs, was destroyed in the crash. Equally fortunate was that the aircraft did not catch on fire. Jet fuel poured out over the still-running engine from a punctured fuel tank. Staggs briefly stayed with the aircraft after the crash in order to turn off all electrical switches, and the wind was so strong that the fumes were likely dissipated immediately.

On a rescue incident on June 25, 1994, at 8:49 p.m., a Bell 206A helicopter sustained substantial damage when the pilot attempted to land at 11,800 feet near Hallett Peak. The helicopter was moving rescue crews back and forth as part of the rescue of an injured hiker. The pilot and two passengers were not injured, but the helicopter had to be dismantled and removed in pieces.

Aircraft Accidents

August 29, 1948	Lt. Cranston Dodd—pilot, 23	**Below Tundra Curves** Fatal crash of Corsair fighter plane. Pilot *unable to bank and gain altitude* in upper Fall River Canyon.
April 9, 1967	Jack Hernander—pilot, 28 William Elrod, 55 Charles DeNovellis, 54	**South Signal Mountain** Fatal crash of Piper aircraft. Plane with 6 occupants was returning to Colorado from Wyoming fishing trip. *Poor weather/visibility. Ice on wings.* 3 survivors, 3 fatalities.
August 16, 1977	Martin Ryan—pilot, 23 Janet Bonneville, 19	**Fall River Canyon Road** Fatal crash with 2 occupants. Single engine plane flew too low up Fall River Canyon westbound. *Insufficient elevation/power* to climb over the ridgeline.
December 23, 1979	Virginia Krieger, 62	**Never Summer Range** Emergency landing at 12,000 feet. Twin engine Piper Apache with 5 occupants had *insufficient power/ elevation* to clear ridgeline. 1 fatality.
April 4, 1989	Jerome Bentley—pilot, age unknown	**Rowe Glacier** Fatal single engine Cessna Skylane crash in *storm. Off course.* Bentley only occupant. The wreckage was not found for 2 months.
January 31, 1996	Peter Smith—pilot, age unknown	**Ypsilon Mountain** Fatal twin engine Piper Seneca crash 200 feet below summit. Westbound plane made *unexplained descent, resulting in crash.* Smith only occupant. Wreckage found 6 weeks later.
April 30, 2000	Rob Donoho—pilot, 52 Terry Donoho, 47	**Comanche Peak** Donoho and his wife were eastbound in a Smith Aerostar 601 twin engine aircraft en route to a Ft. Collins airport. Fatal crash 100 feet below summit in *poor weather/visibility.*

Second Chances—Non-fatal Crashes

October 12, 1945	Andrew Herczeg—pilot	**Milner Pass** *Ran out of fuel.* Emergency landing on Trail Ridge Road.
November 10, 1947	Ollie O. Smith—pilot	**Above Lulu City** *Unable to gain altitude.* All three occupants survived.
March 1, 1967	Virgil Jones—pilot	**Horseshoe Park** During an elk roundup, 3 occupants survived a hard helicopter landing caused by *avoiding a telephone wire.*
August 11, 1978	Mike Staggs—pilot	**Grants Pass near the Boulderfield** Four rangers and the pilot miraculously survived the crash and roll of a Llama helicopter. Trail maintenance project. *Strong winds.*
June 25, 1994	Paul Bennett—pilot	**Hallett Peak** A Bell 206A helicopter made a hard landing during a rescue operation. Helicopter disabled. No injuries to the three occupants.

ELEVEN

Lightning

An Internet search for "Lightning" or "Lightning Safety" brings you to an excellent website posted by the National Weather Service. The stated goal of this site is "Safeguarding U.S. residents from dangerous lightning. The campaign is designed to lower lightning death and injury rates and America's vulnerability to one of nature's deadliest hazards." In the United States, an average of 44 people a year have died from lightning strikes over the last 10 years. There are roughly 300 injuries per year. Approximately 43 percent of these victims were out in the open; 29 percent were taking shelter under a tree. In 2009, there were 33 lightning deaths. The following information is copied from the NWS site:

The lightning safety community reminds you that there is NO safe place to be outside in a thunderstorm. If you absolutely can't get to safety, this information is designed to help you lessen the threat of being struck by lightning while outside. Don't kid yourself—you are NOT safe outside.

Being stranded outdoors when lightning is striking nearby is a harrowing experience. Your first and only truly safe choice is to get to a safe building or vehicle. If you are camping, hiking, climbing, on a motorcycle or bicycle, boating, scuba diving, or enjoying other outdoor activities and cannot get to a safe vehicle or shelter, follow these last resort tips. These will not prevent you from being hit, just slightly lessen the odds.

Do NOT seek shelter under tall isolated trees. The tree may help you stay dry but will significantly increase your risk of being struck by lightning. Rain will not kill you, but the lightning can!

If lightning is in the immediate area, and there is no safe location nearby, stay at least 15 feet apart from other members of your group so the lightning won't travel between you if hit. Keep your feet together and sit on the ground out in the open. If you can possibly run to a vehicle or building, DO so. Sitting or crouching on the ground is not safe and should be a last resort.

Wet ropes can make excellent conductors. This is BAD news when it comes to lightning activity. If you are mountain climbing and see lightning, and can do so safely, remove unnecessary ropes extended or attached to you. If a rope is extended across a mountain face and lightning makes contact with it, the electrical current will likely travel along the rope, especially if it is wet.

Stay away from metal objects, such as fences, poles, and backpacks. Metal is an excellent conductor.

Do NOT seek shelter under partially enclosed buildings.

Stay away from tall, isolated objects. Lightning typically strikes the tallest object. That may be you in an open field or clearing.

Know the weather patterns of the area. For example, in mountainous areas, thunderstorms typically develop in the early afternoon, so plan to hike early in the day and be down the mountain by noon.

Know the weather forecast. If there is a high chance of thunderstorms, curtail your outdoor activities.

Do not place your campsite in an open field on the top of a hill or on a ridge top. Keep your site away from tall isolated trees or other tall objects. If you are in a forest, stay near a lower stand of trees. If you are camping in an open area, set up camp in a valley, ravine, or other low area. A tent offers NO protection from lighting.

In Colorado, between 1980 and 2008, 87 people have been killed and 391 injured by lightning. With its many peaks and trails above timberline, and Trail Ridge Road, Rocky Mountain National Park has unfortunately contributed to the list of Colorado lightning fatalities with eleven known deaths and numerous non-fatal strikes.

More than a hundred years ago, and before the park was established, lightning killed one of the area's early settlers. Donald MacGregor and Abner Sprague described Mr. Alexander Q. MacGregor's death to Superintendent Roger Toll in April 1925. MacGregor, age 50, had settled in the Black Canyon area in the fall of 1873.

In the early 1870s, the infamous Earl of Dunraven bought up most of the land in the Estes Valley for his private hunting reserve. However, the Earl and his American associate, Theodore Whyte, overlooked several productive tracts of land in Black Canyon, Moraine Park, and Beaver Meadows. Into this void came some of the early settlers, such as Abner Sprague, Elkanah Lamb, and MacGregor. MacGregor first visited Estes Park in 1872 on a camping trip. He and his new wife Clara returned in late 1873 or early 1874 and staked a 160-acre claim in the Black Canyon area below Lumpy Ridge. They recognized that the beauty of the Estes Park region would soon attract tourists and more settlers, so one of MacGregor's first actions was to build an improved wagon toll road from Longmont, through what is now Pinewood Springs, to Estes Park during the winter of 1874–75. In January, 1875, their first son, George, was born. By the summer of 1876, MacGregor had built a series of log buildings on his property, including a water-powered saw mill, and the family began to take in guests for $1 a day. The MacGregor Ranch also boasted the first local Post Office in 1876, with Clara as postmistress. By 1884, the ranch grew to 1,500 acres, and they were grazing over a hundred head of cattle. During the 1880s, Alexander and Clara elected to be absentee winter landlords, returning each summer from Ft. Collins and then Denver, where Alexander practiced law.

During the autumn of 1895, Alexander made a fishing trip to the west side of the divide. Along the way, he collected rock samples, and later showed them to his son, George, who was a student at the Colorado School of Mines. The most promising ore sample came from a point just to the west of the head of Forest Canyon, near Poudre Lake. Around June 17, 1896, Alexander and George went up to the site to prospect for a few days. They dug a prospect hole approximately four feet deep, six feet wide, and fifteen to twenty feet in length. Around noon on June 21st, they prepared their first dynamite blast. Alexander stood up in the trench with a drill in one hand and a sledge in another, and lightning suddenly struck and killed him. George, who was down on his hands and knees in the trench, was knocked unconscious and suffered a burn to his right leg from the knee down. When George regained consciousness, he found his father dead. He made his way to the horses and rode along Trail Ridge and down Windy Gulch to Sprague's Ranch, then into Estes Park to get help. Early the following morning, a rescue party consisting of George MacGregor, Abner Sprague, Dr. Homer James, Shep Husted, Jim Ferguson, and Will Golding-Dwyre left town to retrieve Alexander's body. They returned to Sprague's that afternoon.

Donald MacGregor, who described Alexander's death to Superintendent Toll, was the second son of Alexander and Clara MacGregor. Clara MacGregor died in 1901. In 1910, Donald bought out his two brothers, George and Halbert, who had little interest in ranch life. Donald and his wife Maude returned to operate the ranch on a full-time basis. By this time, tourism at the ranch had diminished considerably, and Donald focused on raising a quality Black Angus cattle herd. Donald and Maude had one child, Muriel, born in 1904. Both Donald and Maude died in 1950. Muriel MacGregor died in 1970.

In 1978, the Muriel L. MacGregor Charitable Trust was formed. In 1983, the National Park Service worked with the Trustees to purchase a conservation easement on the main 1,200 acres of the ranch. The site is now maintained in perpetuity as an example of turn-of-the-century, high-mountain ranching. With roots in the 1870s, the MacGregor Ranch Historic District is home to 43 buildings on 1,200 acres. Twenty-eight of the buildings are listed on the National Register of Historic Places. The ranch is the last remaining working cattle ranch in Estes Park and one of the few sites that operates as both a working ranch and youth education center in northern Colorado. It is unique in that its historic collection and structures are original to the 1873 homestead family, and the collection is completely intact. On the north side of Estes Park, the ranch and museum are open to visitors.

One last note: For some unexplained reason, Alexander MacGregor changed the spelling of his last name from McGregor to MacGregor in the early 1870s. Most maps show a "McGregor Mountain" and "McGregor Falls," which are assumed to be named for Alexander, the original settler.

In another story told to Superintendent Toll in February 1925, Max Giesecke and George C. Bernard recalled the lightning death of Dr. Dillingham on August 17, 1914.

Dr. Dillingham, his wife, and their nine-year-old son were from Mead, Colorado. They, and another couple, left Camp Wheeler (Squeaky Bob's) around August 17th and were heading east over Fall River Pass. Around 1:00 or 2:00 p.m., a thunderstorm came up. Dr. Dillingham was walking and leading a horse ridden by his son. They were a short distance ahead of the rest of the party when lightning struck. Dr. Dillingham and the horse were killed instantly, and the boy, who was probably insulated by the saddle, was knocked unconscious.

A couple days before this accident, the Colorado Mountain Club was in the area with the intention of setting up a camp in Willow Park in Fall River Canyon. The group had left their existing camp at Shipler Park, north of Squeaky Bob's, when a hard hailstorm caused the pack train to stampede helter-skelter. It took two days to find all the animals and gear and restore order. On the 17th, Dr. Max Giesecke and Dr. V.C. (Clyde) Smedley, both of Denver, left the Willow Park camp on horseback to travel west and meet the newly reconstituted pack train. They were near Fall River Pass when lightning struck close by. This was the lightning that killed Dr. Dillingham, as they discovered 15 minutes later.

At the scene, the boy was just regaining consciousness and crying. His right foot was caught under the dead horse, so that he could not get up. Giesecke and Smedley released the boy, and then attempted artificial respiration on Dr. Dillingham without success. Dillingham had been found lying partly under the horse's feet. He had probably been leading the horse with his left hand, as the hand was badly burned. The rest of the party came along and were told what happened, then went directly down to Estes Park, as more lightning seemed imminent. The pack train supporting the

Colorado Mountain Club eventually came along. Shep Husted wrapped the body of Dr. Dillingham in a tent and packed it down to Estes Park.

The next incident occurred August 1, 1922. Greeley resident Jesse E. Kitts, age 22, was struck by lightning on the summit of Longs Peak at approximately 12:30 p.m. and killed instantly. Joe Bullas of Topeka, Kansas, was knocked unconscious and severely burned at the same time. They were standing within a few feet of the summit cairn when the thunderstorm came up. The first stroke of lightning struck Kitts and burned off half his clothes. Bullas was knocked unconscious and his head was badly seared and his shoes burned off his feet. Other hikers tried to revive Bullas, but failed, and then went to the Longs Peak Inn for help. Chief Ranger Allen rushed to the summit with Dr. Wiest. By this time, Bullas had miraculously regained consciousness and was working his way off the summit barefoot. Allen and Wiest dressed Bullas' injuries and helped him down. Superintendent Roger Toll formed a rescue party to remove Kitt's body. They did not return until 4:00 o'clock the following morning.

There was a space of thirty years before the next lightning fatality occurred in the park. On August 15, 1956, Mrs. Rena Hoffman, age 33, was on a day hike with her husband and another couple from Chicago, Illinois, Mr. and Mrs. Paul Hartrich. They had lodged at the YMCA for a week. About 2:30 p.m., the two couples were on the Timberline Ridge, just east of Chasm Lake, when an electrical storm struck. Rena Hoffman was struck dead, and Mr. Hoffman was knocked unconscious. Mr. and Mrs. Hartrich suffered only minor injuries and sent an unidentified hiker down to the Longs Peak Ranger Station for help. Ranger Dunbar Susong returned and unsuccessfully attempted artificial respiration for about an hour on Rena Hoffman.

The next two deaths by lightning occurred along roadways in the park. On August 6, 1964, 46-year-old Leola H. Swain of Archie, Missouri, stood on the retaining wall at Medicine Bow Curve on Trail Ridge Road. Remember the warnings listed above from the National Weather Service? Don't be the highest object around! Swain was struck and killed by a bolt of lightning. Her husband Fred was about 100 feet away and was unhurt.

In another incident on Trail Ridge Road, 17-year-old Barbara Gully of Farmington Hills, Michigan, was on an outing with her family. On July 1, 1974, at approximately 1:00 p.m., lightning struck her near the Lava Cliffs parking area. She was taken to the Alpine Visitor Center, and then flown to a Denver hospital. Sadly, she died at 5:45 the following morning.

Many visitors are exposed to lightning on Trail Ridge Road, but they have the option to retreat to the safety of their vehicles. Thus, only two of the eleven lightning fatalities were along roadways. The remaining four fatalities were again in backcountry settings. On August 24, 1979, Boulder, Colorado, resident Andrew W. Paton, age 15, was killed by lightning above treeline on Twin Sisters.

On June 28, 1992, 31-year-old Glenn R. McDonald of Troy, Ohio, and Wayne Smart, 51, of Boulder, Colorado, completed a climb on Hallett's Chimney, a technical climbing route on the 12,713-foot Hallett Peak. The two climbers were descending along a ridge above treeline when McDonald was struck around 9:00 p.m. Smart was not injured because the two climbers separated themselves due to the lightning threat. Smart reached the trailhead at Bear Lake and notified park rangers at approximately 2:30 a.m. Monday. McDonald's body was removed by helicopter that afternoon.

There are times when lightning travels horizontally many miles away from the thunderstorm cloud. The National Weather Service refers to these types of lightning flashes as "bolts from the blue" because they seem to come out of a clear blue sky. Although these flashes are rare, they have caused fatalities.

While the weather was not perfectly clear at the time, lightning did not seem imminent in yet another one of those incidents that just makes you wonder why. John Retting, age 35, was killed by lightning on July 21, 1999. The Retting family was from Brooklyn, New York. John Retting was carrying his young daughter in a child backpack. Retting, his wife, and other family members were hiking approximately one-half mile west of the Alpine Visitor Center when they were struck by lightning. John Retting was killed instantly. Amazingly, his daughter in the backpack survived despite suffering burns and wounds. Retting's wife was stunned, but did not lose consciousness. A family member took the daughter to the visitor center for first aid and to notify rangers. Ranger staff responded immediately and performed CPR on John Retting for 50 minutes without success.

In a similar incident just three weeks later, lightning struck Michael Hines, age 35. August 7, 1999, dawned bright and beautiful. Hines was part of a church group hiking the Cow Creek Trail from McGraw Ranch to Bridal Veil Falls. Along the way, the group mingled with the Karnes family from Arlington, Texas, who were enjoying a family reunion at the Lane Guest Ranch in the Tahosa Valley. Sharing stories and idle banter back and forth, they noted clouds gathering to the west and heard thunder, but there was no rain or sense of danger where they were in the semi-wooded valley, well below treeline. On the return hike near the Gem Lake trail junction, lightning struck the group about 1:00 p.m. Michael Hines was struck directly and was unconscious and not breathing. Members of the two groups immediately started CPR, but they were unsuccessful in reviving Hines. Another member of the group, Bryant Karnes, 17, stood three to five feet from Hines when the lightning struck and then traveled through the ground to melt the tops of his socks. Karnes was knocked down and had no feeling in his legs, but did not lose consciousness. A third victim in the group was Linda Lloyd of Ft. Collins. She was able to walk out to the trailhead on her own and refused treatment. Rangers evacuated Karnes to the Estes Park Medical Center for observation before being released. Bryant's mother, Susan Karnes, later said "I don't know why Bryant was spared. We're trying to make sense of something that is pretty senseless."

Yes, lightning is senseless and indiscriminate, as in the unusual death of climber Andy Haberkorn on July 12, 2000. The 28-year-old Boulder, Colorado, resident was climbing with Stan Smigel on the Casual Route on the Diamond of Longs Peak. Smigel and Haberkorn got a 3:00 a.m. start from the Longs Peak Trailhead. They stashed gear below Mills Glacier and made good time on their climb. About 2:30 p.m., the weather deteriorated, with a storm cloud in the area and increased winds. Considering their location,

the two climbers elected to continue up the route. Smigel had been leading the climb and was belaying Haberkorn on a crux 5.10 pitch around
3:00 p.m. when there was a "bright flash of light," but no sound.

Smigel felt Haberkorn fall and immediately arrested the falling climber
below him. Haberkorn told Smigel that he thought he had been struck by
lightning, but he wasn't very coherent. Smigel lowered Haberkorn 40 feet
to the Yellow Wall Bivouac Ledge and yelled at him to clip into an anchor,
but Haberkorn didn't seem to understand what he was being told. In ar-
ranging his equipment to rappel to Haberkorn, Smigel felt him fall again,
and he again arrested the fall. He then tied the rope holding Haberkorn to
an anchor and rappelled down to assist him. This took almost ten minutes. When Smigel reached Haberkorn, he was hanging from his harness,
face up, with arms and legs sprawled out. He was blue in color, with no
pulse or respirations. Smigel recalled that he struck Haberkorn in the chest
twice, but could not do CPR because of their positions on the vertical face.

During this time, Smigel had been yelling for help. His calls were
heard by campers in the Boulderfield, who hiked over to the Chasm View
overlook. They used a cell phone to contact the park dispatch office and
report the accident. In turn, they were able to yell across the chasm to
Smigel that a helicopter was en route. Smigel told them it was no use, in-
ferring that Haberkorn was dead, and rappelled to Mills Glacier to retrieve his gear. He later met a ranger on the Longs Peak Trail and was
escorted to the Incident Command Post.

That afternoon around 5:50 p.m., rangers Bill Alexander and Mark
Ronca did a reconnaissance flight of the climbing route in a contract helicopter. They observed Haberkorn hanging motionless from a rope in the
position described above. By 6:07 p.m., they landed in the Boulderfield
and interviewed the hikers who had called in on the cell phone. An hour
later, Alexander and Ronca went to the top of the Camel formation and observed Haberkorn for 15 minutes through binoculars. Based on witness
statements and the lack of any movement in the body position, it was determined that Haberkorn was deceased. At this time, the rangers also recommended to the Incident Commander that Haberkorn's body be

removed by raising him to the summit and flying his body off with a helicopter. This incident helps illustrate the complexity of rescue operations.

The following morning, a briefing was held at 6:00 a.m. Assignments were made and gear was organized. By 8:00 a.m., the first three rangers were flown to the summit of Longs Peak to begin the recovery phase of the incident. Nine people would be flown to the summit to manage the rope systems for the recovery. Rangers Alexander and Ronca would be the investigators/recovery team lowered over the edge of the Diamond wall. As the morning progressed, fixed lines and anchor points were placed but the weather again deteriorated with winds and hail. As lightning was again a strong possibility, the recovery team was flown off the summit of Longs Peak back to the Upper Beaver Meadows heliport.

On the morning of the 14th, the team was again flown to the summit of Longs Peak. Building on the rope work completed the previous day, Alexander rappelled the 200 feet from the Casual Route/Table Ledge belay location down to Haberkorn. Alexander noted that Haberkorn was in the same position as before with his body suspended from his harness in a downward supine position. His head was extended back and both arms extended and hanging down. Alexander noted what appeared to be an electrical injury as there was a small burned area of skin centered on the sternum. After securing Haberkorn to the belay and haul lines, Alexander jumared back to the Yellow Wall Bivouac Ledge where Ronca provided a belay for him. Haberkorn was then raised by the support team to Alexander and Ronca's location. They placed Haberkorn into a skid litter and it was raised the rest of the way to the summit. By 4:00 p.m., Haberkorn's body had been flown off the summit and turned over to the Boulder County Coroner. By 6:10 p.m., all personnel and equipment had been flown off the summit of Longs Peak and all climbing routes reopened.

Lightning is common in the Colorado high country during summer, and this period in July was particularly unsettled. As noted in the warnings listed earlier, lightning usually strikes the summit or protruding points on ridges. Also, lightning normally strikes the leader or higher individual in a group. It is difficult to explain why Andy Haberkorn was struck and

Smigel was unaffected, or why there apparently was no thunder clap or sound associated with the strike. Considering the circumstances, rangers commended Smigel for his efforts in tending to Haberkorn and getting off the Diamond alone under difficult conditions.

In concluding this chapter, I offer a second chance incident where experience and good judgment contributed to two ladies' success. On September 4, 1923, Ethel Ridenour, from Kansas City, and a Miss Edwards, a doctor friend from New York City, were hiking among the rocks at the base of Longs Peak when a severe electrical storm came on quickly. Being familiar with mountain conditions, Ridenour suggested to Dr. Edwards that they separate in the event one of them should be struck by lightning, then the other could render assistance. Dr. Edwards apparently did not give much thought to the suggestion, but Ridenour insisted. They had only gone a few steps when a lightning bolt struck and knocked them both unconscious. The bolt struck Ridenour on the left side of her head and went down her spine and out her feet. The lightning's path was marked on her body by broad burned streaks. All breathing and heart action ceased. All of Dr. Edwards' clothing was shredded by the electrical blast, but she quickly regained consciousness. Still dazed, she at once started artificial respiration on Ridenour and began screaming for help. By sheer miracle, Ridenour regained consciousness and survived. The fact that Ridenour insisted they separate a distance while hiking undoubtedly contributed to the survival of both women.

Lightning

June 21, 1896	Alexander Q. MacGregor, 50	Struck while prospecting with his son on ridge *above treeline east of Poudre Lake.*
August 17, 1914	Dr. Dillingham, age unknown	Heading east *above treeline over Fall River Pass.* Struck while walking and leading a horse, which was also killed. Rider of the horse survived.
August 1, 1922	Jesse E. Kitts, 22	Struck while on the *summit of Longs Peak* and died instantly.

August 15, 1956	Mrs. Rena Hoffman, 33	Struck while hiking along the *Timberline Ridge east of Chasm Lake*.
August 6, 1964	Leola H. Swain, 46	Struck while standing on the retaining wall at *Medicine Bow Curve on Trail Ridge Road*.
July 1, 1974	Barbara Gully, 17	Struck near the *Lava Cliffs parking area* on Trail Ridge Road.
August 24, 1979	Andrew W. Paton, 15	Struck while *above timberline on Twin Sisters*.
June 28, 1992	Glen R. McDonald, 31	After successful *Hallet Peak* climb, struck while descending along ridge *above treeline*.
July 21, 1999	John Retting, 35	Struck while hiking above timberline *west of Alpine Visitor Center*. Infant daughter in child pack survived.
August 7, 1999	Michael Hines, 35	Struck by "bolt from the blue" while hiking below treeline on the *Bridal Veil Falls Trail*.
July 20, 2000	Andy Haberkorn, 28	Climber struck while on the Casual Route on the *Longs Peak Diamond*.

TWELVE
Snow Play
Incidents

Winter sports such as skiing, tubing, and sledding are heaps of fun. The problem is that speed and gravity play major roles in drawing the thin line between having a great time and being out of control on a snow slope. This is particularly true with tubing and sledding. Most participants don't practice the activity, and only enjoy the sport once or twice a winter, so they are not in tune to the potential danger.

As with many things in life, moderation is the key. But it sure looks like fun as participants squeal with delight when they bounce and fly down a slope! In reality, these snow play sports are high risk activities. While there have been a number of injuries over the years, fortunately, there have only been five fatalities, as recounted below.

On Sunday morning, June 26, 1927, Miss Flora Napier became the park's first sledding fatality in what was actually an early summer incident. Napier was 38 years old and a stenographer with the Continental Oil Company in Denver. The day before, a large party of employees from the oil company, known as the Conoco Club, came up to Estes Park and stayed at the Cascade Lodge in Horseshoe Park. On the morning of the 26th, a group of about 25, guided by Irvin Dawson from the lodge, went up the Hidden Valley Trail on horseback to a point just below timberline, where some large snow banks remained. This was probably in the upper Hidden Valley area where the current Trail Ridge Road crosses the creek.

(Remember, Trail Ridge Road or the Hidden Valley Ski Area didn't exist at the time.) The group hauled a toboggan with them and were soon sliding on fast runs down the slope.

As they took turns with four or five people to the toboggan, the group perfected a method to stop on a level stretch of snow before a sharper descent into a patch of timber. At a command, all the sledders leaned to one side and the individual at the rear would fall off. This person held the rope attached to the front of the toboggan and essentially served as an anchor in the snow.

On the fatal run, Irwin Dawson sat in the rear with Napier in front of him. At the moment Dawson discharged himself from the back of the sled, he noticed the rope was wound around Napier's arm. He later recalled that his first thought was that he would break her arm if he pulled on the rope. In that moment of hesitation, the rope slipped through his hands, and the toboggan failed to lose its momentum. It slid another 100 feet, turned on its side, and struck a tree. The four remaining occupants of the toboggan, including Flora Napier, were knocked unconscious. All but Napier regained consciousness.

A member of the party jumped on a horse and galloped five miles back to Horseshoe Park, where he notified ranger R.V. Dondanville at 11:45 a.m. Dondanville notified the superintendent's office and Dr. Henry Reid in Estes Park. Rangers Dondanville, Allen, and Garrison met Dr. Reid and his assistant, Dr. Bonesteel, and others at the end of the automobile road in Hidden Valley and hiked up the trail. After about a mile, they met the group carrying Napier on the toboggan. Napier had a pulse and was breathing, but had not regained consciousness. Dr. Reid and Dr. Bonesteel tried unsuccessfully to restore Napier's consciousness. She was then carried on a stretcher to the automobiles, but died on the way to Estes Park. Her skull was fractured, her left arm broken in two places, her hip was probably broken, and her left ankle was broken.

Fifty-eight years later, another individual died in winter recreation. On February 3, 1985, 21-year-old Scott T. Anderson, a Mason City, Iowa, resident, died in a skiing accident at Hidden Valley Ski Area. Anderson was described as an intermediate skier. He and his brother spent the morning skiing the lower part of the mountain below Trail Ridge Road. In the afternoon, they decided to try the main run on the upper slope, which was considered an expert run. Several skiers near the loading ramp for the T-bar lift saw Anderson skiing extremely fast and out of control, as if he didn't know how to stop or brake at the speed he was going. These witnesses stated that he shot over the loading ramp, flew over fifty feet in the air, and landed on the surface of Trail Ridge Road. (In those days, the road was plowed to the upper slope and a bus shuttled skiers up to the lift.)

The Ski Patrol arrived immediately and found Anderson unconscious, but breathing. His breathing soon stopped, and CPR was initiated as Anderson was transported to the Estes Park Medical Center, where he was pronounced dead. Anderson was the only skiing fatality in the 36-year (1955–1991) history of Hidden Valley Ski Area.

Tragedy struck a Longmont, Colorado, family on January 24, 1988, when wife and mother Brenda K. Butrick, age 30, died from traumatic head injuries resulting from a tubing accident. She was tubing with her husband and two children on a hill just east of the Beaver Meadows Entrance Station. The Butrick family intended to go up to Bear Lake, where they had tubed before, but saw others enjoying this area and decided to stop. After a number of runs, Brenda Butrick made a run by herself, during which she slid head-first into a tree. Other sledders in the area went for help at the Beaver Meadows Entrance Station. Rangers and an ambulance responded, and Butrick was taken to the Estes Park Medical Center, where she was pronounced dead.

In another tubing accident, Omar Mehdawi, age 17, was critically injured at Bear Lake. On February 27, 2005, Mehdawi had come up to Bear Lake with friends from the Islamic Center in Ft. Collins to play on the snow and ice. Mehdawi was a popular senior at Rocky Mountain High School in Ft. Collins. He was shorter than most of his classmates, but excelled in indoor soccer and basketball. He planned to attend Colorado State University to study electrical engineering.

It was the first time Mehdawi had been tubing. The group first tubed on the north side of the lake, but later moved to a steeper, less used area on the southwest side of the lake. It was also narrower and more dangerous. Mehdawi was one of the first to try the new slope. Sadly, he gained too much speed, lost control, and then slid into a tree and struck his head. Five rangers responded to the accident scene and immediately recognized the seriousness of his injuries. Mehdawi was unconscious with labored breathing and had likely sustained a closed head injury. Speed was critical in getting Mehdawi to a hospital, and a helicopter was ordered through the dispatch office. While Mehdawi was being stabilized, rangers kept his friends busy foot packing a firm helicopter landing pad on the snow and ice on the lake. They elected to have the St. Anthony's Flight for Life helicopter land on the ice at Bear Lake. This type of ice landing had only been done a few times before on a rescue in the park, but reflected the nimble risk assessment all rescuers need to make. It was the right decision. The helicopter landed and flew Mehdawi to Poudre Valley Hospital in Ft. Collins. Unfortunately, he did not regain consciousness. He was pronounced brain dead and removed from life support a week later on March 5, 2005.

Mehdawi and his family were part of the small, tightly knit Islamic community in Ft. Collins. Though Omar was born in Ft. Collins, many of his friends since childhood did not have a true sense of the strength of his Islamic faith. In the aftermath of his death, the Mehdawi family became the comforters to many of Omar's friends. While deeply saddened by the loss of Omar, his family showed remarkable strength through their acceptance of Omar's fatal collision as God's will. In the Fort Collins *Coloradoan*, teacher Mike Dyer and principal Tom Lopez reflected that "Omar's death had been a positive learning experience for many students and staff who were unfamiliar with the Islamic culture and traditions."

In a late summer incident, 40-year-old Matthew Chesaux of Boulder, Colorado, died while attempting a solo ski down Taylor Glacier, between Taylor and Powell Peaks along the Continental Divide. Chesaux apparently had a goal of skiing every month of the year. On the evening of September 30, 2008, the park dispatch office was notified by concerned friends that Chesaux was overdue from his planned one day ski trip. An initial search began that night centering on probable trailheads and confirmed that his vehicle was parked and unoccupied at Glacier Gorge Trailhead. Rangers began a search the next morning. His body was found near the bottom of the steep face of Taylor Glacier and lifted out by helicopter that afternoon.

The high alpine snow fields are particularly dangerous during this time of year. The previous winter's snows had melted off by late autumn, leaving exposed the hard pack ice formations underneath, often referred to as "black ice." These surfaces are littered with rock debris and are very slick. Chesaux was skiing alone, and his fall was not witnessed, but it appeared he fell and slid a considerable distance.

THIRTEEN

Lost

Lost, and never found

The park usually gives up its dead. Sometimes it takes a few months. In the case of the Reverend Thornton Sampson, it took seventeen years for his remains to be found. It was also roughly seventeen years before the bones of "Billy Bones" were found, though we still don't know who he was. The same can be said for the unidentified skull found above Lost Lake in 1927. The following are short vignettes of four individuals who are still missing in the park's backcountry and presumed to be dead.

Joseph L. Halpern, age 22, was a University of Chicago doctoral student from Chicago, Illinois. According to his father, he was writing a thesis titled "Meteors and Shooting Stars." Joseph Halpern was camping with his parents and a college friend, Samuel Garrick, in Glacier Basin Campground. On the morning of August 15, 1933, Halpern and Garrick drove to Bear Lake and hiked from Bear Lake to the summit of Flattop Mountain and on to the head of Tyndall Glacier. According to the report by Chief Ranger John McLaughlin, around 2:00 p.m. a fellow camper from the campground ran into Halpern and Garrick west of the summit of Hallett Peak. This hiker had come up through Loch Vale and Andrews Glacier. Apparently, Halpern was interested in going to the summit of Taylor Peak, and the hiker mistakenly pointed out the Chiefs Head Peak as being Taylor Peak. According to Garrick, Halpern said he wanted to return by Taylor Peak and Andrews Glacier to Loch Vale and thence to Bear Lake. They parted company around 2:30 p.m., with Garrick heading back down the Flattop Mountain Trail and Halpern hiking southeast towards Andrews Glacier. When Halpern failed to return to Bear Lake by 9:00 p.m., Garrick reported the incident to temporary ranger Bradford at the Bear Lake Ranger Station. Several rangers searched that evening with no success. The following day, a large search was initiated, but ultimately it proved unsuccessful.

The search involved dozens of searchers, with the same key areas gone over extensively several times. Chief Ranger McLaughlin suspended the search the evening of August 21st. Ranger Jack Moomaw wrote in *Recollections of a Rocky Mountain Ranger*, "It was a matter of wandering in a general direction over the boulder fields, and anyone who has seen this country knows that a hundred men might search the entire region for an entire summer and still miss an object as small as a man lying down." No trace of Joseph Halpern has ever been found.

A more disturbing incident occurred on October 9, 1949. Dale Devitt, age 21, of Arvada, Colorado, and Bruce Gerling, 20, of Phoenix, Arizona, were part of a group of eighteen Colorado A&M (Colorado State University) students on an Aggies Hiking Club outing. Devitt and Gerling hoped to qualify for membership into the club on this trip. Thirteen students, including Gerling and Devitt, drove to Grand Lake via Trail Ridge Road and planned to hike back over to Bear Lake by way of Flattop Mountain on the North Inlet Trail. The other five students left from Bear Lake to hike in the opposite direction. Both groups met at the North Inlet ranger cabin.

Following a discussion of the deteriorating weather conditions, eleven members of the eastbound group decided to continue on to Bear Lake. These men were known to be experienced mountain climbers and advised Gerling and Devitt to turn back to Grand Lake and return to Ft. Collins with the westbound group. Initially they agreed, but apparently changed their minds after the westbound group left. After resting, it appears they unsuccessfully tried to catch up with the eastbound group. Both groups thought Gerling and Devitt were with the other group.

After waiting a while at Grand Lake, that group of five returned to Ft. Collins via Berthoud Pass because Trail Ridge Road was closed due to blowing snow. They did not arrive in Ft. Collins until 3:00 a.m. Monday morning. It was not until the hiking club got together Monday afternoon in Ft. Collins that they realized that Devitt and Gerling were missing. It was then that they notified the National Park Service. Tuesday morning, a twenty person search party of rangers and A&M students struggled in poor visibility against blowing, drifting snow. On the 13th, fifteen men from the Camp Carson 14th Regimental Combat Team joined the search effort. Trail Ridge Road was closed from Sunday night, the 9th, until Thursday, the 13th, due to snow and wind.

During this period, a west wind averaging 80 mph blew down thousands of trees and blocked or obliterated twenty-five miles of trails. Rangers Fred McLaren and Hugh Elbert coordinated the search from the Grand Lake side. Assistant Chief Ranger Ernst Fields coordinated the overall search, which covered seven days and involved over 1,000 man hours in near blizzard conditions. Despite intensive searches over the succeeding years, no trace of the boys has ever been found.

The most recent disappearance occurred on February 19, 1983, when Rudi Moder, a 27-year-old backcountry skier was lost. Of this incident, ranger Charlie Logan wrote in the 1984 edition of *Accidents in North American Mountaineering*:

> On February 13, 1983, Rudi Moder, 27, departed the Zimmerman Lake Trailhead on Colorado Highway 14 near Cameron Pass for a two to three night ski mountaineering trip over Thunder Pass and down into the Ditch Camp 3 area of Rocky Mountain National Park. According to his friends, Moder was planning to take day trips from a base camp he planned to establish in the area. He was last seen by friends in the Zimmerman Lake area that morning, as he headed up alone, while his friends skied back to the trailhead. Moder, a West German, was described as an experienced winter mountaineer, with two years experience in the German Army Mountain Corps and two Himalayan expeditions, very fit, and a strong ski mountaineer.
>
> On February 19th, Hans Moosmueller, Moder's roommate, reported that Moder was overdue to the Larimer County Sheriff's Office. Search plans and further investigation were initiated, and search teams were in the field early on February 20th.
>
> A food cache belonging to Moder was found at the mouth of Box Canyon, in the extreme northwest corner of the park. On February

Helicopters unload searchers in Box Canyon on Moder search. Photo courtesy of Ray Miller

*21st, a snow cave was found about 45 feet from the food cache. Only
a small hole was evident due to heavy snow on the 19th. These were
the only positive clues found during the intensive four day search.*
Moder is still missing and presumed dead.

Lost … and found. Yep, alive!

In the introduction to this book, I promised to sprinkle in some success
stories of those who were given a second chance and survived their or-
deals. We can learn just as much from the actions of those who survived,
as those who died.

I use the term "SAR" to describe an incident of searching for a missing person(s) or a rescue of someone found. Therein lies the key difference,
in that a rescue can follow a search, once the victim is found, but rarely
does a search follow a rescue. The other key difference is the obvious tac-
tics deployed. The benefit of a rescue is that you know where the person
is, their condition, and the general area of the park, all of which dictates
the response. In a search, the SAR team tries to find someone in a general
area. It is not easy—in fact, it is extraordinary how difficult, frustrating,

Fire, Lost Hikers Reported

Lost hikers and a minor fire near Sheep Lakes kept Rocky Mountain National Park rangers busy over the weekend.

Ranger Tom Morgan extinguished the fire, which was in a tree stump, with a hand extinguisher.

Rangers searched for a missing nine-year-old girl, Karelle Tauger, who became separated from her hiking group in the area of the junction of the Lawn Lake and Ypsilon Lake trails on Saturday afternoon.

They located the missing girl approximately one hour after she was reported mssing and returned her to her group.

Friday evening backcountry rangers, with help from the St. Anthony's Flight for Life helicopter, assisted three young girls from the YMCA of the Rockies who had become stranded on technical terrain southeast of Lake of Glass.

The girls, none of whom was injured, were lowered to safer ground after the helicopter transported rescue personnel and equipment to their location.

On Sunday an injured girl named Shirley Rabner was transported to Elizabeth Knutsson Memorial Hospital with burns received after having hot water poured on her.

A Park employe transported the girl from the Moraine Park Campground.

Ms. Rabner was transferred from EKMH to the Boulder Community Hospital with first and second degree burns, and she was listed in satisfactory condition Tuesday.

Typical summer weekend in RMNP, July 22, 1981. Courtesy of Estes Park *Trail Gazette*.

and draining a major search can be for the park staff. Such was the exhausted state of the staff, and particularly the ranger division, after the Jeff Christensen search in August 2005. Yet barely 3 weeks later, the park dispatch office received an afternoon cell phone call from Hillel Ben-Avi, who said he was lost in the Mummy Range. This was in the same area where the park staff had just spent eight days looking for Jeff Christensen.

Hillel Ben-Avi was a 45-year-old radiologist from Austin, Texas, who was hiking with his brother Doran Ben-Avi. They frequently hiked together and had been to Rocky Mountain National Park a half dozen times, but had never hiked in the Mummy Range. While ranger Christensen had started his hike from Chapin Pass on the Old Fall River Road, the Ben-Avi brothers came up the Lawn Lake Trail, passed Lawn Lake and Crystal Lake, and headed toward the summit of 13,502-foot Fairchild Mountain. Being the stronger hiker, Hillel was ahead of his brother and was near the summit of Fairchild when Doran last saw him. When Doran himself reached the summit, he found no sign of his brother. As it turns out, when Hillel had seen his brother so far behind on the climb up Fairchild, he decided to descend rather than wait for his brother—thus violating one of the basic safety rules of backcountry travel: stay together!

Hillel descended too far to the west and apparently missed the saddle that would have taken him back toward Lawn Lake. Realizing he was lost, he called his wife in Texas on his cell phone, and she gave him a park phone number. He contacted the park at 4:30 p.m., and again a half hour later before his phone battery faded. The only information he could offer was that he hiked by three lakes and summited Fairchild Mountain. Thinking Hillel had dropped in to the Fay Lakes area, an initial search party headed there that evening, but without success. The days were warm, but the evening temperatures in late August were near freezing at that elevation. It had also been determined that Hillel had limited clothing and food, as the brothers had only planned to be out for the day.

On Sunday, August 28, 2005, the search effort accelerated, and again on the 29th. By the morning of August 30th, over a hundred searchers from the park staff, Larimer County Search and Rescue, Rocky Mountain Rescue Group, Alpine Rescue Group, Front Range SAR dogs, SAR dogs of Colorado, and 2 helicopters combed the area. Over 20 searchers camped in the backcountry near Lawn Lake and Fey Lakes to save time getting into the search area. Finally, on Wednesday, the 31st, rangers spotted Hillel from a helicopter. He was above treeline in the Hague Creek drainage, northwest of the Fairchild Mountain summit. When he realized he was lost, Hillel wisely stayed where he was. He was picked up and flown out to an ambulance at Upper Beaver Meadows. Before returning to Texas, Hillel repeatedly thanked the search teams and offered that "this instance has not soured me on walking around in God's country. It's not going to stop me from hiking; I'll just go about it a little safer." With a second chance, we certainly hope so.

An earlier search incident also took place in the Mummy Range. Retired ranger

> **Safety Lessons:**
> 1. **Stay together,** particularly if hiking in unfamiliar terrain.
> 2. **Always carry at least minimal overnight gear and food.**
> 3. **If lost, stay put.** It is rarely a good idea to try and rescue yourself.

Doug Ridley and I collaborated on the following story, which was published in the 2007 edition of *Oh, Ranger! True Stories from our National Parks.*

While outside pressures have no effect on the missing subject, they can indirectly influence search urgency. Concern from relatives and demands from the media sometimes create an unwelcome burden—an overriding level of stress. The longer an incident lasts, the more public interest is generated. A consequence of this publicity is that more of the unusual offers for assistance or advice come in, such as palm readers, clairvoyants, and anyone with a sixth sense or premonition. Frequently, as Chief Ranger, I intercepted these contacts, so as not to distract the field rangers from running the SAR incident. Over the years, I thought I had seen and heard it all. With this in mind, I looked with suspicion at the telephone receiver in my hand. I was told I was on hold for the White House. My first thought was that my ranger staff was up to another of their practical jokes … or was the White House really on the line?

It was August 11, 1995, and we were in the second day of a search for Hayley Green in the Mummy Range. Rocky Mountain National Park's mountainous panorama, glacial moraines, and tundra covering one-third of the alpine high country, beckon over three million visitors annually. The more vigorous outdoor enthusiasts leave their automobiles behind to climb and hike the trails, seek solace and self fulfillment among the peaks, and push themselves to dizzying heights, far from civilization, roads, and even established trails.

It was just such an experience that Cheley Camp employee Hayley Green sought. At 16 years of age, Hayley came from her home in Tennessee to work at the eastside youth camp in the summer of 1995. She enjoyed hiking the trails, bagging peaks, and showing the boys at camp she could keep up. An unwritten rite of passage among the guys challenged employees worth their salt to accomplish what is known as "The Mummy Kill." A successful Mummy Kill requires a solo hiker to traverse the Mummy Range, including the six summits of Chapin, Chiquita, Ypsilon, Fairchild, Hagues, and Mummy Mountains, all in one day. The average height of these peaks is 13,255 feet! This 16-mile, cross-country trip is not to be taken lightly. Physical strength and stamina are required. Map and compass skills, along with an ability to travel long hours in steep terrain in the dark, are absolute necessities. By August, Hayley Green was ready. She was physically fit, possessed the necessary survival gear, and she understood the challenges of route finding … or so she thought.

On August 10, 1995, at 6:30 a.m., the dispatch office received an overdue party notification from James Green of Nashville, Tennessee. A two-day search in rugged terrain was about to begin for Hayley Green. When the phone rang at the Bighorn Ranger Station, district ranger Doug Ridley was apprised of the overdue report. Hayley had departed Chapin Pass Trailhead the day before, alone and in the dark, at 3:30 a.m., intent on completing the Mummy Kill. Her visiting parents had camped out in the Roaring River drainage, anticipating her appearance after the hike. She didn't arrive. They waited beside the trail in sleeping bags until first light, and then hiked out to contact a ranger.

Determining search urgency is based on many factors, including terrain hazards, subject profile, experience, available equipment, and weather. As Ridley arrived at the operations center, he assumed the role of incident commander, a search team of one. With the information available, he placed the Green search on the urgent side of the scale. The terrain was horrible, she carried limited equipment for multiple nights out, her knowledge of the area was questionable, and she was alone! The weather factor was the remaining catalyst for an urgent response. The day before had been typical for August, late afternoon thunder and lightning, gusty winds, and snow and hail above 12,000 feet.

Ridley gathered an incident command team to manage the incident. He then activated several field teams to the point where Haley was last seen, to retrace her steps. They searched her intended path and keyed on areas where previous cross-country hikers had become disoriented. Field teams concentrated on the Roaring River Trail, Chapin Pass to the summit of Mt. Ypsilon, and egress points toward Mt. Fairchild, the most difficult part of the traverse. This took time. A Forest Service helicopter conducted three sorties, flying the intended travel route and inserting teams for positioning. The search team now numbered 45.

Most of the 200 annual SAR incidents are resolved within the first 24 hours. We were not so lucky. Despite the best efforts of rangers in the field, search dogs, helicopter pilots, observers, and command personnel, Hayley was nowhere to be found. Ridley's command staff segmented the search area and brainstormed all possibilities for Hayley's location. Fortified with take-out pizza and hot coffee, they settled in for a night of planning and speculation. The next morning came quickly. Seventy-five searchers were now engaged in the effort. The helicopter was temporarily grounded due to weather. Field teams deployed with instructions to stay out all night if necessary.

It was about this time, while I was working in my office, that the phone rang. Kris in dispatch said she was forwarding a call from the White House. A moment later a no-nonsense voice said, "This is the White House; please hold for the Vice President." Three things went through my mind: 1) What's Ridley up to now? 2) Who is this, really? and 3) Dang, what if it is the White House! As it turned out, the Gore family was close personal friends of the Greens in Tennessee. The Vice President was calling to offer any necessary assistance and, shall we say, unbridled encouragement.

A few minutes later, I walked down to the incident command post and asked to speak to Doug privately outside. I explained that I had just talked to Vice President Gore in the White House. They wanted to make sure this one has a favorable outcome. "Yeah right Chief, that's a good one," he said.

"I'm not making this up!" I replied, as Doug searched my face for a hint of a smile.

You see, humor is often used in the ranger ranks to relieve tension, especially in a situation like this. Rangers love a good scam, and Doug was most upset because he hadn't thought of calling my office and claiming to be the White House! Once Doug realized I was serious, we agreed that I would run interference with the White House as needed, and we would rely on the talented professionals we had in the field to find the missing girl. One remaining concern was whether or not to relate the White House connection to the incident team. Doug and I decided against it for the time being. The field teams had enough to worry about without this.

Fortunately, it wasn't long before we received welcome news. To the relief of family, friends, and, I'm sure, Vice President Gore, Hayley Green was located deep in the Hague's Creek drainage that afternoon. Searchers, directed by the helicopter, heard a shrieking whistle and followed it to Hayley's location at treeline. She told her story at the debriefing. A hail storm forced her to abandon Ypsilon Ridge and seek shelter in the trees. She selected what seemed to be the safest descent, but one that drew her northwest toward Desolation Peaks, away from the primary search area.

To her credit, Hayley Green did what lost people are supposed to do.

She hunkered down in one spot, used pieces of clothing to signal the helicopter, and carried enough gear to survive two cold, wet nights alone in the Rocky Mountain wilderness.

Oh, and we asked the Greens to convey our thanks to the Vice President for his concern.

In a rare case where self rescue successfully worked out, John Dalie walked into the Meeker Park Campground along Highway 7 six days later and sixty pounds lighter than when he disappeared on Longs Peak on August 22, 1954. Dalie was a first year law student at Denver University and an avid hiker. August 22nd was a Sunday outing for 32 members of the Colorado Mountain Club. Dalie climbed the 14,259-foot Longs Peak for the first time by the standard Cables Route. He later told *The Denver Post*, "There was a lot of hail and some snow, and I was having trouble with my eyes. When I got to the top, I looked for the rest of the gang. There was no one there. I looked around for the register to put my name on it. I couldn't find it ... That was about 1:00 p.m. It was storming, and I had my knapsack. A gust of wind got hold of it and blew it over the side of the peak." In almost zero visibility, Dalie descended by a different route, most likely the Keyhole Route, and got lost. That night, with little protection above treeline, Dalie shivered among the rocks. It was not until 9:30 that same evening that members of the club realized that Dalie was missing and contacted Longs Peak ranger Bob Frauson. He and district ranger Ed Kurtz immediately organized a major search effort.

For five days, search teams crisscrossed the area. Three SA-16 search planes from nearby Lowery Air Force Base took aerial photos. Frauson and Kurtz thought Dalie might have plunged over the edge of the peak in the whiteout conditions, so the East Face of Longs was closed while climbers searched the base of the wall. After the fifth day of searching, most had given up finding Dalie alive. So it was a bit of a shock on the sixth day when Dalie walked into the Meeker Park Campground and asked, "What's been going on in the world?" Dalie later lamented, "The planes must have flown over me a dozen times. I waved my jacket, but they never saw me. I walked in high places and in low places. Up the mountain and back down."

FOURTEEN

Falls from a Horse

There have been few fatal accidents in the park caused by falls from horses. Unfortunately, for Emily Russell, Albert Furch, and Herbert Kuhn, an accident while horseback riding resulted in their demise.

Mrs. Emily Foster Russell was from Webster Grove, Missouri. On July 28, 1938, she was riding with a friend on the Deer Mountain Trail, west of the Elkhorn Lodge. As is fairly common for weather in July, a sudden rainstorm caught up with them. Her friend later reported that Russell tried to put on a rain slicker while she was still in the saddle. This spooked the horse, who threw her off, and she fractured her skull. Her friend went for help, but Emily Russell died eight hours later without ever regaining consciousness.

Forty-nine-year-old Albert W. Furch and his family, visitors from Chicago, Illinois, were staying at the Bear Lake Lodge. On July 13, 1945, he and his daughter MaryAnn were in a train of horses enjoying an outing to Loch Vale. After lunch, a storm swept through the area, and the party delayed their return to Bear Lake until the storm cleared. The *Estes Park Trail* reported that "the horses were a bit restive from the storm and the delay in going home." On the return trip, Furch's horse unexpectedly wheeled and reared on a switchback. Furch was thrown approximately 70 feet down a steep embankment and died instantly of a basal skull fracture.

Herbert D. "Pat" Kuhn, age 42, died of a cerebral vascular hemorrhage on July 24, 1969. He was on a pack trip to Lost Lake in the northeast corner of the park when he got bucked off his horse and struck his head. Pat Kuhn had lived in Colorado most of his life. In 1966, he and his family moved to Estes Park. That autumn, he purchased Buckskin Bo's Livery Stables in Glen Haven. Kuhn was active in both the Estes Park and Glen Haven communities. He was instrumental in the formation of the Glen Haven Volunteer Fire Department and served as the Fire Captain. He was survived by his wife and seven children.

FIFTEEN

Death from Above—
Falling Rocks

In such a vertical environment as Rocky Mountain National Park, falling rocks are a reality. This is particularly hazardous along some of the popular climbing routes in the park, where two or more parties may be strung out along the same route. The climbing community is generally well aware of this danger. Many climbers wear helmets and communicate between groups to shout warnings. Two of the three deaths by rock fall were caused by careless hikers, not by climbers.

In the earliest incident, 41-year-old Robert F. Smith of Indianapolis, Indiana, who was the General Manager of the American Legion Publishing Company, was instantly killed on July 18, 1932. He was struck by a falling rock at Chasm View below the North Face Cables Route on Longs Peak. Smith was in a party of six, including his wife, who had left Bear Lake at 4:00 a.m. on horseback. The party left their horses at the Boulderfield shelter and intended to go up the Cables Route with a hired guide. At approximately 11:45 a.m., they paused to enjoy the scenery at Chasm View.

Hull Cook, a climbing guide on Longs Peak in the 1930s and guide for the group, vividly recalled the incident over 60 years later in an oral history narrative:

As we progressed across the Boulderfield ... we were passed by several vigorous teenagers who were three or four hundred feet above us by the time we reached Chasm View, where everyone stopped to enjoy the spec-

tacular view across the east face. Mr. Smith was standing next to me, asking questions about the hazards that he felt were inherent in rescue work, and, although I explained that most rescues were not dangerous, he modestly expressed a lack of interest in such activities. In fact, his very last words were "I'd rather be a live coward than a dead hero."

Seconds later, as I was looking at him there was a flash of some dark object in the air above him, and most of his head just disappeared. Instantly he was on the ground, having been struck by a rock the size of a football. I jerked off my pack and laid it over his gruesome injury before Mrs. Smith could witness a macabre sight that would have tormented her memory for the rest of her life.

She at once asked about a doctor, and I had to explain that her husband was absolutely beyond all possible hope. This was to her a shockingly unfathomable fact. Seconds before, he had been standing there in the prime of his life. I waited until I saw them depart ... before shouldering the body and carrying it down.

Hull and the other guides believed the rock had been dislodged by the boys above, though it could not be proven.

In a mid-winter double fatality, 28-year-old Mark Frevert of Boulder, Colorado, and 19-year-old Colorado State University student Samuel Mitchell, from Lafayette, Louisiana, were reported missing Sunday evening, February 6, 1983. This story was briefly mentioned in chapter nine, concerning deaths by hypothermia.

Frevert and Mitchell failed to return from a Saturday climb of the Spiral Route on Notchtop Mountain. Rangers found the climbers' car at Bear Lake parking lot that evening and initiated a search. Rangers Charlie Logan and Mark Magnuson were the initial search team sent out, later followed by others rangers, along with staff from the Fantasy Ridge Climbing School, Rocky Mountain Rescue, and Larimer County Search and Rescue. At the time, the weather was described as nasty, with high winds, low visibility, and a wind chill well below zero. As Logan and Magnuson made their way up toward the descent gully on the west side of Notchtop

Mountain, the wind swept down from the gully, and they noticed small sand grain–size ice pellets that were red. This turned out to be blood. The wind scoured the accident site and swept red grains of snow and ice downhill quite a distance. Not a good sign for a search team. As they started up the descent gully, they moved just above an ice bulge and found Frevert's body. He was tied in to one end of a climbing rope, with the other end still tied to a climbing harness, but there was no other climber. Logan and Magnuson surveyed the scene and noticed fresh rock sitting on top of hard snow, indicating that the rock fall had come down from above, causing Frevert's head injuries.

The searchers also noticed faint footprints moving downhill in the direction of Lake Helene. The other searchers keyed into these leads and found Mitchell's body about 100 yards east of Lake Helene and about a mile from Frevert. Mitchell had suffered a head injury, and he had discarded a pair of wind pants, crampons, an ice axe, and a day pack in his attempt to make his way to the trailhead. Blizzard conditions hampered the investigation into the cause of the incident. The on scene evidence in-

Frevert body recovery in blizzard conditions. Courtesy of Joe Arnold

dicated that the two were struck by rock fall during their descent, as opposed to causing the rock fall themselves and tumbling down with the debris. Frevert was killed instantly. Mitchell died of hypothermia complicated by exhaustion and other serious injuries from the rock fall. They were not wearing helmets. Mitchell's body was brought out Monday evening. Blowing snow, winds up to 45 mph, and an estimated wind chill factor of 30 to 40 below zero prevented searchers from removing Frevert's body until Tuesday.

Another senseless tragedy occurred on August 17, 1983, when Edward R. Griess, age 14, scrambled around on the rocks approximately 500 to 600 feet below Trail Ridge Road at Rock Cut. He was with several companions from the Christ Bars None youth group from Noble, Oklahoma. Griess was struck in the head by a small, loose rock accidentally dislodged on the steep slope by one of his companions above. When the rock struck him, he fell another 50–100 feet. He died from the head and neck injuries from the fall.

SIXTEEN

The Odd
and Unusual

Falling Tree

Bizarre circumstances befell William N. Hudson, age 68, and his friend, Carl Cox, also 68, who enjoyed hiking together in the park.

There was nobody else on the trail on November 27, 2007. It was cold and windy, with gusts estimated at 40–50 mph at the time of the accident. A skiff of snow blanketed the Sand Beach Lake Trail out of Wild Basin. Hudson and Cox were aware of the wind and the potential for trees falling or branches breaking, but felt confident in their awareness and experience. The accident just happened too quickly. In this fatality, the cause of the accident was clearly the torque of the wind on the top of a dead tree that forced it to break and fall at a precise moment and knock William Hudson to the ground, causing his head to strike a rock. After a fatality, it is common practice to conduct a post incident review to try to determine the cause of the death. Usually, there is a specific cause, such as faulty equipment or poor judgment. In this incident, one might wonder why the tree broke at that very moment and struck one of the only two people on the trail for miles in either direction. As park spokesperson Larry Frederick commented, "Five seconds one way or the other, and these gentlemen would have had an interesting story and enjoyable hike." So, why did the tree break at just that moment? It is a question with no good answer.

Guns in High Places

One of the earliest, and most bizarre, tragedies to occur in Rocky Mountain National Park involved young Frank Stryker, age 24, who died on August 28, 1889. Stryker died when a gun in his pocket or belt loop accidentally discharged a bullet through his neck when he stumbled while on a descent from Longs Peak.

Through the lens of today's sensibilities, one may wonder "What the heck were they thinking carrying revolvers to the summit!" But considering the context of that time period, perhaps it was not all that unusual. In 1889, there wasn't even the hint of preserving the area as a national park. The comfortable two-hour drive we enjoy today from Berthoud, where the Stryker clan gathered to the Lamb Ranch in Tahosa Valley, was a long, hard day by wagon or horse. Firearms for protection and putting a meal on the table were still very much a way of life in 1889. So, who is to judge? But, as always, there is more to the story.

Aside from local newspaper accounts found in the August 28, 1889, issue of the *Longmont Ledger* and the August 31, 1889, *Rocky Mountain News*, personal accounts of the incident were later given by two key participants. Frank's father, John Stryker, provided a lengthy story to the Tipton, Iowa, *Advertiser,* dated September 5, 1889. The Rev. Elkanah J. Lamb, father of Carlyle Lamb, wrote of the incident in 1913 in his *Miscellaneous Meditations.*

By all accounts, Frank Stryker was a fine young man. Since March of 1889, he had been operating a straw-baling business near Berthoud, Colorado, which was also the home of his uncle, Cornelius. After a prosperous growing season, Frank's father, John, left Tipton, Iowa, on August 12th to join up with his other brother Henry and to visit with Cornelius and Frank. By August 27th, they made their way to the Lamb ranch and secured the services of young Carlyle to guide them to the summit of Longs Peak the following morning.

Elkanah J. Lamb wrote:

The next morning, after an early breakfast, they started, some of them carrying revolvers, and one of them a bottle of whiskey. Having had

their morning's meal, they departed in high glee, often stopping to im-
bibe by the way the spirits, soon tuning them up to a degree of hilar-
ity. In this manner, they finally reached the summit and observed the
majestic scene as much as it is possible for men under the influence of
megmarilles stew; then after lunch and an hour's rest, they started on
the return trip. When down a few hundred feet, the ones in front said
to those in the rear: "be careful and don't roll any rocks down on us,"
whereas one of them remarked, so my son stated: "The first one that
rolls a stone on me will get shot." Just then, as he (Frank Stryker) slid
from one table rock to another, his revolver somehow caught and
slipped from his pocket, discharging itself and sending a death-dealing
bullet through his body. His companions succeeded in getting him
down as far as the Narrows, and then he expired, as he was bleeding
profusely and they were unable to stop the flow.

John Stryker's transcribed story in the *Advertiser* does not mention any alcohol:

No arms had been carried up the mountain except a revolver which
Frank had in his hip pocket. Before starting downward, for conven-
ience of sliding over the slippery rocks—which at the beginning fall off
like a series of great rough steps—he took it out of his pocket and
slipped it under the band of his overalls, outside his trousers. No one
knows just how it was placed, and still less can anyone explain how it
was exploded, or the fatal direction of the ball attained! But the young
man had only gone a few yards when he slipped and sat violently
down—the revolver exploding with the concussion and a large bullet
tearing upward through his vest, penetrating his neck just above the
collarbone on the right side and lodging beside the spine at the back
of the neck, where it could be felt with the finger.

Frank never lost consciousness, though he bled profusely. His family applied pressure on the wound and stopped the external bleeding, but could not determine the level of internal bleeding. Carlyle was dispatched immediately for help, and so began an extraordinary ten hour struggle for life. At one point, Frank attempted to descend the mountain, but was only able to achieve a couple hundred yards' distance before his strength left him. Those who have been to the summit of Longs Peak can visualize the upper end of the Narrows, where Frank was laid down again as night fell. Imagine his inevitable fate. Poorly clothed, the small party of Henry, John, and Frank suffered greatly as a strong wind blew fresh snow about them. John and Henry lay on the ledge on either side of Frank, trying to keep him warm. The effort was of little consequence, as Frank Stryker died peacefully at 10:00 p.m. Around 4:00 a.m., Carlyle returned with one other man, all he could find at the time, and so began yet another chapter of this epic event as they struggled to remove the body from the mountain. It took them another ten hours to reach the Boulderfield, and a horse to carry the body out.

I'll leave the final word to the Rev. Lamb:

> What strange providence decreed to ... God only knows, but we do know it is very dangerous to carry a gun in mountain climbing; and worse yet, to carry and drink ardent spirits of any kind in high altitudes; for they naturally quicken the already increased action of the heart as it is affected by the rarefied air causing a rush to the head and consequent abnormal brain action; in fact, no man is in a normal condition of mind and body while under the influence of liquor.

Homicide

The shooting death of "Rocky Mountain" Jim Nugent by Griff Evans on June 19, 1874, in Estes Park was one of the most dastardly events to tarnish the fair name of the budding mountain community. Nugent was a character. In 1871, he barely survived a bear mauling in Grand Lake and lost an eye. He supposedly romanced the English author Isabella L. Bird in 1873. Perhaps inspired by the passions of a rumored romance, Bird's writings about Nugent in her classic book, *A Lady's Life in the Rocky Mountains*, helped create a legend bigger than the man. The following year, fueled by jealousy, greed, and likely alcohol, Evans shot Nugent off his horse near

Fish Creek. Though charged with murder, Evans was found innocent due to lack of evidence.

The community of Grand Lake also witnessed a stain on its reputation. The early 1880s were a splendid but turbulent time for Grand Lake. The local citizens had a great deal of optimism about the potential for several mines in the area. Yet, while the State of Colorado had been established in 1876, the structure of the county government was still being developed. Opposing forces of prominent men represented the ranching interests on one side, and mining interests on the other. They sparred over taxes and the location of the county seat, either Hot Sulphur Springs or Grand Lake. Fueled by greed and power, corruption was rampant in the local politics.

The conflict finally boiled over on the morning of July 4, 1883. On this calm, beautiful morning in Grand Lake, three masked men ambushed Grand County Commissioners E.P. Weber, Judd Day, and Thomas Dean, Clerk of the County Court. Weber died almost immediately. Day and Dean were able to return gunfire before being mortally wounded. One of the masked men was killed immediately in the return fire and turned out to be John J. Mills, the Chairman of the Grand County Commissioners. The other two were Charles Royer, the Sheriff of Grand County, and William Redman, his deputy, though this was not known at the time, as they made their escape. Royer confessed two weeks later and committed suicide on July 16th. Redman was also believed to have committed suicide in Utah later that summer. All told, six men died for no good reason. The regional newspapers deplored the senseless killings, and tourism in Grand Lake suffered from the impression of lawlessness in the area. When the mines began to fail that winter, the community endured the first of several troubling years. The final insult occurred when the county seat was moved back to Hot Sulphur Springs in 1888.

What Grand Lake had in its favor, however, was its location on the shores of the beautiful mountain lake. The town's infrastructure was firmly grounded from the mining days, and summer tourists soon returned to the area. The creation of Rocky Mountain National Park in 1915 secured Grand Lake's future as a tourist destination.

These stories provide a glimpse of the rough and tumble growing pains of the two gateway communities, where questionable characters mingled with more reliable citizens. While these murders were outside the park, they help provide the setting for the only documented homicide to occur within the park—the hanging of Fred N. Selak on July 21, 1926. The loot from the subsequent robbery of Selak's cabin led to the capture of the perpetrators of this cold blooded murder. The apparent motive for the murder, however, appeared to be revenge.

Selak was 61 years old and had lived in a cabin on private property since 1907. His property came within the national park boundary when the park was created in 1915. The cabin was near the old Pole Creek Ranger Station, which was about three miles south of Grand Lake. Ranger Fred McLaren lived at Pole Creek and was Selak's nearest neighbor. Some months before the murder, Selak had some trouble with three young men over a right of way across his land. Alonso Osborn, Ray Noakes, and Arthur Osborn attacked Selak and roughed him up pretty good. Selak had them arrested, and they were fined $16.00. Nursing a grudge, Noakes and Arthur Osborn returned to Selak's cabin on July 21st around 9:00 p.m. They held him up with a gun, then tied his hands behind his back and placed a rope around his neck and forced him to walk a half mile through the woods before hanging him. Apparently, Selak pleaded for mercy and promised to give the young men all his possessions, but they hanged him anyway. They returned to the cabin and made off with an estimated $75, including some old coins from a tin trunk in Selak's bedroom.

George Nair was Selak's partner in a sawmill operation. He went to Fred Selak's cabin on July 25th to see why he hadn't shown up for work. Nair found the cabin had been ransacked. Selak was rumored to be wealthy and supposedly kept large sums of money in his cabin. By the thoroughness with which his home had been searched, the authorities initially thought the motive was robbery. Three detectives and a fingerprint expert from Denver were brought in to assist Sheriff Mark Fletcher with the investigation. Ranger Fred McLaren also worked the case. Initially, they didn't have any clues to work on, but as the days went by, Osborn and

Noakes managed to draw suspicion to themselves by making purchases in the community with the rare coins stolen from Selak's cabin.

On August 10th, Sheriff Fletcher arrested Noakes and Osborn for the murder of Selak. Noakes confessed to the crime and implicated Osborn. Noakes took the sheriff and others to the location where the body of Fred Selak was found still hanging from a tree in the southwest corner of the park.

On March 9, 1927, in district court in Hot Sulphur Springs, the two murderers were found guilty in a jury trial and sentenced to die by hanging. In December 1927, the Colorado State Supreme Court affirmed the decision of the district court jury, and Noakes and Osborn were hanged at the Cañon City Penitentiary on or about March 29, 1928. They were 22 years old.

Mountain Lion Attack

Undoubtedly, the furthest thought from the minds of Dave and Katy Miedema was that their ten-year-old son Mark would be attacked by a mountain lion. The family, along with their six-year-old daughter, was returning along the North Inlet Trail from a visit to Cascade Falls on July 17, 1997. They were near Summerland Park, about 2.5 miles from the trailhead in Grand Lake. At about 4:30 p.m., Mark raced down the trail in front of them, maybe only one or two minutes ahead—not unusual for an energetic young boy on a beautiful summer afternoon.

What they did not know was that a young, healthy female mountain lion was hunting for a meal. As noted, it was past the heat of the afternoon, and wildlife are most active as dusk approaches. The meadow area where Mark was attacked was attractive to deer, the lion's primary food source. Possibly the lion had successfully hunted here before and was waiting when young Mark came down the trail. It is doubtful he had been stalked. The attack fit the pattern of a spontaneous reaction of an instinctive natural predator to a small, moving object similar to a deer fawn.

When Dave and Katy came down the trail, they were surprised to see Mark's feet and legs sticking out on the trail from under some trailside brush. Their first thought was that he was fooling around and playing a game. Moments later, they were horrified to see a mountain lion trying to drag Mark's body into the brush. Rushing forward, they scared the 88-pound lion away. Mark was bleeding severely from scratches and puncture wounds on his face, neck, and scalp. Worse, he was not breathing. Katy, a nurse, began CPR, while Dave applied pressure to the bleeding wounds. Within a couple minutes, another family, Joe and Christina Kafka, with their eight-year-old daughter, came upon the scene. Christina, also a nurse, assisted Katy with the CPR. Joe Kafka dropped his pack and ran down the trail to Grand Lake to get help. After fifteen minutes, Christina Kafka thought she detected a weak pulse, but then it was gone. The mothers continued CPR until the first rangers arrived 45 minutes later.

At the report that a young boy had been attacked by a mountain lion, incident commander Chris Ryan's first assumption was that the boy was alive. Ryan needed communications at the scene of the attack and staff to make an assessment and provide initial care for the victim. Within minutes, Ryan dispatched ranger Steve James up the North Inlet Trail from the north side of Grand Lake. It took roughly twenty minutes for him to get to Mark. In the meantime, Ryan and his supervisor Jock Whitworth quickly developed a list of "what ifs": If the victim is alive, what will be the best way to get him out of the backcountry? Litter? Helicopter? Will the lion come back for its prey? Is the lion an immediate threat to others? Closure of the area? Notification to other hikers? The lion will have to be hunted and killed. Where to find an experienced lion hunter? Do we need dogs?

Several response phases to the incident were in motion when ranger James made it to the boy and his family at around 5:10 p.m. With CPR in progress, James scouted for a helicopter landing site. At 5:24 p.m., Grand County Deputy Jeff Houck, ranger/EMT Harry Canon, Kevin Neb—the Director of Grand County Emergency Medical Services, and paramedic Gary Luton arrived and took over resuscitation efforts. Minutes later, another team carrying a wheeled litter arrived. By this time, CPR had been performed for over an hour without a response. Kevin Neb advised the parents that Mark was unlikely to be revived by further efforts. With the parents' approval, resuscitation was stopped at 5:37 p.m.

The unexplainable death of a child as young and innocent as Mark Miedema is a shock to even the most experienced SAR provider. Tears and sadness would come later. For the moment, the focus of the incident switched from a life saving mode to one of managing the incident scene and professionally caring for Mark's family. At the incident command post, rangers Ryan and Whitworth continued to coordinate with the Colorado Division of Wildlife on locating an animal tracker. The lion would have to be tracked and killed for two reasons. The lion would have to be tested to see if it was rabid, out of concern for health consequences to those exposed to blood or saliva during CPR and the rescue operation. The other obvious reason was the lion was now a threat to other hikers.

By 5:52 p.m., most of the rescuers escorted the Kafka and Miedema families back to the trailhead with Mark's body. From the scene of the attack, rangers were sent up and down the trail to warn other hikers of the lion. Hungry, with the taste of fresh blood and frustration of being chased off its victim, it was doubtful the lion had gone far. Ranger Chris Philippi was assigned to stay at the accident scene to preserve evidence for a later investigation. Around 7:17 p.m., waiting alone, Philippi caught sight of the mountain lion slowly stalking toward him at the scene of her kill. Drawing his 9 mm service weapon, Philippi watched as the lion came within fifteen feet of him. Crouching and without a sound, the lion lunged at Philippi. He fired three times, wounding the animal, and it ran off again. Philippi was not harmed. Within minutes, rangers Jim Richardson, Jeff Hodge, and Steve James made it back to Philippi's location and stayed with him.

At the command post, district ranger Bob Love had taken over management responsibilities from Ryan. Ryan and ranger John Taylor were assigned to escort Lyle Willmarth, an experienced animal tracker, and his dogs to the attack scene. They arrived about 7:47 p.m. and began tracking the mountain lion immediately. By 8:00 p.m., the lion was treed by the dogs only 200 yards from the original scene. The rangers shot and killed the lion, and then removed it from the scene.

The North Inlet Trail was closed that evening to allow rangers with Lyle Willmarth and another tracker to return to the attack scene the following morning to determine if there was another lion in the area. Willmarth stated that the dogs could differentiate the scent of different lions. After searching up and down the trail and the rocky hillside above the trail, Willmarth was confident there was not another lion in the area and the trail was reopened.

In the investigation that followed, the mountain lion was taken to Colorado State University's College of Veterinary Medicine for a necropsy. As noted, the female lion was healthy. She weighed 88 pounds and was pregnant with three fetuses an estimated 45 days old. The lion was approximately two-and-a-half to three years old.

Grand County Coroner David Schoenfeld listed Mark Miedema's official cause of death as respiratory failure caused by massive asphyxiation from vomiting during the mountain lion attack. No punctures were significant enough to have caused death.

There have been two confirmed fatal mountain lion attacks on humans in Colorado recorded in the past two decades—Mark Miedema and, in 1991, Scott Lancaster. Lancaster was a high school senior at Clear Creek High School in Idaho Springs. He was on a training run only a few hundred yards from school when he was attacked and killed. While there have been only two fatalities, there have been several attacks resulting in injuries. There

The Colorado Division of Wildlife recommends people take a few simple precautions when in mountain lion habitat to help keep both people and wildlife safe:

- **When venturing into mountain lion habitat, go in groups** and make plenty of noise in an effort to reduce your chances of surprising a lion. Make sure children are close by and under the supervision of adults. Teach children about mountain lions and what to do if they see one.

- **Stay calm if you come upon a lion.** Talk to it in a firm voice in an effort to demonstrate that you are human and not its regular prey. Do not approach lions. Most mountain lions will try to avoid a confrontation. Give the lion a way to escape.

- **Back away slowly.** Running may stimulate a lion's instinct to chase and attack.

- **Face the lion** and make an effort to appear as large as possible. Open your jacket or lift objects to appear like a more formidable opponent. Pick up your children.

- **If the lion behaves aggressively,** throw rocks, sticks, or whatever you can pick up, without turning your back to the lion or bending down.

- **If the lion attacks, fight back.** Lions have been driven away by prey that fights back. Remain standing and keep attempting to get back up if you are brought to the ground.

are an estimated 5,000 mountain lions in Colorado. As residents build more homes in mountain lion habitat and more visitors come to enjoy Colorado's outdoors, it is inevitable that more attacks will occur.

In Rocky Mountain National Park, warning signs had been posted at the trailhead as a lion had been observed in the general North Inlet Trail area before the attack on Mark Miedema.

The Strange Circumstances of J.P. Chitwood

Sad indeed is the person who dies alone. Worse yet, is when no one really cares about the death of the odd drifter or old prospector when his demise is discussed around the campfire or morning coffee session. The final insult is to be buried twice! Such was the fate of drifter J.P. Chitwood, whose true end has never been fully understood.

The tale of J.P. Chitwood began on October 14, 1920, when ranger Eugene Guild, on a routine patrol out of Grand Lake, found "a young collie at large" near the summit of Flattop Mountain. As it frequently does, winter had come early to the Continental Divide. In Guild's report to the Superintendent, he indicated a 12-inch snowfall the day before his patrol. The fresh layer of snow covered any tracks or clues that might have helped Guild figure out how the dog got there or who the dog had been with. Guild took the dog with him back to Grand Lake. With the weather, fresh snow, and no reports of missing people, the unusual discovery was temporarily relegated to the rangers' winter stories told around a fire.

The story picks again on June 28, 1921, when a letter arrived at the park headquarters. The letter was mailed the day before in Denver and was strange in that it was signed only by "a tourist." No name or other address. The letter was as follows:

Dear Sir,

A little time ago, just north of the Tyndall Glacier at the
head of the cliff where the flat-top trail goes nearest to it, I
came across what was evidently the luggage of a miner: sad-
dle bags, provisions, a rifle and revolver, an overcoat, sock,
coat, vest, etc. Same seemed very strange and after some

*thought I concluded that the owner of them had evidently
fallen over a cliff into the glacier below. Feeling that notifications should be made in case of any names or addresses in
his pockets, or in the saddle bags, I went through them and
found 2 letters addressed to J.P. Chitwood—at Grand Lake
and Cheyenne. There were several cards and names, one of
them being J.A. Grout, 1311 South University, which I supposed to be of Denver.*

*Just before leaving, I made a wider search and came
across the body of an old man, perfectly preserved except that
the skin had shrunken somewhat and grown black. He had
evidently fallen and hit his head on a rock. As the last letter
in his pocket was dated sometime in Oct. 1920, I take it
that he must have perished last fall and been preserved in
the snow since.*

*The shock to me was tremendous. Of course I touched
neither him nor the clothing upon him. And I left immediately as it was growing dark and I was not familiar with
the trail or the country.*

*I am notifying J.A. Grout and you so that what ever
should be done will be done.*

A Tourist

The next day, June 29th, rangers Eugene Guild and Richard Wagner
were working on the telephone line over Flattop Mountain when they
found Chitwood's body. They apparently didn't know who he might be at
the time, as they had left Grand Lake the day before and were not aware
of the letter to the superintendent. The superintendent's monthly report
for June 1921 stated that "the body was found about 250 yards south of
the Continental Divide sign, near the Flattop Trail, and on the brink of
the cliff above Tyndall Glacier. The body lay face down, pointing toward
the Glacier, with his head against a rock. The head was crushed on one
side, where he had evidently tripped and fallen on the rock. He had never

moved after he had fallen." The report also indicated that no weapons or other marks of identification were found.

What is interesting is that the report by ranger Guild to the superintendent indicated that Chitwood was found on "the brink" of the cliff above Tyndall Glacier, not over or down a cliff. Yet Chitwood's skull appeared to have been "crushed" when he fell over ... or was he killed? Doesn't it seem unusual to sustain a "crushed head" by tripping on a rock? And as part of the investigation, authorities talked with Mr. E.S. Tedmon, who was the Secretary of the Water and Storage Supply Company of Ft. Collins. Tedmon told authorities that Chitwood was a summer employee of the company working north of Grand Lake. He had left the work crew around October 1, 1920, and had about $400 with him. Yet there was never a mention of money in the tourist letter, Guild's report, or that of the coroner. Suspicious indeed.

Because of the advanced state of decomposition, Guild and Wagner secured a slicker over the body with rocks and awaited further instructions. On July 6th, County Coroner H.M. Balmer, Undersheriff Ira Knapp of Ft. Collins, and rangers McDaniel and Stephens returned to the body to hold an inquest and perform a burial near where it was found. This was not a totally unusual practice during this period, as noted in the burial of Louis Levings on Ypsilon Mountain in 1905 and the Reverend Sampson in 1932 near the Fern Lake Trailhead. It should be noted that the coroner's report did not indicate any suspicion of foul play or that Chitwood's death was nothing more than an accident. Resort owner "Squeaky Bob" Wheeler supported the belief that the body was that of Chitwood. Since 1907, Wheeler had operated a tent resort camp in the Kawuneeche Valley and knew most of the local characters. Sadly, he was quoted in the July 8, 1921, *Loveland Reporter Herald* as saying, "Chitwood was not missed because he had no especial friends in this part of the country and had wandered from one place to another continually."

Normally this story would have ended here. However, later that summer, on September 2, 1921, ranger Cliff Higby was hiking with a group of visitors from Bear Lake up through Tyndall Gorge to Hallett Peak. Near the lower end of Tyndall Glacier, they discovered the carcasses of two horses and assorted personal effects, such as a toothbrush, blankets, pieces of canvas, and a fairly good pair of corduroy pants with the pockets turned wrong side out. It appeared the horses had been traveling together because there was a halter rope tied to the tail of one horse. There was little doubt that these animals had belonged to Chitwood.

Putting the evidence together, it appears that Chitwood traveled from Grand Lake to Estes Park and got caught in an early winter storm, probably on the 12th or 13th of October, 1920. Likely disoriented, it appears that he tripped or fell near the rim of Tyndall Gorge and struck his head. He probably lost consciousness and died of an epidural hematoma or hypothermia. Here, I would like to speculate on another possibility of Chitwood's death. There is the slim possibility that he had been murdered and robbed. To me, the missing money and different versions of finding or not finding identification or weapons is a bit unusual. It also seems unusual, although not impossible, to sustain a crushed skull by tripping and falling on relatively level ground.

I think another possible scenario is that he had an accident with his horses and was violently knocked over. Remember, his horses were found down on Tyndall Glacier in September. Chitwood was up on the rim of the gorge. Anybody who has been around livestock knows when horses panic or spook, you really need to watch out. Many a horseman has been knocked down by an animal weighing several times that of the average person. In blizzard conditions, Chitwood's horses could have spooked at a flapping tarp or blanket and knocked him over with the force necessary to create a "crushed skull." In their panic or confusion, the horses went over the rim to the glacier below.

But wait, there is still more to the Chitwood story. In July 1923, three hikers came across Flattop Mountain west to east and off the marked trail. One of the hikers, Bill Bohn, saw a shoe and, as reported in the *Loveland Reporter Herald*, "reached for the shoe and to his astonishment found it encased a human foot. He excitedly called his companions to the place, and the boys saw the remains of an aged man stretched over the rocks. An

Army blanket and slicker were covered over the body, the body being dressed in a dark blue suit. The dead man had a long grey beard." Apparently, Superintendent Toll presumed that the body was Chitwood. He ordered the remains encased in a concrete vault "in a manner becoming to a pioneer" to prevent further incidents.

For decades, Chitwood's final burial site remained a mystery. One reason may be that most searchers were probably looking for some type of "concrete vault," as supposedly ordered by Superintendent Toll in 1923. In August 2009, using an old photograph as a reference point, two amateur historians from Estes Park found what is believed to be J.D. Chitwood's burial site on Flattop Mountain. A ranger and I went up the following week and confirmed the site. There was no concrete, and the site was difficult to find. This is a good thing. Chitwood left a small, almost indistinguishable mark on the world, but he is no less deserving of being undisturbed in his final resting spot. His burial site is considered a cultural resource and is protected by law. The National Park Service has been notified of the discovery. I have been purposefully vague as to the location. I hope we can all leave him alone.

The Skull Point Story

There are dozens of place names in the national park, and there are good stories about how particular peaks or features are named. Louisa Ward Arps and Elinor E. Kingery documented many of these stories in their excellent book *High Country Names*. One of the park's more interesting stories is about the naming of Skull Point. You can find this landmark on most maps. It is located west of Lost Lake in the north part of the park.

On August 9, 1927, University of Colorado law student Charles R. Hughes and two friends, Fred Nelson and Elwin Watson, left camp at Lost Lake to explore the upper end of the valley to the west. They passed timberline, and on the right was a rocky point on the divide between the watershed of the Big Thompson River and that of the Cache la Poudre River. Hughes parted from his companions to climb to this vantage point, some 600 feet above timberline and about 12,000 feet in elevation. Just short of the summit, he noticed something white in a recess in the jumbled rocks. Reaching in, he drew out a human skull! Hughes unsuccessfully looked around for other bones. He carefully carried the skull back to camp and turned it in to the park staff for further investigation.

The circumference of the skull was small, only 20 inches, whereas the skull of a man of average height is generally between 21 and 23 inches. The lower jaw was missing, and two teeth remained in the upper jaw. Both were first molars with a moderate amount of wear, indicating an adult, not a child. The forehead was prominent, rather than retreating, and there was no indication of an injury that might have led to death.

On September 15th, Superintendent Roger Toll and three rangers returned to the location described by Hughes. In his report, Toll described the location as a "tumbled mass of large boulders anywhere from a few feet to 10 feet or more in size. There was no soil or vegetation." By crawling back into the many small cavities between the rocks, the group recovered 22 other bones—none of them human.

These bones, together with the skull, were taken to the Colorado Museum of Natural History, where Director J.D. Figgins and a Mr. Miller identified most of them as bones from three different bison. There was one mountain sheep bone, a right hind metacarpal. Figgins speculated that the size of the skull was that of an approximately 35-year-old adult, and that the shape of the forehead indicated a woman. He thought the skull had been there for 40 to 50 years, which would have dated it from the 1870s.

Toll sought additional opinions. Dr. I.E. Wallin from the Colorado General Hospital Medical School thought the skull was that of a Caucasian between 20 and 35 years of age, judging from the teeth. He was uncertain as to the sex, and he also thought the skull was approximately 50 years old. A Dr. E.R. Warner, a dentist, put the age at 30 to 35 years old and thought the skull was more likely that of a Caucasian woman. Wallin noted the teeth were sound and had no need for dental work. Generally, the teeth of Native Americans wore more rapidly than those of Caucasians due to a coarser diet requiring more grinding. Superintendent Toll also sent the skull to the Smithsonian Institution in Washington, D.C. Dr. A.

Hrdlicka confidently wrote back to Toll that he believed the skull that of a female, probably less than 30 years old. Hrdlicka was not able to make a positive identification as to race, but believed certain features indicated it was a Caucasian.

How did the skull and other bones get there, particularly without any other bones from a human skeleton? The first thoughts were that it was that of a prospector. Another idea was that the skull dated back to when Native Americans traversed the Rocky Mountains. Before the 1860s, the Front Range of the Rockies was prime hunting grounds for various tribes, and there is evidence of trade and hunting routes across the continental divide through the park from east to west over Flattop Mountain and through Fall River Canyon. The North Fork of the Big Thompson River, near where the skull was found, was another hunting route. In fact, on this trip, Toll's party found a number of Indian flints above treeline around two miles west of Skull Point.

In a later interview, Estes Park pioneer Abner Sprague told of guiding two English hunters in 1877 or 1878 past Lawn Lake around the east slope of Mummy Mountain. On the east slope of Hague's Peak, at an elevation of 12,000 feet, Sprague observed a large, well preserved bison skull and horns. This is in the same area as Skull Point. Sprague had no doubt that bison crossed back and forth over the Continental Divide to follow good grazing, much as did elk and deer, so it is likely the Native Americans also used this as one of many routes across the Divide. Regarding the possibility of the skull being that of a Caucasian, it was possible a lone prospector could have wandered through the area, considering that gold was discovered in Colorado in the late 1850s.

Toll assumed the skull dated from the same period as the bison bones. If this was the case, the bones and skull belonged to a period when Caucasians were much less numerous than Native Americans in the area. The great slaughter of buffalo on the plains took place mostly from 1868 to 1874. Only a few scattered buffalo were noted in the area north of Estes Park in the late 1870s.

Superintendent Toll believed there were two likely scenarios to explain the skull and animal bones. The first was that the site was related to the

Native American culture as a spiritual site, and that the skull was that of a Native American. The other scenario was that a mountain lion used the locality for a den and that the bones had been dragged there to feed the lion kittens. Arguments against the second theory are that a mountain lion would likely bring back bones with meat on them. A humerus or femur bone would seem more likely. If a lion had killed a human, a femur would provide more nourishment than a skull, and remember the skull was undamaged. But if the skull was indeed that of a female Caucasian, where did she come from? In the 1860s and '70s, there were very few Caucasians in the area, other than possibly the lone prospector, let alone females.

Superintendent Roger Toll seemed stumped that the skull was that of a Caucasian woman, and he finished his report thusly:

One can not but wonder how this unknown pioneer met death. If it was a woman, how came she there? Was it a tragedy? Some accident perhaps? Did she meet a solitary death, or was she one of a party? Did she die near or far from the point where the skull was found? A human skull, white and weather-beaten, at the summit of an unnamed point, above timberline, in a remote and unfrequented region. That is the last chapter in the story. Will the preceding chapters ever be known, except in imagination?

What do you think?

Superintendent Toll named this rock feature "Skull Point" in September 1927.

SEVENTEEN

Mutual Aid—
Incidents Outside
the Park

When I arrived as the Chief Ranger for Rocky Mountain National Park in 1991, I was pleased to find a high level of interagency cooperation among the emergency services providers in and around the park. In my research for this book, I found a long history of this cooperation between park staff and local agencies. Then, as now, these relationships tap into the strengths of all organizations to serve everyone safely and efficiently.

In the main body of this book, I mention numerous times when park staff is supported by outside groups on search or rescue incidents within the park. In this section, I have provided a listing of the known fatalities that occurred just outside the park in which rangers assisted the local authorities. The bulk of these incidents occurred on the Grand Lake side of Rocky Mountain National Park, and more specifically in the old Shadow Mountain Recreation Area. This was one of those anomalies of park management, and a minor challenge in analyzing incidents for this book. The boundaries of many of the older western parks, such as Yosemite and Yellowstone, have not changed in 100 years, so it is obviously easier to document the fatalities and incidents within the park. Not so with Rocky Mountain National Park, whose boundary has continued to change over the years. In particular, the Shadow Mountain Recreation Area (primarily Lake Granby and Shadow Mountain Lake) on the west side of the park was administered by the park staff from 1952 to 1979 through an agreement with the Bureau of Reclamation. In other words, the National Park Service managed the area, but did not own it. This responsibility was transferred to the United States Forest Service in October 1979, and the area is now known as the Arapaho National Recreation Area.

As the author, I have elected to include the Shadow Mountain incidents in this section of the book, as the incidents were technically not on park property. Yet these incidents help demonstrate the complexity of work for the ranger staff and deserve to be mentioned. Yes, it could be argued both ways. However, I believe separating the incidents that occurred "outside the park" will help the reader to better understand the incidents in the core park area.

In summary, the park staff has responded to 43 incidents outside the park, involving 47 fatalities. Three incidents on the Grand Lake side of the park involved multiple fatalities. (These statistics do not include the 145 people who lost their lives in the Big Thompson River Disaster in 1976, which is the concluding story in this book.)

Incidents around Grand Lake

Over the years, rangers have responded to 34 fatalities outside the park in the Grand Lake area. The majority of fatalities are drownings in Shadow Mountain Lake and Lake Granby. Grand Lake was not under the management of the park, but park staff responded to several incidents there.

Drownings

On July 20, 1933, Louis "Billy" Lipscomb, age 6, drowned in Grand Lake. Sadly, Antonio Basuno, age 30, also drowned in an attempt to save Lipscomb. Both were from San Antonio, Texas.

Gordon Lynch, age 18, drowned in Grand Lake on August 17, 1939.

Sam Osburne, age 22, drowned in Shadow Mountain Lake on November 5, 1946.

In another sad case, Kathleen Read, age seven, drowned at Shadow Mountain Lake Dam on June 20, 1949. Kathleen was the daughter of a Bureau of Reclamation tractor operator who lived near the dam. On the afternoon of the 20th, she either slipped or fell into the water and was carried through the outlet gates of the Shadow Mountain Dam before help could reach her. Her body was recovered from the lake at 9:00 p.m. by rangers and Bureau of Reclamation personnel.

Louis J. Smith, age 59, drowned on August 23, 1955, when his boat capsized in Shadow Mountain Lake.

On August 26, 1957, young Patrick Flanagan, age two, drowned on private property near Grand Lake along the North Fork of the Colorado River.

Neil B. Brewer, age 16, from Wheatridge, Colorado, drowned while boating on Shadow Mountain Lake on August 2, 1958.

On August 9, 1958, George Louderbach, age 54, stepped in a hole while fishing and disappeared 150 yards above the bridge at Arapaho Valley near Shadow Mountain Lake. Remains identified as Louderbach were found seven years later on June 13, 1965.

October 25, 1958, witnessed a double drowning when a boat capsized on Shadow Mountain Lake. Denver residents George Matkovitch and John Cadwell, both 38, lost their lives.

On August 16, 1960, Edward Bird, age 43, drowned in Lake Granby.

On August 24, 1960, Denver resident Harold Reed, age 38, drowned while scuba diving in Shadow Mountain Lake.

On June 10, 1967, Andrew A. Hacker, age unknown, drowned in Lake Granby. He was from Granby, Colorado.

On July 24, 1969, young Tim Rehm, age three, from Dows, Iowa, drowned in a private swimming pool near Shadow Mountain Lake. Chief Ranger Jim Randall recalled the professional way that ranger Al Simonds supported the family in this difficult situation.

Granby, Colorado, resident Rolland L. Novak, age 25, drowned in Lake Granby on September 7, 1969.

On July 7, 1976, Margaret Haskins, age 44, from Shawnee Mission, Kansas, drowned in Shadow Mountain Lake.

On July 11, 1976, Earl Traw, age 19, from Lakewood, Colorado, drowned in Lake Granby.

Heart Attacks

Rangers responded to the Grand Lake Lodge on June 17, 1934. Denver resident Mrs. Francis F. Williamson, age 34, died of apparent heart failure.

On October 27, 1962, Lorin Tackwell, age 54, was out fishing with two friends on Lake Granby. Tackwell apparently suffered a heart attack and, when he collapsed, caused the boat to capsize. The two companions were rescued and Tackwell's body recovered.

In a similar incident, Sydney Shuteran, age 51, of Denver, was fishing on Lake Granby on July 20, 1963. He was believed to have suffered a non-fatal heart attack, but fell in the lake and drowned.

On October 5, 1970, Audrey Kay, age 57, suffered a fatal heart attack at Green Ridge Campground in Shadow Mountain National Recreation Area. Kay was from Sacramento, California.

June 28, 1975, Denver resident Mayme Rawson, age 69, died at the Green Ridge Campground.

Carl J. Fabian, age 66, died of heart failure at the Green River Campground in Shadow Mountain Recreation Area on August 17, 1978. Fabian was from Ponca City, Oklahoma.

Asphyxiation

A triple fatality due to asphyxiation occurred on December 6, 1964. William Widener, age 29, David Widener, age 17, and Douglas Gilreath, age 20, were from Arvada, Colorado. They were camping in the Willow Creek Spillway parking area at Shadow Mountain Lake and died of asphyxiation as a result of faulty heater in their camper.

On August 3, 1965, Ft. Morgan residents Vince McCune, age 44, and his wife, Lorene McCune, age 37, died of asphyxiation from a propane gas leak in a houseboat on Lake Granby.

Firearms

In an unusual incident, David Adams, age unknown, accidentally shot himself to death on October 26, 1946. Adams was cleaning his gun in a private residence west of the Grand Lake Entrance Station area.

Motor Vehicle Accidents

Arthur Purdy, age 60, was from Denver, Colorado. On May, 20, 1967, he died in a motor vehicle accident at Elephant Island turnoff near Lake Granby.

On March 4, 2005, rangers assisted the Grand County Sheriff on a snowmobile collision with a tree on the South Supply Trail in the Arapaho National Forest. Richard J. Jeffords, age 35, from Elizabeth, Colorado, died from blunt trauma to the head. Excessive speed was the primary factor in this accident.

Medical

In another unusual incident, Robert Gill, age 40, died of a cerebral hemorrhage on July 25, 1977. He was an employee of the Kawuneeche Guest Ranch and Resort.

Bear Attack

John Richardson, age 31, was from Denver, Colorado. On July 25, 1971, he and several friends, including his fiancée, Linda Moore, camped on private property just north of Grand Lake and west of the National Park. Richardson and Moore planned to get married in an open air ceremony near where they camped. Richardson and Moore were sleeping in a tent when a 300 pound black bear attacked. Moore was mauled and bit on the buttock, then the bear dragged Richardson from the tent. Their screams awoke nearby friends, who came to their defense. Linda Moore was mauled by the bear, but survived. Another member of the group drove the bear off after hitting it on the head several times with a frying pan. Richardson died later that evening of bite wounds to his neck. Rangers assisted the County Sheriff at the scene. The following day, a professional hunter tracked and killed the bear believed to be responsible for the attack. Colorado State University veterinary scientists determined that the bear was otherwise healthy and not rabid.

Moore had not been menstruating. Food odors, improper food storage, and camping in the area where the bear had previously found food were primary factors in this incident. This was the first fatality from a black bear attack in the history of Colorado. In 1993, a person was killed by a black bear in Fremont County. In August, 2009, Donna Munson, age 74, of Ouray, was killed and eaten by a black bear. Munson had repeatedly been warned about feeding bears in her yard.

Fall—Hiker Scrambling

Phillip A. Connolly, age 27, was a United States Forest Service employee from Ft. Collins, Colorado. On July 22, 1981, he was hiking with fellow employee Ken Thoman after the two had completed trail maintenance work on the Roaring Fork Trail in the Indian Peaks Wilderness Area. This area is just south of the park and east of Grand Lake. This accident occurred as the two were traversing a steep slope about 1 mile east of Watanga Mountain. Thoman later reported that Connolly slipped, then fell and tumbled down the slope. It took an hour for Thoman to reach Connolly, and he did not find any vital signs. Connolly's body was recovered by a joint Forest Service and Park Service team.

Downed Aircraft

On January 30, 1967, 2nd Lt. Eldon C. Hart, age 26, was flying a single seat F-100 Super Sabre jet on a routine training flight with another aircraft out of McConnell Air Force base in Kansas. Hart was part of the 184th Tactical Fighter Squadron. According to the accident report, he had gone into a cloud and lost control while executing a barrel roll around the lead plane. He was believed to have crashed in the Never Summer Range in the northwest corner of the park.

The military and Civil Air Patrol had primary responsibility for the search. The park staff contributed a cross-country ski group and two snow cats (tracked oversnow vehicles), which spent several days searching in the Never Summer Range. The crash site was found several months later on the west side of Mt. Cirrus, just outside the park boundary.

Incidents around Estes Park

Over the years, there have been 13 deaths along the east side of the park that rangers responded to.

Motor Vehicle Accidents

In 1921, there was not yet a Highway 7, also known as the Peak to Peak Highway. The road between Lily Lake and the Longs Peak Inn was simply the Longs Peak Road. On August 14, 1921, Carl W. Hall, age 54, was on an excursion with his wife and friends, who were in two other cars. One of the vehicles had a mechanical problem. The vehicle was jacked up with the front wheel off. Hall was working under the vehicle when it slipped off the jack and crushed his head at the base of the neck. He died 30 minutes later without regaining consciousness. Hall had been a mail carrier in Denver for several years.

In another motor vehicle accident, Estes Park resident Paul Schroeder, age 25, drove off the road about three-quarters of a mile east of the Thompson River Entrance and died. The Superintendent's Monthly Report stated: "Resident of Estes Park was instantly killed about midnight on February 26, 1938, when the car he was driving left the road about ¾ mile east of the Thompson River Entrance and crashed in a tree some distance from the road. Schroeder's three companions suffered no serious injuries. The accident occurred outside the park on the antiquated county road."

Hypothermia

Not much was known about John Vesper, age 37. Originally from Cincinnati, Ohio, he had lived in Estes Park for six years. He was a World War I veteran and was drawing disability compensation due to shell shock and having been gassed. He had married for the second time in June 1927. On the evening of October 2, 1927, Vesper and Edgar Van Gilder drove up Fish Creek Road in a moderate snow storm. About a quarter mile northeast of the junction with the Longs Peak Road (near the present day turnoff to Cheley Camp), their car left the road and struck a fence. Unable to get the car restarted, Vesper elected to walk back to Estes Park, as Van Gilder was handicapped. Vesper never made it. The following morning, Estes Park resident Jac Christian found Van Gilder and gave him a ride into town. The search that afternoon was unsuccessful. Rangers found Vesper's body the following day, October 4th, over three-fourths of a mile from his vehicle, in a marshy meadow. He appeared to have decided to hike cross country directly toward town rather than staying on the road. The coroner gave the cause of death as heart failure, with exposure (hypothermia) likely contributing to his death.

Suicides

On July 8, 1934, Dr. S.C. Bell committed suicide by hanging himself just outside the park boundaries on Deer Mountain above High Drive. Dr. Bell was a dentist from Grand Island, Nebraska. He had come to Estes Park with his wife and son for a two-week holiday. The *Estes Park Trail* stated, "Bell had been an inmate of a psychopathic hospital for many months prior to their Estes Park visit. A few years earlier, his father had killed himself and two of Dr. Bell's brothers. The tragedy played on him."

The young Mary E. Overturf apparently took her own life on Old Man Mountain. Only 19 years old, Overturf was from Greeley, Colorado, and an employee of the Stanley Hotel. The investigation indicated that Overturf may have been contemplating suicide when she fell from Old Man Mountain. She was last seen on Friday morning, June 3, 1988, and was reported missing the next day. Her body was recovered on Sunday, June 5th.

On January 19, 2003, the body of Michael Laudel was found just outside the park near Camp St. Malo. St. Malo is a Catholic Retreat facility along Highway 7 south of Estes Park. Laudel had been the object of a multi-agency search in September and October 2002 after his abandoned vehicle was found in the St. Malo parking area. The 45-year-old Laudel had last been seen in Denver on September 22, 2002, and the Denver Police Department had him listed as missing and possibly suicidal. On Monday, September 30th, a groundskeeper from St. Malo called the Boulder County Sheriff's office about an abandoned vehicle, which turned out to be Laudel's. On October 1st, over thirty searchers, three dog teams, and a helicopter participated in the search. As the park boundary is 200 yards west of the St. Malo facilities, there was a good possibility Laudel had travelled into the park, so park staff supported the Boulder County Sheriff's

Office in the search. Poor winter weather and lack of any evidence led to the search being suspended after several days.

Three months later, on January 19th, a visitor to the area happened to look up and caught sight of Laudel's body hanging from a branch where he hung himself. This incident provides a good lesson for the SAR community. Laudel made the unusual effort to wear a camouflage poncho before he climbed to the top of a large ponderosa pine tree to hang himself. The tree was less than 100 yards from his vehicle, but Laudel was over sixty feet up in the canopy of the tree. The area had been searched extensively the previous autumn. The lesson is that searchers tend to look down as they search for clues and evidence, not necessarily up!

Fall—Hiker Scrambling

In the following three fatalities, park rangers assisted with the body recoveries. On August 23, 1938, 18-year-old YMCA employee Rowland Spencer, from Kansas City, Missouri, was killed in a fall from the west face of "Teddy's Teeth," a popular rock formation on Giant Track Mountain. Spencer and his friend John Barber were climbing on the center tooth. Apparently Barber became stuck, and Spencer was attempting to down climb to help him when he lost his grip and fell past the horrified Barber.

On September 20, 1964, Gary Hartman, 17, fell while rock scrambling on the Thumb formation on Prospect Mountain, just south of Estes Park.

On July 25, 1969, Gregory A. Calohan, 20, fell from a cliff in the Big Thompson Canyon above Big Chief Motel. The Glendora, California, resident died instantly.

Drownings

Once again, I recommend parents visiting the area with young children pay particular attention to this next incident. On May 15, 1987, Dustin R. Milton, age 2, wandered away from his residence on Spur 66, the access road to the Estes Park YMCA. The Miltons' house sat next to the Big Thompson River, and there was a small footbridge out to a small island. In mid-May, the Big Thompson was running close to high water from spring runoff. Dustin enjoyed throwing rocks into the river. Apparently, the boy's mother left him playing in the yard for "just a few minutes" and discovered him missing when she returned at approximately 6:10 p.m. "It happened very, very quickly," she said. It was "not a case of neglect" according to Larimer County Lt. Cy Cole. Searchers scoured the river until dark, as well as the surrounding area, without success. Over 100 people searched for Dustin, including several park employees. Searchers found his body in the river the next morning about two miles downstream and a quarter mile above the Mary's Lake Road bridge.

Heart Attack

The Reverend A.A. Haferman, age 60, from Syracuse, Nebraska, died of a heart attack on the west side of the YMCA near the park boundary on July 22, 1958.

Natural Death

On July 29, 1949, four-year-old Jeanine Cobb died of "natural causes." Her family was from Denver, Colorado. They were vacationing at the old Faulkner's Cabins, southeast of Estes Park, for eighteen days. The child had been ill, possibly with rheumatic fever. She died at the vacation cabin. An autopsy was performed, and the manner of death was determined to be natural. The exact cause was undetermined, but likely associated with the rheumatic fever.

Lightning

Rangers assisted in an extremely unusual incident when Robert J. Faugno, age 22, was struck by lightning while riding as a passenger on the back of a motorcycle on July 8, 1973. The operator of the motorcycle, Greg Drescher, was not seriously hurt. The two were near the intersection of US Highway 36 and Colorado 66.

The Big Thompson River Flood

Recognized as one of Colorado's worst natural disasters, the Big Thompson River flood caused over $35 million in damages (1976 dollars) to 418 homes and businesses, many mobile homes, 438 automobiles, numerous bridges, paved and unpaved roads, power and telephone lines, and other structures. The tragedy claimed the lives of 145 people, including two law enforcement officers trying to evacuate people in danger, and there were 250 reported injuries. Five bodies have never been found. Scores of other people narrowly escaped with their lives. More than 1,000 people were evacuated by helicopter.

On July 31, 1976, the nation was still basking in the glow of its bicentennial celebration. In addition, Colorado was enjoying a three-day weekend in recognition of its 100 years as a state. The national park and private campgrounds and hotels in Estes Park were filled to capacity, as well as those in the Big Thompson Canyon along Highway 34 between Loveland and Estes Park. Many summer homes in the canyon had been in families for generations. That evening, between 6:00 and 10:00 p.m., a near stationary thunderstorm released over ten inches of rain on the eastern side of Estes Park and in the Glen Haven area. These communities straddle the middle reaches of the Big Thompson River Basin. In steep mountain terrain with thin or no soil, this large amount of rainfall in such a short period of time produced a flash flood that caught residents and tourists in the canyon by surprise. In fact, it was hardly raining in the lower stretches of the canyon and only a modest one inch of rain had fallen in the headquarters area of the national park. It was dry in Loveland, Colorado, just outside the mouth of the canyon. Afterwards, it was estimated that this flood was more than four times as strong as any in the 112-year record available in 1976, with a discharge of 1,000 cubic meters per second.

By 8:15 p.m., it was becoming apparent that this was not a normal afternoon thundershower. Reports began coming in that Highway 34, below Estes Park, was washed out. Estes Park Police Officer Bob Miller drove down to investigate. At 8:35 p.m., Miller radioed the first warning that a major flood was possible. Miller's tape recorded transmission was, "We've got to start taking people out. My car's gonna be washed away. I've got a real emergency down here!" Miller was able to make it safely back to Estes Park, and all eastbound traffic was blocked. At this same time, the order was given to stop all westbound traffic at the Dam Store, west of Loveland. At 8:46 p.m. Colorado State Patrol Sgt. Hugh Purdy, from Loveland, began heading up the canyon to assess the threat. Remember, it was dry in Loveland. Around 9:00 p.m., Purdy radioed that he was about 2 miles east of Drake. At 9:15 p.m., Officer Purdy radioed that he was one-half mile east of Drake. "I am stuck. I am right in the middle of it. I can't get out." At 9:35 p.m., Highway Patrol Dispatch in Greeley tried to contact Purdy several times. There was no answer.

About this time, Lt. Leo Baker of the Larimer County Sheriff's Office in Estes Park realized that he and Estes Park were cut off from support from Front Range cities. Highway 36 to Lyons was closed six miles east of town by a washout 150 feet across and 50 feet deep. Highway 34 was closed, as was the road past Glen Haven. The Larimer County deputies and Estes Park Police Department had their hands full. At 9:46 p.m., Baker requested support and heavy equipment from Rocky Mountain National Park. Fifty-five National Park Service personnel responded in two groups: heavy equipment operators under the direction of maintenance chief Ron Cotten and rangers trained in search and rescue led by Chief Ranger Dave Essex.

The park crews focused on Highway 34, east of town, to determine damage and assist stranded people. Below the first road bend to the left, east of Estes Park, the crews ran into high water and washed-out sections of road from side gullies running perpendicular across Highway 34. The heavy equipment led the cautious rescuers down the canyon, where flood waters and wreckage stopped them near the Glen Comfort Store area, about three miles east of Estes Park. They found an estimated 30 to 40 people stranded there. The relentless rain continued all this time, and Essex remembered he could barely see a foot in front of himself at times. By 1:00 a.m., the crews headed back up the canyon, but were trapped by high water. They placed ropes on the nearby slopes to provide a way to evacuate to higher ground, if the water kept rising. Fortunately, it did not. By 3:00 a.m., the rainfall slackened and it looked like the water level was dropping. Chief Ranger Essex and others made a tentative effort to drive back up the canyon toward Estes Park, followed by a few private vehicles.

Near the Tuckaway Cabins, Essex was stopped by a rampant cascade across the highway from a side gully. Mr. and Mrs. Fred Woodring, Tuckaway residents, were behind Essex in a four-wheel-drive International Scout. Apparently, they thought their vehicle could cross the torrent in front of the rangers, and they swung around in front of them. The rangers watched helplessly through the lightning flashes as the floodwaters swept the Scout from the roadway and into a pile of debris. Awash in the surging water, Fred Woodring managed to climb onto the top of the car. Debris built up in the stream flow and caused temporary dams, which soon gave way and released a two to three foot surge of water and debris above the flood level, causing a significant hazard to the rescuers. As surges of water rushed down the canyon, Essex and his crew tried several times to throw a rope to Woodring, but he was soon washed away into the darkness and drowned. Mrs. Woodring was later found dead, pinned underneath the vehicle.

Big Thompson Canyon Flood damage. Photo courtesy of Estes Park Museum

Near daylight at 5:30 a.m. on Sunday, most of the park crews and stranded residents and visitors from the upper end of the canyon made it back to Estes Park. The park crews changed clothes, got a bite to eat, and headed back into the canyon. By now, the waters had receded significantly. In daylight, the mood was grim as everyone surveyed the unbelievable destruction. Around 7:00 a.m., the rangers helped with the first of many body recoveries near Glen Comfort Store. While the maintenance crew pioneered a passable road through the debris, the ranger crews probed farther down canyon, assisting stranded people, identifying bodies for recovery, and setting up helicopter landing areas. By late morning, National Guard helicopters arrived and began landing and flying people out of the canyon. By Monday, over 1,000 people had been airlifted out of the canyon. Over the next two weeks, the park staff continued to support the sheriff's office in managing the post-incident activity. Rangers helped staff a 24-hour-a-day road block at the head of the Big Thompson Canyon, just east of Estes Park. The maintenance staff provided water and port-a-potties for residents and work crews and continued with road construction and debris removal.

The incredible energy and violence of the storm and the level of destruction left in its path will not soon be forgotten by those who experienced the night of July 31, 1976. Also not forgotten will be the high level of cooperation between representatives of the town, county, and national park in coming to the support of those in need.

Of the 145 people who lost their lives that evening, two were law enforcement officers. Colorado State Patrol Sgt. Hugh Purdy died near Drake. He was 53 years old and left behind a wife and three children. Estes Park summer police officer Michael O. Conley also died saving the lives of others. Conley was from Colorado Springs. He was on his day off and drove up the Big Thompson Canyon Saturday evening with his wife. They stopped near Waltonia because of the rising water. Recognizing the danger, Conley began moving people and automobiles to higher ground, including his wife. Witnesses later told Estes Park Police Chief Robert Ault that a surge of water came roaring down the canyon. Michael Conley

Big Thompson Canyon Flood damage. Photo courtesy of Estes Park Museum.

made a run for a light pole to escape the onrush. Sadly, "the pole snapped like a toothpick and he was gone."

For their selfless and often heroic efforts during and after the Big Thompson Flood, the park staff was recognized with the State of Colorado Governor's Citation in September 1976. The staff was also recognized with a Department of Interior Unit Valor Award in December 1976.

Conclusion

On March 30, 2009, President Barack Obama signed legislation that designated close to 250,000 acres of Rocky Mountain National Park as wilderness. This is roughly 93 percent of the park's 265,770 acres.

Congress passed the Wilderness Act in 1964, which defines wilderness as "an area of undeveloped federal land retaining its primeval character and influence, without permanent improvements or human habitation, which is protected and managed so as to preserve its natural conditions." In 1974, wilderness designation was first proposed for Rocky Mountain National Park, and the park has been managed as wilderness ever since. Still, it was nice to get this official stamp of wildness on the books. Yes, I did say wildness, not wilderness.

A few days later, in early April, I drove to the park to see if anything had changed. As I stood alone at Many Parks Curve overlook, snow banners streamed off the high peaks, and the trees swayed as they have for centuries as the wind swept down from the Continental Divide. I felt comfortable knowing that the view before me was not much different than if I had been here 500 years earlier. In a simple sort of way, this was a good thing. It was still wild. I could still sense "its primeval character and influence." So while we pat ourselves on the back for managing and preserving wildness for the greater good, the sad fact is that the love is not returned. Let me be frank. Nature, wilderness, wildness simply does not care about you or me. The "primeval character" of a mountain lion or bear is that you are a potential threat or meal. Nothing more, nothing less. The seductive beauty of a waterfall or the majesty of Longs Peak is in our eyes only. The water is simply finding the path of least resistance to the ocean. Longs Peak is cold granite.

Visitors need to reconcile this detachment when they visit public lands, and particularly wilderness areas. Yes, it is still okay to attach human feelings and emotions to park experiences, to write eloquent tomes to the grandeur of national parks and wilderness areas, and to send glowing postcards to distant relatives. That is what parks are there for, to stimulate and challenge us, to make us feel better, to help us bond with our families or friends. But don't lose sight of the detachment that nature has for you, and be soberly grounded to the dangers before you, as you step off the pavement and onto the trail. These dangers are the essence of wildness in wilderness. The unregulated, take-it-as-it-comes danger is what makes a wilderness or park experience whole.

Safety Tips
Your Safety is Your Responsibility

Preparation

1. **Packing.** Know and carry the "Ten Essentials" in your pack: waterproof map, compass or GPS unit, headlamp, food and water, extra clothes including a warm wool hat (over 50 percent of body heat is lost through the head and neck), sunglasses and sunscreen, knife, first-aid kit, matches and fire starter, and raingear. Also consider an emergency blanket or large garbage bag, a signal mirror and/or whistle, and an 8-inch square of heavy foil for making a cup or cook pot.

2. **Planning.** Know your limits and plan trips that feature mileage, elevation gain, and terrain that you can handle. Be aware of potential hazards and dangers. Consult those with local knowledge at land management agencies. Follow your plan.

   ALWAYS leave a detailed plan of your route with friends, family, or rangers when you go into the backcountry, including the anticipated return time. This information should include what equipment you have, the color of your pack, etc.

3. **Don't go alone.** Unless you have a fair amount of experience, it is rarely a good idea to go into the backcountry alone. At the very least, leave a note on your dashboard or seat. See #2 above. Example: July 30th. Solo day hike to Black Lake.

4. **Technology.** National park rangers are seeing more backcountry visitors relying on technological devices such as cell phones and GPS units. These tools can be fun and valuable. However, they are not always reliable. They are no substitute for common sense and good trip planning.

On the Trail

1. **Hiking the trail.** Look up often to orient yourself to prominent features. Also look behind you to see where you have come from. Often this will be your return route. Periodically verify your location on a map. Don't focus and depend on a GPS unit.

2. **Layer your clothing**. Most of the trails in Rocky Mountain National Park quickly rise in elevation from the trailhead. Many hikers get overheated quickly with the exertion. Pace yourself. Shed layers of clothing as your body heats up. You want to avoid excessive sweating. The wetter you get, the more you will cool off and chill when you stop for a break. Educate yourself to the signs and symptoms of hypothermia.

3. **Be aware of falling trees.** This is a very real hazard that is emerging in the national park due to the extensive beetle kill of trees. Stay alert as you pass through swaths of dead forest, particularly on windy days.

4. **Lightning.** Lightning is always a possibility during afternoon storms. Watch for approaching storms and try to get below treeline. Be familiar with how to respond if caught by a lightning storm. Space the members of your hiking party. See chapter eleven.

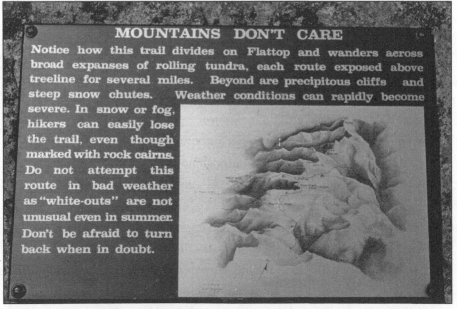

Warning sign along the Flattop Mountain Trail above Emerald Lake overlook. Courtesy of RMNP

5. **Stay together.** Try to pick a hiking partner of similar ability. At the least, always stay within sight of each other. Never leave anybody alone.

6. **Altitude Sickness.** Most visitors to Rocky Mountain National Park experience some symptoms of altitude sickness. Symptoms range from headache and dizziness to nausea and unconsciousness. High elevation can also aggravate existing medical conditions such as heart or lung disease. The only cure is to descend to a lower elevation.

7. **Lost.** If you find yourself lost, it is usually better if you stop and safely prepare yourself to be found. Stay warm, dry, and visible if you can.

8. **Swift water.** Rocks at streamside are often slippery due to algae and mosses growing in the warmer water near the water's edge. Mountain streams are particularly dangerous during the high runoff of May and June. Half of the drowning fatalities involved children under the supervision of adults. Remember that water is like a magnet to children.

The "Ten Essentials"

The "Ten Essentials" is a list of essential items recommended for safe travel in the backcountry. This list was first described in the 1930s by The Mountaineers, a hiking and mountain climbing club in Seattle, Washington. It is still very relevant to today's backcountry user.

As found in the classic book, *Mountaineering: The Freedom of the Hills*, the ten essentials are:

1. **Map.** Always carry a detailed map of the area you will be visiting. The point is to carry a map appropriate for the area you will be in and the activity you will be undertaking—and know how to use it!

2. **Compass.** (optionally supplemented with a GPS receiver)

3. **Sunglasses and sunscreen.** Your eyes can experience damage from the intensity of ultraviolet light in the park. As elevation increases, so does the intensity of ultraviolet rays. Adequate eye protection is a must!

4. **Extra food and water.** Whenever you go out, even for a day trip, bring extra food in case you are delayed by emergencies or foul weather, or you just get lost. A one-day supply is recommended. Carry plenty of fresh water. Unfortunately, giardia is fairly common in the waters of Rocky Mountain National Park. Use a water filter, purifier, chemical tablets, or boiling to treat any water before consuming

5. **Extra clothes.** In addition to the basic layers you would normally take, bring extra clothing that can get you through an unplanned night out or through the worst conditions you might come up against. In addition to the extra clothes, carry an emergency shelter such as a space blanket. A space blanket weighs about 3 ounces, but will completely encase you and keep you warm and dry. Insulation should allow you to

survive the worst conditions that can be realistically expected. A wool hat provides more warmth for its weight than any piece of clothing. Adequate rain gear is critical in the Colorado high country. Many a novice hiker has been fooled by the crystal clear Colorado mornings, and later drenched by the afternoon thundershowers.

6. **Headlamp/flashlight.** Flashlights and/or headlamps are important even on day trips. You never know when you might need to spend the night or make that last mile or so after sunset. It's a good idea to carry a small, lightweight hand-held light in addition to a headlamp. In the hand-held light, use a regular bulb which requires less battery juice than the bright-beam bulbs. Use this light for simple chores around the camp to conserve batteries. In the headlamp, use a halogen (or other bright-beam bulb), and use this light when you are pathfinding or otherwise require a bright beam.

7. **First aid kit.** Carry first-aid supplies for minor injuries. In particular, carry plenty of adhesive band-aids and sterilized bandages because they can't be easily improvised in the woods.

8. **Fire starter.** Fire starters are useful for quickly starting a fire, especially in emergency situations. They are also useful for igniting wet wood. There are several commercial fire starters available: magnesium blocks with striking flint, chemically-treated fire sticks, etc.

9. **Matches.** Carry matches that have been waterproofed or wind- and waterproofed, or else carry extra strike-anywhere matches—along with something to strike them on—in a waterproof container.

10. **Knife.** A good example of a single piece of gear which has multiple uses. The simple knife, which still is essential, can be part of a multi-tool device popular with many backcountry users today.

Many publications recommend supplementing the Ten Essentials with:
- Water treatment device (water filter or chemicals) and water bottles.
- Ice axe for glacier or snowfield travel (if necessary).
- Repair kit, including duct tape and basic sewing materials.
- Insect repellent (or clothing designed for this purpose).

- Signaling devices, such as a whistle, cell phone, two-way radio, satellite phone, unbreakable signal mirror, or flare.
- Plastic tarp and rope for expedient field shelter.

Not every outing will require the use of an essential item. Carrying these basic items improves the chances that one is prepared for an unexpected emergency in the outdoors. For instance, if a hiker experiences a sudden snow storm, fresh clothes and fire starter may be used to keep warm, or the map and compass and headlamp will allow them to exit the wilderness quickly. Otherwise hypothermia becomes a prominent possibility, perhaps even death.

Use common sense and good judgment. Know when to turn back. Be leery of "summit fever"—don't be too destination or goal oriented. Enjoy the experience! There will always be another day.

Chronology of Deaths in Rocky Mountain National Park

1884 – Carrie Welton (hypothermia)

1889 – Frank Stryker (gunshot)

1896 – Alexander MacGregor (lightning)

1905 – Louis Levings (fall)

1914 – Dr. Dillingham (lightning)

1915 – Rocky Mountain National Park established.
Dr. Thornton R. Sampson (hypothermia)

1916

1917 – Eula Frost (fall on snow)

1918 – Mrs. C.W. Wood (auto accident); Mrs. E.F. Kimmelshuhe
and two sons (auto accident)

1919

1920 – J.P. Chitwood (hypothermia)

1921 – H.F. Targett (fall); Gregory Aubuchon (fall)

1922 – Jesse E. Kitts (lightning)

1923

1924

1925 – Agnes W. Vaille (hypothermia); Herbert Sortland (hypothermia)

1926 – Charles Hupp (heart attack); Forrest Ketring (fall); Fred N.
Selak (murder)

1927 – Flora Napier (sledding accident); William N. Vaile (heart attack);
unidentified skull (cause unknown)

1928

1929 – Charles W. Thiemeyer (fall)

1930

1931 – R.B. Key (fall)

1932 – Robert F. Smith (struck by falling rock); Mary S. Day and Lucille Day (auto accident); Gray Secor, Jr. (fall)

1933 – Joseph L. Halpern (lost and never found)

1934 – C.F. Peyton (auto accident); Kenneth Meenan (auto accident)

1935

1936 – James Fifer (auto accident); Ben Servey (heart attack); Forrest Hein (fall)

1937 – William S. Moore (heart attack);

1938 – Emily F. Russell (fall from horse); John A. Fuller (fall); Nola Morris (auto accident); Alfred Beilhartz (drowned)

1939 – Gerald J. Clark (hypothermia); Raymond Johnson (auto accident)

1940 – Hoyt White (fall)

1941 – Wesley F. Diem (heart attack)

1942

1943

1944

1945 – Albert W. Furch (fall from horse); Shelley Heimbichner (auto accident)

1946 – Thomas H. Evans (fall); John E. Barney (heart attack); Charles Grant (fall)

1947 – Robert Briggs (drowned); Raymond Young (auto accident); Oscar Jacobson (auto accident); Wilmer S. Holley (drowned)

1948 – L.C. Ingram (heart attack); Lt. Cranston Dodd (plane crash); Edward Schneiderhahn (heart attack)

1949 – Dale Devitt and Bruce Gerling (lost and never found)

1950 – Lorena Pauley (suicide); Kenneth Swisher (auto accident); Earl S. Davis (heart attack)

1951

1952 – B.R. Schabarum (heart attack); John H. Tallmadge (fall); Wayne J. Kurtz (heart attack); Ralph Corlew (heart attack)

1953 – Abe Brown (heart attack); A.J. Canino (heart attack); Kathryn Rees (fall); Sandra Miller (fall); Robin A. Howarth (drowned)

1954 – Earl F. Harvey (fall); A.J. McPhillips (suicide); Harold Grey (heart attack); Richard Williams (auto accident) Mrs. R.G. Van Blarican (medical—hemorrhagic anemia)

1955 – Jack Roberts (heart attack); Irwin C. Oderkirk (auto accident)

1956 – Robert Salt (medical—acute diabetic shock); George Bloom (fall); Mrs. Rena Hoffman (lightning)

1957 – Cecil F. Hall (heart attack)

1958 – O.E. Kinnaman (heart attack); Edwin V. Drake (heart attack); Bobby Bizup (hypothermia); George F. Wellman (heart attack)

1959 – Edith Zockett (stroke/heart attack) Raymond Harrington (heart attack); Jeanne Gillett (fall on snow)

1960 – David L. Jones and Prince D. Willmon (fall); Charles Raidy (auto accident); Lester Reeble (fall); George W. Krah (heart attack)

1961 – Myron M. Fritts (fall)

1962 – Patricia L. Beatty (fall on snow); Gerald R. Noland (fall on snow); Ken Murphy (fall); James S. O'Toole (fall)

1963

1964 – James L. Keller (drowned); Norris C. Livoni (suicide); Leola H. Swain (lightning); "Billy Bones" (suicide—never identified)

1965 – Robert E. Brown (fall); Rev. Alvin Whittemore (heart attack)

1966 – Jay DuPont (fall); Nathaniel R. Lacy (auto accident); Ms. Xana Schurene (heart attack); Walter Stentzil (heart attack); John Rapchak (heart attack); C. Blake Hiester (fall)

1967 – Jack D. Henander, William P. Elrod, and Charles DeNovellis (plane crash); James B. Clifford (heart attack)

1968 – Marshal Wrubel (heart attack)

1969 – Jerry P. Johnson (fall); Herbert D. Kuhn (fall from horse); James D. Majors (heart attack)

1970

1971 – Walter G. Seabold (heart attack); Roy C. Handshew (heart attack); Rudolph Postweiler (heart attack); William Frechtling (heart attack)

1972 – Fred Stone and Joan Jardine (hypothermia); Paul F. Russell (fall); Steve Day (fall); Gregory Holzer (lost—hypothermia); Danny Saucier (drowned); Gerald Murphy (heart attack); Lilie E. Brown (heart attack); John Kruppa (heart attack); Harry J. Sears (heart attack)

1973 – Jay Van Stavern (fall); Lois L. Matthews (drowned); Sherran Haley (drowned); Kurt Primosch (drowned); Michael Egan (drowned); Joseph Holub (fall); Jonathan Williams (lost—hypothermia); Robert Fritz and David Emerick (avalanche)

1974 – Barbara Gully (lightning); John Berger (fall)

1975 – Richard Ankanbrandt (heart attack); Diana Hunter (fall); Chris Rejeske (fall on snow); Allan Jacobs (fall); Domingo Alvarez (heart attack); William Gizzie (hypothermia); Laurene S. Nuzzo (auto accident); Virgil Munsinger (heart attack); Don Mullett (heart attack); William A. Pistorio (fall)

1976 – James Boicourt (fall)

1977 – Asuncion Navaretti (fall); Harold Holtzendorf (fall); Michael Neri (fall); Sam Friedman (heart attack); Martin Ryan and Janet Bonneville (plane crash); Jason E. Quest (auto accident); Eric Rumsey (suicide)

1978 – Christopher Ermijo (drowned); John White-Lance (auto accident); Lawrence Berman (fall on snow/ice); Herman Milner (heart attack); Grete E. Wignall (heart attack); Harvey Schneider (fall); Denzel Baker (heart attack)

1979 – Andrew W. Paton (lightning); Coy Conley (fall on snow); Virginia Krieger (plane crash); Dr. Edward Sujansky (heart attack); Charles O. Nesbit (fall); Kris Gedney (suicide)

1980 – Ruth Magnuson (hypothermia); Robert Silver (fall); Bernard F. Conway (heart attack); John Link (fall); Christine M. Ulbricht (fall); James S. Johnston (fall)

1981 – Robert Elliott (fall); James P. Duffy (hypothermia)

1982 – Robert Baldeshwiler (fall); Steven See, Terry W. Coates, and Bridget Dorris (drowned); John W. Daly (heart attack); Audrey G. Day (auto accident)

1983 – Mark D. Frevert (struck by falling rock); Samuel Mitchell (hypothermia): Rudi Moder (lost and never found); Edward Griess (fall)

1984 – Cecelea Mulvihill (heart attack); David P. Ormsby (fall); Lee S. Jamieson (fall); Gilbert Hana (heart attack); Ruth L. Bruso (heart attack)

1985 – Scott Anderson (skiing accident/head injury); Nancy Garbs (undetermined medical); Alice A. Philbrick (heart attack); William Becker (suicide); Edna M. Digman (suicide)

1986 – Ellen Marx (drowned); Lawrence Farrell (fall)

1987 – Francis Murray (suicide); J.D. Burger (heart attack); Charles Housman (natural causes); Rey Dermody (drowned); David D. Felts (fall); John R. Schnakenberg (fall)

1988 – Brenda K. Butrick (tubing accident on snow); Kevin Hardwick (fall); George C. Ogden (fall); Roger A. Boyce (suicide)

1989 – Jerome H. Bentley (plane crash); Evan R. Corbett (suicide); Albert Fincham (heart attack)

1990 – Andrew Tufly (fall); Timothy Fromalt (fall); William W. Carson (fall)

1991 – John R. Thomas (suicide); Joe Massari (avalanche); Wilburn J. Parks (suicide); Lawrence Taylor (heart attack)

1992 – Kurt Witbeck (suicide); Glenn McDonald (lightning); Lon L. Egbert (suicide); Sarah Wolenetz (fall); Gary Boyer (fall); Bruce Anderson (suicide); Jon M. Hofstra (fall); Todd Martin and Brad Farnan (avalanche)

1993 – Carl E. Siegel (fall); Glenn M. Hayes (drowned); Kelly Thomas (hypothermia)

1994 – Kip Lloyd (suicide); Alison Bierma (suicide); Jack L. McConnell (fall); Robert Baker (heart attack); Noel Jarrell (heart attack); Eugene Gomolka (heart attack); Jack E. Keene (heart attack); Richard Smith (suicide)

1995 – Alan B. Farwell and Forrest Sprague (auto accident); Jun Kamimura (fall)

1996 – Peter Smith (plane crash); Robert C. Drury (heart attack)

1997 – Francis W. Clyde (heart attack); Todd Marshall (fall); Mark Miedema (mountain lion attack); Hayes W. Reid (suicide); Mona Barlow (heart attack); Timothy Maron (fall)

1998 – William C. Heflin (heart attack); Raymond C. Barbknecht (heart attack); Richard Ladue (fall)

1999 – Charlie Harrison (fall); Michael J. Fritzen (heart attack); John Retting (lightning); Raymond Decker (fall); James D. Page (fall); Michael B. Hines (lightning); Gregory J. Koczanski (fall)

2000 – Erin C. Sharp (fall); Claude and Terri Donoho (plane crash); Cameron Tague (fall); Andy Haberkorn (lightning); Edward Calloway (heart attack)

2001 – Melanie Wood (suicide); Scott Johnson (drowned); Michael P. Carter (suicide); John C. Hodge (suicide/hypothermia)

2002 – Robert Whittington (heart attack)

2003 – Kurt Zollers (fall); Jonathan J. Rozecki (suicide); Robert Chu (heart Attack)

2004 – Shannon Thomas (suicide); Abigail Walter (fall); Marilyn Frongillo (heart attack); Sudheer Averineni (hypothermia)

2005 – Omar Mehdawi (tubing accident on snow); Jeff Christensen (fall); John Whatmough (auto accident)

2006 – Clayton Smith (fall)

2007 – William N. Hudson (struck by falling tree)

2008 – Richard Frisbie (fall on snow/ice); Robert Bacon (heart attack); Matthew Chesaux (fall while skiing on snow/ice)

2009 – Albert Langemann (heart attack); Connie Fanning (auto accident); Maynard Brandsma (heart attack); Carol Nicolaidis (fall); John Bramley (fall)

Summary of Deaths in Rocky Mountain National Park, 1884–2009

Accidental Deaths

Incident Type	Male Victims	Female Victims	Total
Falls—Hiking/Scrambling	50	9	59
Falls—Technical Climbing	25	1	26
Motor Vehicle Accidents	18	9	27
Drownings (children under 13 yrs old)	15 (8)	3 (1)	18 (9)
Hypothermia (exposure)	12	4	16
Aircraft Accidents	8	3	11
Lightning	8	3	11
Avalanches	6		6
Snow Play Accidents	3	2	5
Lost … and never found	4		4
Falls from a Horse	2	1	3
Falling Rocks	3		3
Falling Tree	1		1
Accidental Gunshot	1		1
Mountain Lion Attack	1		1
J.P. Chitwood	1		1
Skull Point		1(?)	1
Subtotal—Accidental deaths	158 (81%)	36 (19%)	194

Non-accidental Deaths

Incident Type	Male Victims	Female Victims	Total
Heart Attacks	64	8	72
Other medical deaths	2	3	5
Suicides	20	5	25
Homicide	1		1
Subtotal—Non-accidents	87 (84%)	16 (16%)	103
GRAND TOTAL	245 (82%)	52 (18%)	297

Bibliography

Arps, Louisa Ward, and Elinor E. Kingery, *High Country Names*. Rocky Mountain Nature Association. 1972

Buchholtz, C.W. *Rocky Mountain National Park: A History*. Colorado Associated University Press. Boulder, CO. 1983

Bueler, William M. *Roof of the Rockies, A History of Mountaineering in Colorado*. Pruett Publishing Co. Boulder, CO. 1974

Currie, Jr., Thomas W. *Austin Presbyterian Theological Seminary: A Seventy-fifth Anniversary History*. Trinity University Press, San Antonio, TX. 1978

Dunning, Harold M. *Facts about Longs Peak*. Johnson Publishing Company. Boulder, CO. 1970

Dunning, Harold M. *Over Hill and Vale*. Johnson Publishing Co. Boulder, CO. 1956

Farabee, Charles R. *Death, Daring and Disaster*. Taylor Trade Publishing. Lanham, MD. 2005

Farabee, Charles R., and Ghiglieri, Michael. *Off the Wall: Death in Yosemite*. Puma Press. Flagstaff, AZ. 2007

Geary, Michael M., *A Quick History of Grand Lake*. Western Reflections. Ouray, CO. 1999

Ghiglieri, Michael, and Myers, Thomas M. *Over the Edge: Death in Grand Canyon*. Puma Press. Flagstaff, AZ. 2001

Gillett, Bernard. *Rocky Mountain National Park: The Climber's Guide*. Earthbound Sports, Inc. Chapel Hill, NC. 2001

Gorby, John D. *The Stettner Way. The Life and Climbs of Joe and Paul Stettner*. Colorado Mountain Club Press. Golden, CO. 2003

Jessen, Kenneth. *A Quick History of Estes Park*. Self published. 1996

Jones, Arthur G. *Thornton R. Sampson, D.D., LL.D., 1852–1915: A Biographical Sketch*. Richmond Press, Inc. Richmond, VA. 1917

Judkins, Grant, editor. *The Big Thompson Disaster*. Lithographic Press. Loveland, CO.

Lamb, Elkanah J. *Memories of the Past and Thoughts of the Future*. United Brethren Publishing House. 1906

Miscellaneous Meditations. The Publishers' Press Room and Bindery Company. 1913

MacDonald, Dougald. *Longs Peak: The Story of Colorado's Favorite Fourteener*. Westcliffe Publishers. Englewood, CO. 2004

Robertson, Janet. *The Magnificent Mountain Women*. University of Nebraska Press. Lincoln, NE. 1990

Moomaw, Jack. *Recollections of a Rocky Mountain Ranger*. Times-Call Publishing Co. Longmont, CO. 1963

Oh, Ranger! True Stories from our National Parks. American Park Network. New York, NY. 2007

Pedersen, Jr., Henry F. *Sadness in Sunshine: The Flood of Estes Park*. Self published. Estes Park, CO. 1995

Perry, Phyllis J. *It Happened in Rocky Mountain National Park.* The Globe Pequot Press. Guilford, CT. 2008

Pickering, James H. *Early Estes Park Narratives, Vol. IV. Narratives of Exploration and Mountain Adventure.* Alpenaire Publishing, Inc. Estes Park, CO. 2006

———. *The Ways of the Mountains.* Alpenaire Publishing, Inc. Estes Park, CO. 2003

———. *This Blue Hollow: Estes Park, the Early Years, 1859–1915:* University of Colorado Press. Niwot, CO. 1999

Ramaley, William C. *Trails and Trailbuilders of the Rocky Mountain National Park.* Library, Rocky Mountain National Park.

Superintendent's Monthly Reports—Rocky Mountain National Park—1917–1967. Rocky Mountain National Park Research Library.

Toll, Roger. *Mountaineering in Rocky Mountain National Park.* Publisher unknown. 1919

Toll, Oliver W. *Arapaho Names and Trails: A Report of a 1914 Pack Trip.* Estes Park Public Library.

Transcripts of *Longs Peak Reunion Symposium.* August 25, 1991. Estes Park Public Library.

Trimble, Stephen. *Longs Peak, a Rocky Mountain Chronicle.* Rocky Mountain Nature Association. Estes Park, CO. 1984

Whittlesey, Lee H. *Death in Yellowstone: Accidents and Foolhardiness in the First National Park.* Roberts Rinehart Publishers. Boulder, CO. 1995

Newspapers & Magazines

The Tipton Conservative & Advertiser, Tipton, Iowa

Estes Park Trail Gazette, Estes Park, Colorado

Rocky Mountain News, Denver, Colorado

Boulder Daily Camera, Boulder, Colorado

The Coloradoan, Ft. Collins, Colorado

Denver Post, Denver Colorado

Loveland Reporter Herald, Loveland, Colorado

Longmont Times Call, Longmont, Colorado

Trail and Timberline magazine. Colorado Mountain Club. Multiple issues

Accidents in North American Mountaineering. American Alpine Club. Multiple issues

Index

Joe Evans retired in 2006 after thirty-three years as a National Park Ranger. For thirteen years, he was the Chief Ranger of Rocky Mountain National Park. He worked in nine national parks, including assignments in Yosemite, Grand Canyon, and Yellowstone. These parks, along with Rocky Mountain, are recognized as some of the more active parks for search and rescue in the country. He wants you to visit the national parks, and to go home safe and happy. He lives in Estes Park, Colorado.